Change... and BI:
How M... How?

Papers and ... nty-Second
Nat ... nce

Eastern Michigan University

and

Rhonda Fowler
Access Services Librarian
University Library
Eastern Michigan University

Published for Learning Resources and Technologies
Eastern Michigan University
by
Pierian Press
Ann Arbor, Michigan
1996

ISBN 0-87650-342-3
Copyright © 1996, The Pierian Press
All Rights Reserved

The Pierian Press
Box 1808
Ann Arbor, Michigan 48106

LIBRARY ORIENTATION SERIES
(Emphasizing Information Literacy and Bibliographic Instruction)

*   Pierian Press's ISBN identifier is 0-87650. This identifier should precede the number given for a book (e.g., 0-87650-327-X).

Table of Contents

Articles

Instructive Sessions

Poster Sessions

Bibliography

Roster of Participants

PREFACE

The relationship between library instruction and reference is a long one; both try to assist the library user in finding information and in learning to use the library. Most library instruction programs, in fact, grew out of reference departments and many are still a part of the reference function organizationally.

Despite this close relationship—or perhaps because of it—there has often been friction between the two library functions. Philosophies and practices have often been at odds. James Rettig, well known to reference librarians in particular as an expert on reference sources, clearly articulates these conflicts and delineates what he feels the future should hold for both reference and instruction librarians in his keynote address, "The Convergence of the Twain or Titanic Collision? BI and Reference in the 1990s' Sea of Change." Both, he maintains, "are burdened with historical baggage that they must toss overboard." As a participant in recent conferences on rethinking reference, James Rettig is particularly well equipped to tell us what to toss and what to save.

Our other main speaker, Cheryl LaGuardia, returned to practical and immediate concerns and presented her experiences regenerating a library instruction program and course at the University of California-Santa Barbara. A delightful speaker, Cheryl LaGuardia engaged the audience with her experiences, which apparently were familiar to her audience.

A final major presentation was Dan Ream's humorous but realistic "Scratch That Glitch: Or, The Fine Art of Glitch Management." Several nightmare scenarios were explored in detail—all familiar to users of audiovisual or computer equipment in presentations. This presentation was the entertainment highlight of the conference.

In addition to these three excellent speaker, the LOEX Conference was fortunate to again have a full set of excellent presenters of short sessions and poster sessions. New ways of handling the reference and instructional functions were explored.

Linda Shirato

THE CONVERGENCE OF THE TWAIN OR TITANIC COLLISION? BI AND REFERENCE IN THE 1990S' SEA OF CHANGE

James Rettig

It all began a very long time ago, sometime before 1876, that *annus mirabilis* of librarianship during which the American Library Association was founded, *Library Journal* debuted, and Samuel Green published in its pages the first article about reference librarianship.[1] And it continues today. Less than a month ago an unidentified library school student from the State University of New York at Buffalo queried the participants of the LIBREF-L listserv, asking them, "Can you give a summary of the 'hot' library reference issues of the week? I'm working on a project for my Reference course, and would like to find out what is REALLY vital to refernce (*sic*) librarians out there today."[2] I was tempted to reply that all of that week's "hot" issues were identified in Green's 1876 article. In that article describing the phenomenon we today call reference service, Green touched on issues such as the librarian's obligation to provide information without injecting personal values, the inability of any librarian to know everything, the need sometimes to refer a patron to another information agency, SDI services, the value of proactive rather than passive service, the challenges of the reference interview, and, of course, what has come to be called the "information versus instruction debate."

In Green's example of service to a "a citizen [who] is building a house" and looking for information about how "to protect against injury from lightning,"

Rettig is assistant dean of University Libraries for reference and information services at Swem Library, College of William & Mary, Williamsburg, Virginia.

he says the librarian "must get the books which contain the desired information, and hand them to the reader open at the proper pages."[3] In contrast, "A school-boy calls for a history of the Suez Canal. You see at once, probably, that what he needs is a brief account, and refer him to some recently-issued encyclopaedia. At the same time you show him how to use dictionaries and encyclopaedias, and tell him he can often find answers to questions himself by using works of this kind."[4] Beyond these examples, two prescriptive statements illustrate and implicitly define each of Green's seemingly contradictory modes of service. On the one hand he counsels that "A librarian should be as unwilling to allow an inquirer to leave the library with his question unanswered as a shopkeeper is to have a customer go out of his store without making a purchase;"[5] and on the other he cautions, "Be careful not to make inquirers dependent. Give them as much assistance as they need, but try at the same time to teach them to rely upon themselves and become independent."[6]

Both of these modes of service have long histories, especially in academic libraries. For example, Justin Winsor in 1880, then serving as librarian at Harvard, advised his fellow librarians, "It would be a good plan to take the students by sections, and make them acquainted with the bibliographical apparatus."[7] Frances Hopkins has traced the history of instructional efforts and the rationale behind them, giving special attention to the early generation of scholar-librarians such as Winsor.[8] This audience surely knows that history well enough that there is no need to repeat it here. Throughout that history there has been tension between the two modes of service Green identified and described.

Instruction-Information Tension

That tension continues today. During the past year Anne Lipow has conducted three "Rethinking Reference" institutes for academic librarians, the first in Berkeley in March 1993, the second at Duke the following June, and the last at the University of Iowa in February. At the first two institutes, the future role, scope, and nature of bibliographic instruction emerged as a significant unresolved issue. It was the topic of considerable discussion at plenary sessions, especially at the Duke institute. Indeed, it appeared that many of the most vocal participants at the Duke institute fell into one of two polarly opposed groups—those who appeared to believe that BI has no future and those who believe that BI *is* the future. In response to this Anne Lipow commissioned three supplementary essays on the question for the printed proceedings[9] and designed a special BI track for the Iowa institute. Despite these efforts, the "Rethinking Reference" institutes failed to resolve the questions swirling about BI and its role in the future.

I was privileged to participate in the Berkeley and Duke institutes. Since then, the apparent polarity of positions on the BI question has sent me on a quest for an explanation of that polarity. Research by Roma Harris provides a partial explanation.[10] She surveyed public librarians and found considerable ambiguity in this group's responses to a series of questions designed to identify their beliefs about the role of bibliographic instruction in public library service. Like all good research, Harris' study raises more questions than it answers. She suggests that "a fruitful area for future research may be to look at how librarians come to hold their beliefs about practice and how well their beliefs match users' expectations. It would also be interesting to explore what happens when librarians with conflicting ideas about instruction work in the same reference department."[11] She followed up this study with a similar study of academic and special librarians.[12] In it she found considerable difference between the two groups but less ambiguity within each group than within the cohort of public librarians studied earlier. In these studies, "On the information-instruction continuum, the academic librarians fall towards the instruction end and the special librarians toward the information end, while the public librarians fall somewhere in between."[13] Why the differences?

Harris suggests one possible explanation—her "curious findings" that academic librarians by and large did not think that their instructional activities enhanced their status within their institutions whereas many special librarians saw their instructional efforts as having just the opposite effect.[14] It appears that the public librarians did not address this issue. The relation of BI to faculty status for academic librarians has been debated *ad nauseam* without yielding any discernible positive effect for either librarians or library users. Clearly, there must be a better explanation.

Another explanation lies in librarians' genuine desire to do what is best for their patrons; however, differing interpretations of what is best for them and how to provide what is best result in differing reference "philosophies" or "theories." What passes for reference philosophy is embarrassingly thin, especially considering its long history. The prevailing sets of values, masquerading as philosophies, emerge in Harris' research, especially in the comments public librarians made in response to her invitation "to make general comments on bibliographic instruction in public libraries."[15] Their responses, many of them implicit definitions of BI, lie all over the map; some of these implicit definitions are expansive, others very narrow and limited to specific circumstances. It is unfortunate that, even though she gave them the same opportunity, she did not elicit (or chose not to quote) similar implicit definitional statements from the academic and special librarians. Lawrence McCrank, commenting on the squishiness of much of librarianship's specialized lexicon, has observed that "even a supposedly mature area like reference instruction is confounded by the lack of functional, working definitions."[16] Until reference has those, it is unlikely to have a coherent, widely accepted and strongly supported philosophy.

Reference "Philosophies"

What passes for reference philosophy has been described numerous times since Green illustrated it in his practice at the Worcester Free Public Library. In 1930, James Wyer saddled reference librarianship with labels for a question long debated and still unresolved—how best to serve library patrons. In his textbook on reference he posited his so-called "theory" of reference work in which one provides "conservative," "moderate," or "liberal" service.[17] "Conservative" roughly equates to instruction; "liberal "roughly equates to information provision; and, as Rothstein sagely noted, "moderate" is more of a "muddle" than anything approximating a philosophy.[18] Rothstein in 1961 relabeled these "minimum," "middling," and "maximum."[19] Yet even he could not synthesize these divergent modes into a coherent philosophy of reference. Nevertheless when reference librarians are asked to explain their "philosophy" or "theory" of reference service, they almost inevitably express it in terms similar to those used by Wyer or Rothstein.

Harris does not suggest it, but I think a worthwhile follow-up study of reference librarians (including those whose title is instruction librarian or some variant thereof) would be, first, to determine individually each one's position on what she calls the "information-instruction continuum,"[20] and, then, to observe each one in practice while providing reference service. My hypothesis is that an analysis of practice of many individuals would reveal a weak correlation between a librarian's professed position on that continuum and his or her position on it as demonstrated through behavior. Furthermore, I hypothesize that the demonstrated position of each individual would range widely along that continuum, dependent primarily on the discerned needs and most effective course of action in each situation in which service is provided. In other words, I question how much "philosophies," such as they are, actually inform and shape practice in individuals, let alone whole departments. I suspect that librarians' desire to do what is best for each patron makes reference practice highly situational and—or so it would appear to an uninformed observer—highly inconsistent.

Yet these philosophies persist and appear to be in sharp conflict. Why?

A Matter of Belief?

A fruitful explanation for the differences in views among librarians, including the differences among academic librarians that were so evident at the Duke "Rethinking Reference" institute, is to analyze values and to follow up on Harris' suggestion that research is needed to determine how practitioners "come to hold their beliefs;" for, indeed, the debate has been driven for a dozen decades more by assertion than by data. These assertions, either in favor of BI or information provision, or against BI or "spoon feeding," derive from some source, especially when delivered with as much certitude and passion as they sometimes were at Duke. It appears that they are rooted in beliefs, but beliefs held so abstractly that reference service is at most marginally affected by them. As a result, those who hold one belief tend to develop an exaggerated view of the beliefs at the other end of the spectrum. And, to make matters worse, they can find evidence to support their views. Take, for example the out-and-out assertion on behalf of instruction that "from no one other than a librarian is a college or university student likely to learn this fundamental truth: The manner in which you go about obtaining material for research on any single college paper is more important in the long run than the material you obtain."[21] Without a hint of irony the author adds, "This is a difficult statement for some to accept."[22] Take, on the other side, the statement that "One hundred years after Green, academic

librarians have failed to recognize that their mission is to provide information to those who need it."[23] These are significant differences.

Since it appears that the differences are matters of belief, Harris' recommendations for further research ought to be acted upon. Furthermore, the values associated with each belief need to be examined and their implications explored. The lack of a standard received definition of bibliographic instruction exacerbates the problem of apparent polarity, allowing BI's critics to assume an exaggerated definition.

BI Undefined

In his "Immodest Proposals" article in *Library Journal* in 1990, Tom Eadie defined BI as "instructional programs aimed at groups of library users, delivered on schedule, and in anticipation of questions that have not yet been asked."[24] The BI community rejected this definition—along with many of Eadie's other ideas—with howls of protest. The Bibliographic Instruction Committee of ACRL's Community and Junior College Libraries Section published a collective rebuttal (called just that) in which they criticized "his inaccurate definitions of user education, his weak premises, and his omission of recent literature."[25] However the committee did not offer an alternative definition. What, then, is the definition of bibliographic instruction? Perhaps, regardless of one's beliefs about the relative importance of information or instruction, it is analogous to the well-known and very imprecise definition of pornography: "I can't tell you what it is, but I know it when I see it." The term "bibliographic instruction" is fraught with semantic ambiguity. If in any discussion of BI, every participant is operating not only from a unique degree of individual belief but also from a unique definition of the phenomenon being discussed, the quest for consensus seems doomed to failure. Beliefs, as well as semantic ambiguity regarding BI's definition, were strong factors in the discussions at the Duke "Rethinking Reference" institute. This explains the apparent polarity of positions taken there.

Values associated with these beliefs also play a prominent role. Both the proponents of BI and the proponents of information provision value service; however, they interpret it differently. In addition to service, the BI community gives great weight to the value of independence. Indeed, the term and the value have been prominent since Green invoked them in 1876. They recur as constants in the BI literature. Constance Mellon has stated that "the aim of a library instruction program is to produce an independent library user who has developed a successful problem-solving search strategy."[26] Elizabeth Frick has written that the key question in designing BI programs is "how best to give students the ability to acquire their own information, thereby enabling them to become independent learners."[27] And Barbara Wittkopf entitled a recent editorial in *Research Strategies* "Making Our Library Users Increasingly Independent."[28] "Independence," at least in this context, appears to be as fraught with semantic ambiguity as the term "bibliographic instruction." But more on that shortly.

External Forces of Change

Both reference and BI, seemingly divergent strains of librarianship's service impulse, have undergone change and challenge during the past decade. Both have been affected by the same external forces. Given higher education's heavy dependence upon government funding, the past decade has not been kind to colleges and universities. They, and their libraries, have had to grapple with the challenge of doing more with less. Among those for whom they are expected to do more are student bodies that are increasingly heterogeneous and diverse.

Automation of information systems is almost too obvious a change to mention. The jury is divided on whether or not automation has made information handling easier or more complex for library users. There is, however, consensus that it has made information identification and, increasingly, information retrieval faster processes. Thanks to the speed of automated systems and, in some cases, thanks to their broad scope, patrons are identifying more information sources than they identified using manual processes and are expending far less effort to harvest that more bountiful yield. Librarians have worried that users attribute too much power to these new systems, that "if it was created on a computer, exists in a computer, or came out of a computer, some will view it as more valid, up-to-date, and credible than a print format version."[29] However illusory the power and comprehensiveness of these systems may be, they are undeniably popular with our patrons. And the younger they are, the more at ease they seem to be with them. It is well worth noting that this year's college freshmen were in first grade when the Atari craze captured the nation and Pac-Man achieved enough recognition in the popular culture to be enshrined on t-shirts. Now college students, these former first graders who played the simple, linear Atari video games, outfit their residence hall rooms with televisions and much more sophisticated Nintendo and Sega game systems. In the very near future college students will probably routinely be playing virtual reality games. In comparison to these, even the best graphic user interfaces of the most user-friendly information systems will look drab. Students will be attuned to receiving immediate feedback from interactive systems and will have those same expectations for other computer systems they use, including information systems.

Another external force that has gained strength in recent years has been non-library (for want of a better term) information services. Services such as America Online, Prodigy, and CompuServe are growing rapidly and are poised to capitalize on the illusion that computerized information is more comprehensive and more valid than information obtained through other means. Only recently have academic libraries had competitors who advertise on national television. These services and the MCI television ad campaign featuring Anna Paquin making pronouncements about the future and AT&T's similar but less subdued ads may raise users' expectations about the speed with which information can be obtained and the ease with which they can connect to distant resources.

Whether or not students have changed, perceptions of students have. Adam and Eve probably thought their children lacked initiative and drive; finding comparative deficiencies in the next generation seems to be an unavoidable collective characteristic. Today, in our video-permeated age, this has been given a label: Generation X. And a recent *New Yorker* cartoon illustrates it: a bookstore customer tells a puzzled clerk, "It's for a young woman in the generation that knows how to read but doesn't feel like it."[30] These, and surely many who came before them, would, if they were ever to read John Updike's *Brazil*, agree with its heroine who felt, "The acts of learning and reading—all those nagging gray rows of type, scratching her eyes, demanding she go back and forth until some kind of meaning tumbled forth in a gush like an ugly baby—did not please her; the future did not belong to written words. It belonged to music and to flowing pictures, one image sliding colorfully into another."[31] This may well characterize the feelings of many of those enrolled in our colleges and universities today. And we librarians, the university personnel most closely identified with the written word—we must serve them.

Internal Forces of Change—Reference

Both reference and BI have also felt internal pressures and challenges during the past decade. Reference was questioned from within in the mid-1980s. When Bill Miller asked, "What's Wrong with Reference"?,[32] he concluded that reference librarians were feeling stressed out because they were reaching beyond their grasp to provide new services without letting go of any existing services. Charles Bunge concurred that "We have been spread ever more thinly. Hours are lengthened, or special services (whether computer searching, bibliographic instruction, or outreach services to special client groups) are added to our responsibilities, without commensurate increases in staff."[33] He noted that reference librarians perceived a considerable difference between the potential and the reality of service at the reference desk. Most of the issues that concerned Miller and Bunge in 1984 seem to have either resolved themselves or been accepted. Today discussions of reference deal not so much with the psychological well being of the individual reference librarian as with the optimal organization of resources to provide effective reference service.

After Barbara Ford questioned the value of the reference desk as a service vehicle in 1986,[34] she and others held a series of symposia at the University of Texas during which they debated variant models for reference service.[35] These symposia addressed the reference desk question as well as questions about the collection-based paradigm of reference librarianship, the effects an entrepreneurial approach might have on reference service, and the potential effects of electronic and on-demand publishing. By the early 1990s, some were done talking and were taking action. First at Brandeis University and then at Johns Hopkins, Virginia Massey-Burzio replaced the reference desk with a Research Consultation Office.[36] Not everyone expresses enthusiasm for such changes, nor for Jerry Campbell's sweeping proposals to redefine the role of reference librarian as "access engineers."[37] A decade after Miller asked what was wrong with reference, the answer seems to be that it isn't working as well as it should.

Internal Forces of Change—BI

Similarly, bibliographic instruction during this period has also undergone change. It has shifted its emphasis from the teaching of tools and tool-based strategies to teaching critical thinking techniques. For example, in 1982 Mona McCormick urged change, noting that "Somehow in our preoccupation with library procedures, we have ignored the reason for searching—to learn, to make informed decisions, to evaluate applications of knowledge, to find truth."[38] That same year, Brian Nielsen echoed McCormick when he said that "Much of what is being taught in bibliographic instruction programs is mind-deadening."[39] Six years later, Joan Bechtel noted that at Dickinson College "the librarians became more and more restless with traditional bibliographic instruction" and "it became increasingly evident that the impediments to students' scholarly growth had more to do with their underdeveloped, flawed thinking processes than with their inability to find library materials."[40] Librarians, especially those who hold a strong belief in BI, raised the banners of critical thinking and information literacy.

At the same time that some have called for a new direction for BI, others in the BI community have raised issues about the importance of individual patrons' needs. Mary Reichel has said that as academic librarians reassess their services and BI programs, "our vision needs to remain on the individual user."[41] Symptomatic of this emphasis, Karen Becker reported on an individualized approach to the time-honored freshman English BI experience.[42]

Research on Research

The most significant internal forces affecting BI and our understanding of it, however, have been research studies, especially those of Stephen Stoan and Barbara Fister. Shortly after McCormick and Nielsen called for change in the emphasis of BI programs, Stoan delineated the significant differences between library use and the research processes of scholars and scientists.[43] In further work in the same vein, he concluded that "research is normally random, nonlinear, and nonsequential,"[44] and that studies of scholars' behavior confirm "that the best of bibliographies, indexes, and database searches are merely sometimes helpful supplements to other methods of bibliographic retrieval."[45] Fister examined the research behaviors of successful undergraduates and drew similar conclusions about their information seeking and use patterns and said that if we librarians "are to represent the [research] process in a way that mirrors the circularity, the uncertainty, and the creativity involved in research, we need to re-examine our tool-based 'systematic' search model—and develop a new model."[46] While recognizing that it flies "in the face of conventional BI wisdom, which recommends a strategy to process a topic through a succession of tools before any reading or writing is performed,"[47] she noted that "the literature suggests no positive correlation between students' ability to find and evaluate texts and their ability to write effective research papers."[48] Following up on Fister's research, Barbara Valentine has recently noted that in the group of undergraduates she studied, "None of the students used the kind of organized strategy librarians often teach in bibliographic instruction sessions. Instead they used various tactics, often seemingly haphazard, that appeared to be driven more by instrumental and social rewards and punishments encountered along the way than by any premeditated strategy."[49] All of this has significant implications for BI.

However, change in the BI world seems to come no more easily than in the reference world. Despite the forces for change from within and without, many discern a maintenance of the status quo in many places. Only two years ago, Fister said that "the portion of library instruction that deals with finding materials tends to emphasize a sequential, tool-oriented search technique."[50] More recently Virginia Tiefel has recognized the need for change but, despite that, says that "most library instruction that has taken place at the postsecondary level...has focused on using individual sources, including databases, with little if any guidance provided on how to integrate and weigh the usefulness of information obtained from a variety of online and print resources."[51] And less than a year ago in the pages of *Research Strategies*, Fister noted that much library instruction "stresses skills in knowledge of the complex inventory control systems that make available detailed and sophisticated lists of items available locally or through special order."[52]

BI Questioned from Within

Finally, bibliographic instruction has been questioned from within, initially by librarians with admittedly less to lose by their questioning than those whose careers are devoted to instruction, but nonetheless by thoughtful, sincere librarians. In the lead piece in a *Journal of Academic Librarianship* symposium, Joanne Bessler in 1990 suggested that "service, not instruction, should be the hallmark of the profession" and that "a library that devotes its resources to collections and services valued by its patrons will fare better than one that expends its energy on programs to build better patrons."[53] Although they did not agree fully, she received a sympathetic hearing from the six librarians invited to reply to her piece.

More recently and, perhaps, more infamously, Tom Eadie, a former instruction librarian who has come to doubt the efficacy of instruction, stated his reasons for concluding, even in his article title, that "user education for students does not work."[54] The initial response to Eadie has already been characterized. However, at the 1992 ALA annual conference, the American Library Association User Instruction for Information Literacy Committee offered him another opportunity to state his case and for a panel of experts to respond. The haggling over definitions noted earlier was evident in this symposium; but more significantly, figures such as Hannelore Rader and Michael Gorman and Fred Roecker of Ohio State University conceded that some of Eadie's arguments have merit and pointed to a need for an overall rethinking and critical reassessment of bibliographic instruction.[55] Echoing Fister, Nielsen, and others (including Eadie), Ross LaBaugh has asked, "Isn't it time we focus on the reason BI began—to teach students the *process* of discovery, not its mechanics? Think about it for a minute. How many times do you suppose one class of freshman students has been shown how to use a Wilson index, or search

a card catalog? Doesn't the fact that we have to show them over and over again prove that we have missed the mark in our instruction? It's time to move beyond the 'how' and focus on the 'why.'"[56] At the same time that the focus shifts, the external environment and its forces must be considered.

External Environment

Anyone who believes strongly in the value of BI might come to regret the conventional counsel given to students unfamiliar with a topic—that they go to a specialized encyclopedia and read about it to get a grounding. For if a student studying bibliographic instruction heeded that advice and looked at the article on library instruction in the new *Encyclopedia of Library History*, he or she would read John Mark Tucker's concluding assessment that, "despite their achievements in the pedagogical development of library instruction, academic librarians lagged substantially behind school librarians in the work of integrating library use into institutional objectives."[57] One might also ask to what extent reference service in academe has integrated itself into institutional objectives. Rather than assign blame, it would be much healthier to look forward and reformulate goals for BI and reference, goals that are integrated with institutional goals and purpose.

Jerry Campbell, surely academic librarianship's most provocative and challenging voice at present, has unequivocally stated that "This profession must soon make certain deliberate and fundamental changes or be swept away."[58] Acutely aware of the external forces affecting librarianship, he says, "First, we must focus on the core mission of the profession, namely making it possible for people to get information. This core mission—not its means or methods—demands our full allegiance."[59] Yet in giving that mission our full allegiance, we must concern ourselves somewhat with the means and methods for carrying it out. Campbell focuses on organizational models; our tools are also important.

Importance of Systems Design

Those tools will someday, all should urgently hope, look as primitive to our successors as we consider the tools of early hunters and makers of fires. Our tools need our attention. As Brian Nielsen said in 1986, "we may want in the next few years to transfer some of the energies away from teaching to get more directly involved in systems design ourselves."[60] This has happened, but must happen more broadly and more intensely. Perhaps it has not happened more because librarians are taught more about how to comprehend the workings of complex systems than about how to design systems from scratch. Some have begun to rethink our basic tools, what they should be, and how they should work. There has been considerable discussion about what "super catalogs" should be and do. There also needs to be more discussion of how they should do it. Fortunately, principles which guide the effective design of consumer products are applicable to the design of information systems.

Many consumer products suffer from a malady called "the complexity problem," described in an *Atlantic* article by John Sedgwick and defined by Charles Mauro, a design consultant, as "'a fundamental mismatch between the demands of a technology and the capabilities of its user.'"[61] As his prime exhibit Sedgwick selects a device whose problems illustrate the complexity problem at its extreme—the programmable VCR. Were VCRs simpler to program, a supplemental device that programs them by using simple codes published in *TV Guide* would not be such a popular seller. The designers of this supplemental device have succeeded because they have employed the principles of user-centered design, a process as concerned with how a device will be used and who will use it as with its purpose. And now Magnavox advertises a voice-controlled VCR. These devices demonstrate how user-centered design can "enhance a worker's feeling of control instead of depriving him of it."[62] Their simplicity of operation compared to their predecessors' complexity confirms Mauro's assessment that the presence of a "dense instruction manual...[is] the clearest sign of design failure."[63] VCRs come with instructional manuals whose prose, even if not their size, tends to be dense or even impenetrable. In the face of the complexity of the programming commands, in frustration over the density of printed instructions, and after repeated failures during which they recorded a *Simpsons* rerun rather than the concluding episode of a *Masterpiece Theatre* drama (or vice versa), thousands of VCR owners have simply given up trying to program the devices and instead use them only for playback of rented videos.

These considerations bear on the information systems reference librarians use and BI librarians teach. In 1960, Calvin Mooers posited Mooers' Law, which states, "An information retrieval system will tend not to be used whenever it is more painful and troublesome for a customer to have information than for him not to have it."[64] Thirty-three years later Fister confirmed this in her finding that "undergraduates tended to look for the easiest, least painful way to complete a research project in a timely and satisfactory fashion."[65]

BI as Remedy for System Design Failure

All of this, of course, is just a formulation and formalization of common sense and intuition. Nevertheless, library information systems—both manual and electronic (and architectural)—suffer from the complexity problem and, consequently, in keeping with Mooers' Law, are avoided rather than used or are used inefficiently or ineffectively by many of those who do use them. In other words, they are plagued with systemic problems that adversely affect their users. One can, therefore, view BI as a reasonable, but remedial, response to libraries' systemic failures or deficiencies.

One of the most innovative projects in instruction appears to have taken just this view. In designing the Gateway to Information system, a user-friendly front-end to the catalog and a number of other information sources, the Ohio State University (OSU) Office of Library User Education has worked hard to minimize how-to instruction within and about the system. Reportedly Gateway's "narrative is so easy to follow that patrons need no workshops or instructional pamphlets to succeed"[66] and "only instruction absolutely essential to using the system" appears in it.[67] The reason for this strategy echoes Mauro on product design; Tiefel explains that "Few users will read lengthy instructions and some will not read any instructions at all. Users like to feel in control of their searching and they do not want to read instructions on how to do it."[68]

Similar principles appear to have guided commercial information systems such as America Online. Anyone who has struggled with ftp and the gyrations required, once a document has been successfully ftp'ed, to move the document from a local campus server to one's own microcomputer cannot help but compare that torturous process to the simple one-step, point-and-click downloading America Online offers!

Limits of System Design

User-centered design, however, has limits and "can go only so far to make a new technological system seem natural....Some operations simply have to be learned. For instance, does a computer's UP arrow mean that the text goes up (and the screen down) or the screen goes up (and the text down)? Neither mental model is more intuitive than the other; the correct answer has to be memorized."[69] Good design of a consumer device minimizes the operations that *must* be learned.

In this, too, there are lessons for librarians. We need to identify those things that *must* be learned in order to make effective use of our information systems. But that is not enough. We lack the luxury in most cases of developing entirely new systems and must instead retrofit existing systems to incorporate evolving technological capabilities. At the same time we must also follow OSU's example and heed Nielsen's advice to devote energy to making systems easier to use and thereby minimize the need for compensatory user instruction. As Bechtel has said about catalog design, "it is no longer sufficient to invent new access points, faster machines, and ever more clever uses for keyword searching, Boolean logic, and authority control. In the academic setting the conceptual framework for development, and for teaching the use of the resulting catalog, must grow primarily out of the needs of students and faculty engaged in learning and research."[70] Designing systems in which these needs are paramount, designing systems that don't require instructional manuals, designing systems that give users a feeling of control over their work, will certainly serve our users' needs. And it will equally serve our needs and aspirations, for it will allow us to shift efforts from teaching the mechanical how-to of information systems to higher, more intellectually challenging and longer-term issues such as teaching the need for critical thinking.

Independence, Again

OSU's Gateway encourages users to evaluate the sources it helps them to retrieve. While it undoubtedly affords many OSU students independence, a value Green blessed in 1876, Gateway more importantly affords them freedom. The semantic ambiguity of "independence" is as great as that of "bibliographic instruction;" and it and its opposite—dependence—can conjure up the same extreme images as information and instruction. Independence appears to be a strongly held, albeit ill-defined, value. The "Draft Statement of Values" of the Strategic Visions group formed by Sue Martin of Georgetown University states that "In facilitating access, we value...users' ability to find information independently."[71] One can imagine the scene in the *Publishers Weekly* cartoon where the book shop owner tells the customer in the self-help section, "No! No! No questions! In this section you're on your own."[72] To the extent that reference librarians, especially those with strong beliefs in information delivery, perceive that this is the meaning of "independence," independence is a value that will inevitably clash with their value of service. This problem is avoidable if the value of independence is replaced by the value of freedom.

Freedom is a fundamental value that any librarian at any position on the "information-instruction continuum" can endorse, a value in no way incompatible with individual belief along that continuum. It is a necessary value for both effective reference service and effective

instruction, whether the setting is a library, a classroom, or the end of the proverbial log opposite a brilliant thinker. It is an equally necessary value for critical thinking and the exercise of judgment. The value of "independence" went well with older approaches to BI, which emphasized processes resulting in physical retrieval of materials. Indeed, early writings on BI extolled the value of the open stacks arrangement as a means of giving students independence and, thereby, of acquainting them with books. Thus the value of "independence" is inextricably linked with physical retrieval of materials, hardly a high-level cognitive skill. For a modern BI world more concerned with instilling the skills required to make informed judgments of information than with teaching identification and retrieval routines, independence falls short as a core value.

Two years ago, I took the bold step of embellishing Ranganathan's immortal Five Laws of Library Science by positing a Sixth Law: "Every reader his freedom."[73] This law, articulating the centrality of the value of freedom, reinforces Mary Reichel's reminder that "our vision needs to remain on the individual user." The Sixth Law allows a librarian latitude along the "information-instruction continuum" in responding to individual needs as appropriate to each situation. For its fullest exercise freedom requires that a patron possess critical thinking skills. Whether or not they profess it as a goal, students come to college to develop and hone these skills.

Critical Thinking

McCormick has described critical thinkers as those who "identify main issues; recognize underlying assumptions; evaluate evidence; evaluate authorities, people, publications; recognize bias, emotional appeals, relevant facts, propaganda, generalities, language problems; question whether facts support conclusions; question the adequacy of data; see relationships among ideas; know their own attitudes and blind spots; and suspend judgment until the search is ended."[74] In light of Stoan's and Fister's findings about the circularity and iterative nature of the research process and the back-and-forth relationships among information seeking, reading, and writing in that process, one might question the validity of the final characteristic in McCormick's list, but surely not the others. Freedom, with its implicit, inherent requirement for individual responsibility, is a value much more intimately allied to these mental faculties than is independence.

Freedom implies the need and responsibility to exercise judgment; independence could also imply this, but in many minds probably does not. Anyone who has been the parent of a teenager can appreciate the difference. It is vital, even though they lack independence during those years, that teens develop freedom and its concomitant responsibility to make informed decisions. Freedom to make critical decisions must be a constant in users' interactions with the library and its information sources and pathways. Users' independence will inevitably vary greatly from individual to individual, and from situation to situation for a given individual. But freedom is far more important than independence and must be absolute for every user. This is consonant with the changed focus of BI, for as Reichel has said,

> The goals of library instruction have moved from a pragmatic approach of teaching- or learning-specific skills for finding and using access tools to a global approach of emphasizing the value of finding information and utilizing it. A part of this shift is that evaluation of information has become a larger part of library instruction goals. Another part of this shift is that librarians are explicitly focusing on the value of information literacy as giving learners more control over decision making.[75]

This sounds a good deal like the purpose of user-centered design for consumer products. The increasingly user-friendly nature of information systems simplifies the source-identification process, gives library users the control Reichel commends, and allows them to focus their time and energies on the all-important assessment of information rather than on its identification or retrieval.

By endorsing and sharing the value of freedom, by allowing the value of independence to fade, librarians, regardless of their beliefs about the relative importance of information or instruction, can put users' needs first and foremost and develop practice that will serve those needs effectively. This will preserve, indeed enhance, users' freedom. Changes in both BI and reference ought to provide fertile soil in which the value of freedom will flourish.

Resolution of the Tension, Convergence of the Twain

The apparent conflict between information and instruction may seem as irresolvable as the preordained conflict Thomas Hardy saw between the roles of the *Titanic* and that most famous of Atlantic icebergs. In his "The Convergence of the Twain," he described their fateful meeting thus:

> And as the smart ship grew
> In stature, grace, and hue,
> In shadowy silent distance grew the Iceberg too.

> Alien they seemed to be:
> No mortal eye could see
> The intimate welding of their later history,
> Or sign that they were bent
> By paths coincident
> On being anon twin halves of one august event,
> Till the Spinner of Years
> Said "Now!" And each one hears,
> And consummation comes, and jars two hemispheres.[76]

It isn't clear what icebergs loom in the information sea; however, one cannot avoid uneasy feelings and foreboding premonitions that both the good ship *Reference* and the good ship *BI* are headed towards one. Whether it is commercial information services and their user-friendly interfaces that enhance users' sense of control and power, whether it is clinging to archaic values rather than adopting others more in tune with the times, or whether it is some other force, both reference and BI must surely change to avoid a titanic collision with one of those forces. As Jerry Campbell has noted, sounding a prophetic warning while providing reassurance, "I do not mean to imply that our role is in jeopardy; it is only to be determined whether we will continue to play the role."[77]

Both reference and BI need a strategy to navigate these uncharted waters safely. The best strategy will be to capitalize on clearly emerging trends in both academic librarianship and society at large. Automated information systems are clearly reducing and simplifying what users must learn in order to identify information sources relevant to their needs. More work needs to be done and it would be premature to view without at least a tad of irony the *Chronicle of Higher Education* cartoon in which one extraterrestrial says to another as they cruise past our planet in their spacecraft, "'I've finally accessed something that I hope has a simple, straightforward, orderly, easy-to-understand and user-friendly approach to all of their knowledge, They call it the "Internet".'"[78] Yet OSU's Gateway demonstrates the validity of this hope and, as Brian Nielsen has said of Gateway, "I felt like I was seeing the future, or at least a piece of it, and it worked!"[79] Indeed it does for, as Tiefel has reported, "Gateway had an impact on both students and library staff. The Undergraduate Library...experienced a...30 percent drop in instructional questions, a 62 percent drop in questions about the online catalog...and a 45 percent drop in directional questions."[80] Tools such as OSU's Gateway remind us that "In a little book of 1911 entitled *An Introduction to Mathematics*, the English philosopher and scientist Alfred North Whitehead pointed out that 'civilization advances by extending the number of important operations we can perform without thinking about them.'"[81] This is the task Jerry

Campbell has challenged access engineers to carry out in libraries; and both reference and BI librarians should hope for its speedy completion, for it serves their shared goal of helping users find, judge, and use information.

It may be easier for the BI community to shift its energies in this direction, since the momentum—at least regarding concepts—among its members seems to be greater. There are, however, leaders in the reference field pushing things along in promising directions. Virginia Massey-Burzio, designer of the radical changes at Brandeis and Johns Hopkins, has said that "The traditional reference desk looks like a service that does not expect to be taken seriously."[82] Thelma Friedes has said that it "conveys an implicit promise never to let the reader go unserved, but it also pegs the service at a low level."[83] The approach adopted at Brandeis and Hopkins dovetails nicely with projects such as Gateway and furthers their goals. As systems such as Gateway assume more and more of the burden of identifying relevant information sources, services such as the Hopkins research consultation allow reference librarians to focus on higher-level skills such as those enumerated by McCormick. The twain, happily, is converging, not colliding.

A Shared Value, a Common Goal

Reference or BI might suffer a titanic collision in the future, but it should not be with the other. More than a decade ago, Nielsen described the "competition between those who advocate the intermediary role and those who advocate the teaching role" as "unfortunate and unnecessary."[84] Now it should end, the two brought together in the shared value of freedom and the common goal of helping users make the best possible use of information sources by judging them critically. If our user populations are made up of information-literate individuals and of individuals who are systematically developing the skills associated with information literacy, what shape will our programs take? Surely there will be ever less of the sort of instruction that Eadie considers questionable and more of the sort of instruction (if that is even the appropriate term for it) imbedded in systems inspired by the success of Gateway and sleek commercial services. As McCormick has said, "If we set goals which describe intellectual curiosity and critical thinking as values in an educated person, we have to figure out ways to move students toward those goals by giving them the *experience* of thinking while they are in an educational setting."[85] Gateway's ever-present options to retrieve evaluative information and the research consultation's inherent opportunities to question assumptions and help students clarify their thinking both further this common goal.

To the extent that students are information-literate, they will know when they can rely on information systems and when they need to seek individual consultations. In either environment, the needs to think critically and to evaluate will be reinforced continually.

We cannot, however, do this alone. Fortunately, freedom as a value and critical thinking as a goal—a value and goal that BI and reference ought to share—are already fundamental to the institutions we serve. If they were not, our efforts would be doomed and we would be able to identify the iceberg that sank us as a titanic lack of synchronicity of goals and values between librarians and the academy at large. Working alone, academic librarians' efforts to educate students to be critical thinkers capable of recognizing and describing their information needs and of judging information's value would be as futile as if our colleagues in public libraries attempted to solve the homeless problem on their own. We need not worry, however, *if* we successfully communicate our interests to faculty and *if* we demonstrate to them that we have something new to offer and that our goals and theirs are similar; for the environment is changing in ways that make collaboration between librarians and faculty mutually beneficial and especially beneficial to the students whom both they and we serve.

John Casteen, president of the University of Virginia, recently said that the electronic revolution now underway means that the "division between classroom and library is no longer relevant;"[86] and "Stanford University's President Gerhard Casper agrees that the latest technology will transform both the content and delivery of higher education to an extent not yet fully understood or appreciated on most campuses."[87] Surely librarians have much to offer and can help assure that this transformation furthers the value of freedom and the development of critical thinking skills.

Impact of Societal Trends

As we collaborate with faculty and computer wizards on that transformation, we can bring to bear not just our experience, but also our appreciation of trends in the wider world. One trend futurist Faith Popcorn calls 99 Lives is definitely universal. We all feel pressed for time and have too many things to do. In response to this, Popcorn says, "The watchword for the streamlined '90s will be multi-function. Products that accomplish two or three things at once, or that allow you to get more than one job done at a time."[88] Our emerging super catalogs with access to multiple databases typify this trend. Popcorn, almost outlining in neon the importance of critical thinking skills, says that "The biggest technological achievement of the 99

Lives era will be a way to *edit down* all the information that assaults us daily."[89] That's exactly what our services, at their best, are intended to help people do!

Shared Task for Reference and BI of the Future

The tasks for reference and BI are clear:

- To identify those things that users *must* learn in order to use our libraries;

- To eliminate as many barriers to their use of our libraries as we possibly can;

- To redesign our systems and service delivery mechanisms to minimize that which they must learn;

- To form alliances with faculty and computer center personnel to devise information systems that will help develop students' critical thinking skills;

- To supplement these systems with reference service that allows individual students and librarians to collaborate on fulfilling students' information needs;

- To reallocate time and resources to developing and improving information systems; and

- To make sure the services offered are in sync with major societal trends and respond to users' expressed needs.

And we must do these things together.

Let me, therefore, add one more item to that rather daunting list of shared tasks reference and BI must do. It would be helpful to find a new name, or at least a new, synthetic definition for the services we should provide—not a new name for an ACRL section, but a new name for a new form of library service that no longer suffers from the bifurcation between reference and instruction that has plagued practice and hobbled theory since the time of Green and before. Although she was arguing strongly for the instructional side of the information-instruction debate, Hannelore Rader's words from 1980 apply:

> the services provided by reference librarians vary greatly, based on their library's and their own professional objectives. Some reference librarians may emphasize the teaching function of reference work; others, the function of providing information. This is unfortunate, because such variance will ultimately confuse the users as to what to expect from reference services. This, in turn, will complicate the communication process between user and reference librarian, and may also lead to increased hesitancy on the part of the user to ask for assistance from the reference librarian. Such complications can be avoided if reference librarians exhibit consistent behavior in their dealings with users and follow clearly stated objectives for reference service.[90]

One could not ask for worthier objectives for either BI or reference service than Ranganathan's "Every reader his book" and "Save the time of the reader," supplemented by the Sixth Law, "Every reader his freedom."

Both reference and BI, however, are burdened with historical baggage that they must toss overboard. Reference needs to get rid of all-purpose reference desks and organizational patterns that militate against consultative, collaborative work with patrons—work that encourages the development and exercise of critical thinking skills. BI needs to get rid of its rock-hard belief in independence in favor of a belief in freedom. We need a single service that furthers the university's broader educational goals, that allows for dependence when individuals are not comfortable with independence, that zealously protects users' freedom to make decisions, that helps them learn what they *must* know to identify and retrieve information, and that encourages them to apply critical thinking skills to their use of information. Both reference and BI must change and the twain must converge. As Barbara Wittkopf has said, "the more libraries change, the more BI must change. We must learn to respond to the forces of change rather than fight them, lest we get carried out to sea."[91] Good advice, especially considering that ominous icebergs lurk out there.

NOTES

1. Samuel S. Green, "Personal Relations Between Librarians and Readers," *American Library Journal* 1 (30 November 1876): 74-81.

2. (19 April 1994) "Help." V122J8ZB@UBVMS. BITNET e-mail to LIBREF-L@KENTVM.BITNET], [Online]. Emphasis in original.

3. Green, "Personal Relations Between Librarians and Readers," 75-76.

4. Green, 75.

5. Green, 79.

6. Green, 80.

7. Justin Winsor, "College Libraries as Aids to Instruction: The College Library," in *User Instruction in Academic Libraries: A Century of Selected Readings*, comp. by Larry L. Hardesty, John P. Schmitt, and John Mark Tucker (Metuchen, NJ: Scarecrow Press, 1986), 8.

8. Frances L. Hopkins, "A Century of Bibliographic Instruction: The Historical Claim to Professional and Academic Legitimacy," *College and Research Libraries* 43 (May 1982): 192-198.

9. Kenneth B. Berger, Johannah Sherrer, and Rich Hines, "Rethinking Information Access," in *Rethinking Reference in Academic Libraries*, ed. by Anne Grodzins Lipow (Berkeley, CA: Library Solutions Press, 1993), 127-33; Karen Williams, "A Response to 'Rethinking Information Access,'" in *Rethinking Reference in Academic Libraries*, 135-137; James Rettig, "To BI or Not to BI? That Is the Question, " in *Rethinking Reference in Academic Libraries*, 139-151.

10. Roma M. Harris, "Bibliographic Instruction in Public Libraries: A Question of Philosophy," *RQ* 29 (Fall 1989): 92-98.

11. Harris, "Bibliographic Instruction in Public Libraries," 98.

12. Roma M. Harris, "Bibliographic Instruction: The Views of Academic, Special, and Public Librarians," *College and Research Libraries* 53 (May 1992): 249-256.

13. Harris, "Bibliographic Instruction: The Views," 253.

14. Harris, "Bibliographic Instruction: The Views," 255.

15. Harris, "Bibliographic Instruction in Public Libraries," 96-97.

16. Lawrence J. McCrank, "Information Literacy: A Bogus Bandwagon?" *Library Journal* 116 (1 May 1991): 40.

17. James I. Wyer, *Reference Work: A Textbook for Students of Library Work and Librarians* (Chicago: American Library Association, 1930), 6-13.

18. Samuel Rothstein, "Reference Service: The New Dimension in Librarianship," *College and Research Libraries* 22 (January 1961): 14.

19. Rothstein.

20. Harris, "Bibliographic Instruction: The Views," 253.

21. Elizabeth Frick, "Teaching Information Structure: Turning Dependent Researchers into Self-Teachers," in

Theories of Bibliographic Education: Designs for Teaching, ed. by Cerise Oberman and Katina Strauch (New York: R.R. Bowker, 1982), 205.

22. Frick.

23. Connie Miller and Patricia Tegler, "In Pursuit of Windmills: Librarians and the Determination to Instruct," *Reference Librarian*, no. 18 (Summer 1987): 122.

24. Tom Eadie, "Immodest Proposals: User Instruction for Students Does Not Work," *Library Journal* 115 (15 October 1990): 43.

25. Wanda K. Johnston, et al., "Immodest Rebuttal: A Community College Perspective," *Research Strategies* 11 (Spring 1993): 101.

26. Constance A. Mellon, "Information Problem-Solving: A Developmental Approach to Library Instruction," in *Theories of Bibliographic Education: Designs for Teaching*, ed. by Cerise Oberman and Katina Strauch (New York: R.R. Bowker, 1982), 80.

27. Frick, 194.

28. Barbara Wittkopf, "Making Our Library Users Increasingly Independent," *Research Strategies* 11 (Summer 1993): 122-123.

29. Ross T. LaBaugh, "BI Is a Proper Noun," *Research Strategies* 10 (Winter 1992): 32.

30. Cartoon, *New Yorker* (18 April 1994): 66.

31. John Updike, *Brazil* (New York: Alfred A. Knopf, 1994), 100.

32. William Miller, "What's Wrong with Reference: Coping with Success and Failure at the Reference Desk," *American Libraries* 15 (May 1984): 303-306, 321-322.

33. Charles A. Bunge, "Potential and Reality at the Reference Desk: Reflections on a 'Return to the Field,'" *Journal of Academic Librarianship* 10 (July 1984): 130.

34. Barbara J. Ford, "Reference beyond (and without) the Reference Desk," *College and Research Libraries* 47 (September 1987): 491-494.

35. "The Future of Reference," *College and Research Libraries News* 49 (October 1988): 578-589; "The Future of Reference II," *College and Research Libraries News* 50 (October 1989): 780-799; "The Future of Reference III," *College and Research Libraries News* 51 (December 1990): 1,044-1,058; "The Future of Reference IV," *College and Research Libraries News* 53 (September 1992): 508-514.

36. Virginia Massey-Burzio, "Reference Encounters of a Different Kind: A Symposium," *Journal of Academic Librarianship* 18 (November 1992): 276-286.

37. Jerry D. Campbell, "Shaking the Conceptual Foundations of Reference: A Perspective," *Reference Services Review* 20:4 (Winter 1992): 29-35; Jerry D. Campbell, "In Search of New Foundations for Reference," in *Rethinking Reference in Academic Libraries*, ed. by Anne Grodzins Lipow (Berkeley, CA: Library Solutions Press, 1993), 3-14.

38. Mona McCormick, "Critical Thinking and Library Instruction," *RQ* 22 (Summer 1983): 339.

39. Brian Nielsen, "Teacher or Intermediary: Alternative Professional Models for the Information Age," *College and Research Libraries* 43 (May 1982): 188.

40. Joan Bechtel, "Developing and Using the Online Catalog to Teach Critical Thinking," *Information Technology and Libraries* 7 (March 1988): 31.

41. Mary Reichel, "Twenty-Five Year Retrospective: The Importance of What We Do," *RQ* 33 (Fall 1993): 30.

42. Karen A. Becker, "Individual Library Research Clinics for College Freshmen," *Research Strategies* 11 (Fall 1993): 202-210.

43. Stephen K. Stoan, "Research and Library Skills: An Analysis and Interpretation," *College and Research Libraries* 45 (March 1984): 99-109.

44. Stephen K. Stoan, "Research and Information Retrieval among Academic Researchers: Implications for Library Instruction," *Library Trends* 39 (Winter 1991): 248.

45. Stoan, 253.

46. Barbara Fister, "The Research Processes of Undergraduate Students," *Journal of Academic Librarianship* 18 (July 1992): 169.

47. Barbara Fister, "Teaching the Rhetorical Dimensions of Research," *Research Strategies* 11 (Fall 1993): 218.

48. Fister, "Teaching," 212.

49. Barbara Valentine, "Undergraduate Research Behavior: Using Focus Groups to Generate Theory," *Journal of Academic Librarianship* 19 (November 1993): 320.

50. Fister, "The Research Processes," 163.

51. Virginia Tiefel, "The Gateway to Information: The Future of Information Access...Today," *Library Hi Tech* 11 (1993): 57.

52. Fister, "Teaching," 212.

53. Joanne Bessler, "Do Library Patrons Know What's Good for Them?" *Journal of Academic Librarianship* 16 (May 1990): 77.

54. Eadie, 42.

55. Barbara MacAdam, et al., "Redefining BI for a New Information Environment: A Symposium," *Research Strategies* 10 (Summer 1992): 104-121.

56. LaBaugh, "BI Is a Proper Noun," 39; italics in original.

57. John Mark Tucker, "Library Instruction," in *Encyclopedia of Library History*, ed. by Wayne A. Wiegand and Donald G. Davis, Jr. (New York: Garland Publishing, 1994), 366.

58. Jerry D. Campbell, "Choosing to Have a Future," *American Libraries* 24 (June 1993): 560.

59. Campbell, "Choosing."

60. Brian Nielsen, "What They Say They Do and What They Do: Assessing Online Catalog Use Instruction through Transaction Monitoring," *Information Technology and Libraries* 5 (March 1986): 33.

61. John Sedgwick, "The Complexity Problem," *Atlantic* 271 (March 1993): 96.

62. Sedgwick, 103.

63. Sedgwick, 98.

64. Calvin N. Mooers, "Mooers' Law, or, Why Some Retrieval Systems Are Used and Others Are Not," *American Documentation* 11 (July 1960): 204.

65. Fister, "Teaching," 302

66. Tiefel, 58.

67. Tiefel, 62.

68. Tiefel, 62.

69. Sedgwick, 104.

70. Bechtel, 32.

71. Strategic Vision Steering Committee, "A Strategic Vision for Librarianship," in *Rethinking Reference in Academic Libraries*, ed. by Anne Grodzins Lipow (Berkeley, CA: Library Solutions Press, 1993), 199.

72. Mort Gerberg, "Out of Line," [cartoon] *Publishers Weekly* 239 (3 February 1992): 10.

73. James Rettig, "Self-Determining Information Seekers," *RQ* 32 (Winter 1992): 162.

74. McCormick, 340.

75. Reichel, 31.

76. Thomas Hardy, "The Convergence of the Twain," stanzas VIII-XI, in *The Variorum Edition of the Complete Poems of Thomas Hardy*, ed. by James Gibson (London: Macmillan, 1979), 307.

77. Campbell, "Choosing," 562.

78. Cartoon, *Chronicle of Higher Education* XL (16 March 1994): B3.

79. Brian Nielsen, "Roll Your Own Interface: Public Access to CD-ROMs," *Database* 12 (December 1989): 105.

80. Tiefel, 61.

81. Charles Scribner, Jr., *In the Web of Ideas* (New York: Charles Scribner's Sons, 1993), 89.

82. Virgina Massey-Burzio, "Rethinking the Reference Desk," in *Rethinking Reference in Academic Libraries*, ed. by Anne Grodzins Lipow (Berkeley, CA: Library Solutions Press, 1993), 43.

83. Thelma Freides, "Current Trends in Academic Libraries," *Library Trends* 31 (Winter 1983): 467.

84. Nielsen, "Teacher or Intermediary," 188.

85. McCormick, 341; italics in original.

86. John Casteen, Welcoming remarks, meeting of Virginia academic librarians, Charlottesville, VA, 25 April 1994.

87. Robert L. Jacobson, "The Coming Revolution," *Chronicle of Higher Education* XL (27 April 1994): A26.

88. Faith Popcorn, *The Popcorn Report* (New York: Doubleday, 1991), 83.

89. Popcorn, 98; italics in original.

90. Hannelore B. Rader, "Reference Services as a Teaching Function," *Library Trends* 29 (Summer 1980): 101.

91. Barbara Wittkopf, "Change," *Research Startegies* 11 (Summer 1993): 59.

REGENERATING A LIBRARY INSTRUCTION PROGRAM: ONE SURVIVOR'S EXPERIENCE: OR, BROKEN FIELD RUNNING AT TWILIGHT

Cheryl LaGuardia

The Set Up

"Regenerating a Library Instruction Program: One Survivor's Experience: or, Broken Field Running at Twilight." When I told a couple of colleagues what I proposed to call my talk here today, I got unmixed reactions: they all thought it was terrible. Too wordy, too ambiguous (the chemistry librarian said something to the effect of, "Just like a humanist!"), too implicit, too explicit (the unmixed reactions were uniformly critical, but not necessarily consistent), too dry, too flippant, and what in God's name was I talking about, anyway?

I was stunned by their collective response. It seemed so obvious; how much clearer could I make it? In two short lines I'd spelled out what I'd spent the last four years of my life doing; not only spelled it out, but characterized it as closely as I could to a familiar experience (familiar, that is, to kids and military personnel everywhere: running pell mell over rutted unfamiliar ground in dim, uncertain light). Think about it. Does that description sound familiar to any of you, as instruction librarians?

Just in case I haven't been explicit enough (no matter what those pre-talk critics may have said), I did not scamper eagerly into the field of library instruction.

LaGuardia was assistant head of reference for library instruction at University of California-Santa Barbara. She is now coordinator of the Electronic Teaching Center at Harvard University, Cambridge, Massachusetts.

I did not even enter it willingly. I didn't exactly kick and scream; it was more like passive resisters going limp as they're carried into the paddy wagon: I was dragged into the instruction fray.

What happened was this: a few years ago I was offered the chance to be head of data services (as it was then called) at the University of California at Santa Barbara (UCSB) Library by my then-boss, who had decided it was time to parole me out of interlibrary loan (where I had spent several quite exhilarating years reorganizing, updating, and automating operations to the point where I was memorizing the OCLC and RLIN library symbols and reciting them in a litany as I went to sleep at night). I was excited at the prospect of digging even further into computers—this was at a time, after all, when online was just entering information hyperspace—so I was ready to jump at the opportunity.

Having waved the electronic carrot under my nose and gotten the hoped-for salivating response from me, my boss delivered the coup de grace, the flaw in the golden ring: "Okay, you get data services, but you've got to take THE CLASSES with it."

BOOM! The boot dropped directly on my head. Eeuugggchh...the classes...the dreaded classes. Two credit-bearing courses, one called "Library Skills," the other "Library Research," that had been taught for years and years and years, unvaryingly, by a small cadre of librarians. The library skills class was workbook-based, while library research met twice weekly and was a series of deadly lectures. "Teaching" skills was considered mindless drudgery by most of the reference librarians—after all, there was no teaching involved, just going over with students the logistics of where to buy the workbook and how much it cost the first day of "class." Library research had devolved into an incredibly labor-intensive exercise in which one librarian devoted approximately 10 to 15 hours per week of his or her time to teaching the intricacies of bibliography-building to two or three students per term.

The classes. I'd have to take the classes. I wouldn't be teaching them all, but I'd be administering the program. But I'd also get data services, wonderful, lovely, exciting data services. What to do? What to do?

It was a foregone conclusion what I'd do, of course. I'd given everything I had to give to interlibrary loan, and I wanted to investigate new electronic terrain. That meant taking data services on. And the classes must inevitably follow.

"Oh, yes," my boss added after I'd verbally signed on the dotted line, "I want you to rewrite the skills class this summer so we can teach an entirely new course this fall."

Kapow! The other boot (they do come in pairs, after all) landed neatly on my noggin.

I would have backed out of the deal right then and there, but for the fact I could see data services passing before my very eyes: keyboards, monitors, DIALOG blue sheets, CD-ROMs galore—visions of them skimmed past my blurred vision in a wide, high-reaching arc, spinning further and further out of reach, till I heard myself saying, in a voice that sounded very, very far away, "Ah... Okay. Well, I'll do that then."

That was the last thing I remembered clearly for a long time; I believe I passed into reference never-never land for the remainder of the term, because I didn't really come to until mid-summer, when I handed the reins of ILL over to my successor and the boss, said, "So, what are your plans for the new course?" It started to hit me then: I was going into the library instruction business.

The Plan?

I, of course, had no plan. I was not exactly terrified of getting up in front of a class (not exactly), but I had little or no experience doing so. I never have been (and daresay I never will be) a pedagogically-formal person, and the thought of attacking a stack of books on educational theory in order to rewrite the skills class *did* terrify me: I think I was traumatized by an educational theory at an early academic age.

Being the daughter of an accountant, however, I decided to tote up whatever assets I might have on my side of the balance sheet. I had been a reference librarian for over ten years, having worked in several college and university libraries during that period of time, and having done some of all kinds of reference:

arts and humanities, social science, science, government documents, business.

Having worked steadily at reference desks ever since I got my MLS, giving public service to undergraduates, graduates, faculty, and community users, I had considerable firsthand knowledge of the kinds of questions that came up most frequently and the kinds of skills patrons needed to attain in order to answer those questions. So I did have a fairly broad grasp of what might be covered in a syllabus (and it took me some time getting comfortable with using that word, I can tell you).

More than anything else, perhaps, I had some keen personal motivations to come up with an effective skills course. Things were getting incredibly hectic at the desk as there were fewer of us around to provide service. We were undergoing the first of several early retirement programs that have, over the past four years, cut the number of librarians at UCSB from 62 to 30. We went from routinely having three people at busy times at the desk to having a maximum of two there (now providing consolidated main reference desk service with the previously separately-staffed government publications desk service).

At the same time we were being radically downsized, we were bringing up our new online public access catalog, as well as new article databases on the systemwide online union catalog. Our patrons were mostly not computer-literate: most shunned touching a keyboard like it was the plague. I'd been fortunate enough to enjoy some success in helping people overcome some of their computer phobia one-on-one at the reference desk, so I had some confidence about my potential to teach basic computer searching skills effectively to students. What was needed, however, was mass instruction.

We reference librarians felt in desperate need of reaching large numbers of the information-retrieval uninformed at a time, We were certain that the effectiveness of our desk service would be improved if we could reach a large slice of the undergraduate population at UCSB in classes and teach them to fend for themselves for their basic information-seeking needs.

The library skills classes could be just the ticket to reaching large numbers: we taught ten sections of the class per term, three terms per year. With luck we could "get at" nearly 1,000 students a year. It would be one way in which we could cope with rising enrollments amid staff number declines.

On the debit side of the balance sheet, I had no teaching experience to speak of, absolutely no experience developing a course curriculum, and had been given very little direction on what to teach. That was one (rather scary) way of looking at the assignment I'd been handed. On the other hand...I had been given very little direction on what to teach...that could mean (at least if I decided to look at it this way) that I had been given carte blanche.

Carte blanche. For the first time in my entire professional life, I was being given carte blanche. Admittedly, it was being proffered more as a challenge—"Here's what we want—a class—just do it"—than as a gift, but which of us really expects to find a gift handed to us in the workplace these days? (Anyone who answers yes to that question please come up and see me afterwards—I want the name of your library and the titles of any job vacancies you may have....)

It's hard to describe the alternating feelings of overwhelming responsibility and exhilarating freedom that I experienced that summer as I was rewriting the library skills class. The responsibility outweighed the freedom at first, as I tossed and turned over the knowledge that whatever I came up with, we'd be offering it as a one-credit course in an ARL Library in the fall. Since I was the only one working on the rewrite at this point, it would be pretty clear who had really messed up if the class was unteachable, unworkable, or unfathomable. Oddly enough, it was the full realization that it was my goose cooking in the summer oven that made me stop worrying about the outcome and concentrate instead on what I thought undergraduate students needed to learn. It was, after all, my goose.

I decided to view the problem from the point of view of a reference librarian at the desk, naturally enough. What were the greatest needs from my point of view? What had I learned was needed at the desk?

A crash course in computer skills was high on the list, for a number of reasons. As I mentioned earlier, we were bringing up our NOTIS catalog, as well as a number of enhanced article index databases on our systemwide union catalog, so anyone using the library pretty much had to master the rudiments of these two systems, at least. We were also installing CD-ROMs at an alarming rate: the government had jumped on the bandwagon and was offering scads of titles only on CD-ROM, and we'd made a financial commitment to the technology by cancelling many print subscriptions for which we'd obtained disk copies.

I should note that our user population was largely undergraduates from California. The mandated mission of the University of California is to educate the top 12 1/2 percent of the state's graduating high school senior classes. This is becoming more and more difficult as funding to the university diminishes. It is especially difficult to bring these students up to speed in library research, because of a little phenomenon that occurred a few years ago called Proposition 13, which, in effect, eliminated elementary and high school librarian positions from California public schools.

What that translated into in very real terms in the UCSB library classroom was that, in response to my usual questions to freshmen classes, "How many of you have used *Readers' Guide*" or "How many of you have used a card catalog before?" one or two hands went up at most. These were kids at a university who had *no* library skills. And here we were throwing two online catalogs and hundreds of different CD-ROMs at them.

So the computer systems were high on my list for things to include on my syllabus. We were about to close the last remaining portions of the card catalog that summer, so I decided *not* to cover card catalog use in-depth (there went a good half of the content of the previous library skills class: filing order had filled ten pages of the workbook). Since neither of the online catalogs had keyword searching capability, I was resigned to the idea that somehow we would have to discuss Library of Congress Subject Headings (LCSH) with these naive souls, and I cringed at the thought (remember that their library skills were non-existent, for the most part). Since many indexes were not yet represented in any electronic format, I also put printed indexes on my list.

Computers, LCSH, printed indexes, no card catalog. Not a very detailed syllabus, is it? I was still groping around for the unifying concept that would bring the class together and make it gel somehow in my mind. And the summer was moving on apace.

Then Comes a Raison D'Etre

Then one day at the reference desk, I was working with a freshman who wanted to find a book. So I brought her over to a PEGASUS terminal and showed her the welcome screen, which looks like what you see in figure 1 (or at least this is how it looked to me):

I'd like you all to take a good look at this screen. Nothing very remarkable about it, is there, from a librarian's point of view? Take a good look at it: there's about to be a test in ten to 15 seconds. Okay? Now, I take the transparency away, and what can you tell me that you saw?

PAUSE FOR ANSWERS

Fine, that's what we, the librarians, see. But as I worked with this student, who was pretty representative of most of the students I'm working with every day—she wasn't unusually ill-informed by comparison—it became clear that she wasn't seeing on that screen what I was seeing.

```
┌─────────────────────────────────────────────────────────────────────────┐
│ ┌─────────────────────────────────────────────────────────────────────┐ │
│ │              Pegasus                    Davidson Library              │ │
│ │                                         Introduction                  │ │
│ ├─────────────────────────────────────────────────────────────────────┤ │
│ │  The UCSB Library Catalog and Information System                      │ │
│ │                                                                       │ │
│ │  Use the following command:    To search by:     Examples:           │ │
│ │       A=                           Author          A=hull gloria      │ │
│ │       T=                           Title           T=gone with the wind│ │
│ │       S=                           Subject         S=fog--coastal     │ │
│ │       K=                           Keyword         K=climate          │ │
│ │       C=                           Call Number     C=JK40s S42        │ │
│ │                                                                       │ │
│ │                                                                       │ │
│ │  For examples and more information on searching the Catalog, press<return>│ │
│ │  ------------------------------------------ + Page 1 of 2 ----------------│ │
│ │  STArt over    Enter search command              <F8> FORward page    │ │
│ │                                                                       │ │
│ │   NEXT COMMAND:                                                       │ │
│ │                                                                       │ │
│ ├─────────────────────────────────────────────────────────────────────┤ │
│ │                                                                       │ │
│ └─────────────────────────────────────────────────────────────────────┘ │
└─────────────────────────────────────────────────────────────────────────┘
```

Figure 1: Sample Library OPAC Screen: What the Librarian Sees

For one thing, she had a hard time even reading the screen, she was so busy clenching her fists into white knuckle mounds whenever I suggested she type something at the keyboard. And as the reference interview progressed, I found myself defining, redefining, and re-redefining the words I was trying to use to explain how the system worked. Pressing ENTER took her several tries to master, for example. After we'd sweated it out at the terminal and she had a couple of call numbers to look up, I asked her if she'd worked with computers much. "All the time," she replied. This surprised me no end, given the difficulty she'd had maneuvering through an author search, and she saw my surprise. "I've got a Mac," she explained, "and it's a lot different from this."

That was my first real lesson in looking at our computers from an outsider's viewpoint. By this time I was starting to review CD-ROMs regularly, and I began to look differently at what I saw on the search screens every time I loaded a new product. Now I was asking myself, was this something in which a novice with little or no computer knowledge could find his or her way around? Or was the CD-ROM designed for use by someone with a librarian's level of bibliographic

knowledge? My reviewer's eye became more critical, more consumer-oriented.

I was dealing with the issue of user instruction on a day-to-day basis myself: I had a real, vested interest in finding the systems that weren't labor-intensive to use or to teach the use of, because there were fewer and fewer librarians at UCSB as the months went by, and I could reach only so many people at the desk. The bottom line was clear to me as a practicing librarian: were my students going to be able to use CD-ROMs on their own or was I going to have to spoon-feed the disks' use to them? If I have to teach them the basics in using a disk one-on-one, the product is simply unacceptable. Period.

So over the rest of that summer of the library skills rewrite, as I worked with students at the desk trying to help them get accustomed to the new OPAC, I usually asked them what they saw on that same computer screen when first they approached it. Figure 2 is an approximation of the results of my informal survey:

Most of these are actual phrases quoted to me by students, particularly that one at the top, which came from a dispirited (and well-read) political science major

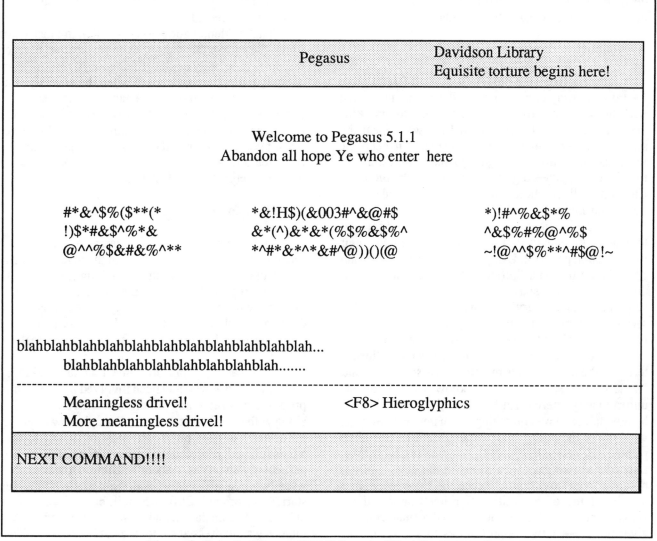

Figure 2: Sample Library OPAC Screen: What the Patron Sees

who'd been struggling for weeks on his own before "giving up" and finally approaching the desk for help.

Looking at the systems now as the students did, rather than as librarians do, I decided to give myself an assignment: to walk into the library not as a reference librarian, but as a new student, assuming that I knew nothing about using anything at all. I decided that for this assignment, I would be a freshman who had a five-page sociology paper on environmental racism to do (in record time, of course, since I wanted this to be a fairly realistic assignment).

Why a paper on environmental racism? Because I wanted something that would require that I use a number of different service points and collections, and in my library that topic takes you all over the map.

I started my "research" early one morning, walking through the library as a sort of split personality, knowing, as a reference librarian, where all I had

to go to get information for this paper but wondering, as that *tabula rasa* freshman, how in heaven's name I was ever going to find anything.

The number of bewildering things I encountered in my student persona was truly overwhelming. Just finding the reference desk, which at that time was located on the second floor of the library near none of the entrances, was a treasure hunt. As I wandered from desk to desk, and through collection after collection, I was amazed that students ever found anything without a reference librarian at their elbows: this was a building with three different wings with anywhere from two to eight floors, over two million volumes, and over 22,000 journal subscriptions, none of them arranged as you might expect to find them (e.g., at your fingertips). In student mode I got more and more frustrated as the morning wore on, but as a course designer I got more excited as a picture of the class began to emerge clearly in my mind.

A Syllabus

Starting from the student's frame of reference, I sat down at my computer that afternoon and drafted what became the syllabus for the revised library skills class. It wrote itself, because all I did was repeat the steps any undergraduate would have to take to get basic information on this issue, going from main reference to sciences-engineering reference, to black studies to Chicano studies to the serials desk, even special collections, and more.

The course goal was now clearly defined for me: to enable students to find the basic materials for their first research papers at UCSB. As a reference librarian I had found material literally all over the library. So the course would start with a tour of the building, stopping at all the service points and describing what services they provided (following a handout that would reiterate all this information for future reference).

As soon as possible I'd add a glossary of library terms to the handouts for that first class so when I said "serials" the students would know what I meant; unfortunately, there wasn't time at this point to do one: by now fall term was breathing down my neck. So next we'd cover the online book catalogs and LCSH, then printed indexes, online indexes, and finally CD-ROMs. I scheduled two review sessions in the class outline, because even my limited teaching experience had convinced me of the utility of reiteration for these skills. I included, too, a midterm and a final exam to give me at least two opportunities to see what was getting across and what wasn't.

It really was a crash course, and obviously it left out large portions of library knowledge that could have gone in. But I didn't have the luxury of including everything, because in less than a month, streams of students *would* be coming in to do five-page papers on every topic under the sun, and this class had to be up and running and teachable.

Teaching the Library Skills Course

Three of us taught the ten sections of the course that first term, and to my amazement, it went well. The students caught on to using the online systems, transferred some of the skills they used on the computers to finding things in printed sources, and, if the tests were any indication of what was going on (and I admit that's somewhat open to question) these kids were making the right connections: they were going to be able to walk into the building and find some basic

sources for those first papers My major course goal was being achieved.

The incidental good news was that the instructors found the course fairly easy, even rewarding, to teach: it didn't completely deplete their energy resources and actually paid them back some when the class dynamic went well, as it often did. I taught four sections of library skills that term, and my two veteran instructor colleagues each taught three apiece. It looked like I wasn't going to bomb out on this assignment completely, after all. And then Fate, in the form of another early retirement, raised its head.

The Hunt for Raw Recruits

In November of that fall term, a second early retirement was announced. Both of the veteran instructors decided (not as a result of teaching the new class, they both repeatedly assured me) to take it. They'd be there for winter term, but gone by spring. I was staring down a tunnel of ten sections of library skills to teach in spring term by myself, unless I did some real fast talking.

Fortunately, I can do some real fast talking. I looked around at who had been involved in the teaching program before: many of them were retiring, right along with my two co-teachers. A couple new reference librarians had been hired, but most of them had their hands full with project deadlines and none of them were particularly enthusiastic about teaching. However, there were two new affirmative action interns who had just started to work at UCSB in the fall, both of whom were upbeat and enthusiastic, and both of whom had, in their interviews, expressed some interest in teaching. They had not committed to working in any particular area of the library as yet. I decided to approach them and see just how interested in teaching they were.

Both of them were about equally excited and intimidated by the prospect of teaching the course. Neither had any teaching experience and both were anxious to gain some, but they were a little leery of jumping off the cliff into a credit-bearing class for their first experience. So I proposed that we team-teach some one-shot classes together during the winter term to let them get their feet wet and see how they liked going into the classroom. They agreed, the library administration agreed, and we started team-teaching introductory composition classes together.

The Team-Teaching Technique

Please remember that at this time, I had exactly one ten-week term under my belt as library instruction administrator, with the same amount of experience as an instructor. I was still learning myself, and here I'd offered to teach two new professionals the ins and outs of the field (a certain amount of cheeky effrontery has come in handy in all my library experiences, and in this project I would have crashed and burned in a week without it).

I was desperate to keep the program running, and fortunately, my two new colleagues (Chris Oka and Lisa Melendez) were capable and eager, so we sallied forth in search of one-shot classes to teach, trying to get as much experience as we could in as short a time as possible. Word got around (we helped spread it) that we were available for library instruction, and the instructors in our writing program eagerly brought their classes to us, then told their friends to do the same. You know how success breeds success? By the end of winter term, we had team-taught a total of over 125 one-shot classes together.

It felt like trial by firing squad: we'd sometimes book four classes a day (the individual record was seven), and after the first two weeks we traded off the partnerships. Sometimes I'd teach with one or the other of them, sometimes they'd teach together. Sometimes we were terrific, other times we'd fall flat on our faces (I remember one class in particular where not just one student, but the entire back two rows fell asleep on us—including the faculty member whose class we were teaching), and other times we were too bone-tired even to know how it was going: we were gibbering the library tour at the desk, at meals, at the supermarket. Even now Chris, Lisa, and I refer to this as "those days when we taught in our sleep." But the day-after-day experience paid off: any one of us now can walk into a classroom and teach a composition class with a total of maybe 30 seconds preparation. And for new classes we may have to prepare a whole 20 minutes or so. As many of you can attest, you learn lots of effective short cuts when you're doing 125 classes in ten weeks. Or you check into a home. There's no third way.

By the end of that term, I knew from student and faculty response that I was a much better teacher, and that I had learned a lot from working with my two partners. Each of them felt like old pros by now. After having taught all those classes, they were very confident about signing on for the credit-bearing classes: I was having to hold them back from teaching a class whenever they saw four or more students standing together in the reference collection. So now there were three of us ready to tackle the library skills classes for spring. During the brief winter intersession I asked Chris and Lisa to look over the course syllabus and tell me what they thought. What they thought was that the assignments could use some rewriting.

They suggested using search questions and examples that would be more directly relevant to the experience of a wider, more diverse population of UCSB students, an increasing number of whom were Latinas/Latinos and Asian Americans. My interest was in making the class as accessible as possible to the largest segment of our user population as possible, so I asked Chris and Lisa to try rewriting the assignments in question as they'd like to see them, which they did. They also wrote some of the critically important pieces of the course there hadn't been time to include before, like the glossary of terms.

These course revisions were very well received: during spring term students and librarians alike complimented us on the evolving makeup of the course—it was drawing the attention of the library administration and of our colleagues, some of whom were expressing interest in finding out what was going on. I figured it was time to capitalize on this burgeoning interest.

Expanding the Program

The word of mouth about the successful team-teaching Chris, Lisa, and I had been doing was a potentially powerful hook for enlisting new instructors, I thought. I started shopping the idea of joining the team around to other librarians, and I approached not just reference librarians, but catalogers and bibliographers: I had seen some of these folks in action at the reference desk and behind the scenes training colleagues and noted that they had excellent teaching skills.

Their initial response was almost uniformly shock and refusal: many of the technical service librarians did not want to go into the classroom and wouldn't even entertain the idea. But a couple of them were intrigued at the idea, although they expressed concern about their lack of classroom experience. So I offered to let them get their feet wet first by just watching a couple of us team-teach a class. Then, if they felt comfortable afterwards, I suggested they could wade in and team-teach a class with one of us to see how it went.

This incremental approach worked like a charm. It was a question of getting people comfortable with being in the classroom and being around other librarians who were confident at what they were doing. Lisa, Chris, and I compared notes about what happened in these "observation" sessions, and the same thing had happened to each of us with several different colleagues. After observing a team-taught class a time or two, and seeing how the two instructors worked off each other, tossing the instructional ball back and forth cooperatively, the new folks would chime in from the back of the room where they were "observing"—sometimes they'd even join us at the computer-projection station to try a different search strategy we hadn't thought of, but they had. They were comfortable with us, we were comfortable with the class, so they gradually, too, became comfortable with the class. Their resistance was breaking down. Now we had to add some other incentives for teaching.

Gaining Administrative Support

Every one of you in this room knows that libraries are not the innocuous, quiet, staid places often wrongly depicted in films and books. They are, as we know, hotbeds of political intrigue that can make situations like those in films like "Room at the Top" and "The Carpetbaggers" look tame by comparison. Even if you don't want to get involved in internecine battles and jockeying for power, the reality is that you have to develop some political savvy just to survive in a library (again, anyone who doesn't experience this in your library, please be sure to see me afterwards).

One of the things I had recognized about the library instructional program at UCSB early on was that it was not seen as a "choice" assignment (big news, right? when I practically had to blackmail people into joining the program). I also realized that bringing a little high-profile success to the program would capture the administration's attention and support. That would translate into support not just for the program, but for the individuals working within it (again, nothing Machiavellian about these surmises).

It was a natural progression to go from carrying out the project to writing and speaking about it. So a group of us who were then working in the program decided to record some of our experiences. As of this writing, members of the team have written individually and collectively over 20 articles, book chapters, conference papers, and poster sessions on the various aspects of our teaching program: on learning to teach through team-teaching; on how the diversity of our teaching team influenced our instructional approach and reached new users; on how to market a library instructional program; how to create computerized collections, budget for them, and teach their use; and more.

We got our administration's attention, all right. When we wrote a grant for a library electronic classroom that was partially funded by the UCSB Foundation, our library administration ponied up the more than $75,000 difference that was needed to create and install the classroom, because they were by now that committed to and supportive of our instruction program.

And when they saw all the publications being generated by the team, our administration rewarded us even more concretely: several team members have earned accelerated salary increases on the basis of our extensive teaching involvement combined with the publications and presentations that arose out of our experiences.

The extent of our administration's interest in the teaching program became even clearer last year when they came to us to urge us strongly to put on a library instruction conference focused on coping with downsizing, the issue that shaped our own instructional scheme. I'm happy to report that our conference went off well just over a month ago, and I can only say after the work it took that Linda Shirato and Company must be Wonder Woman and all the other Super Heroes in disguise to put on this national conference annually).

Where We Are Now

Library instruction is alive, well, and thriving at UCSB now. The library skills class is in its sixth incarnation or so, having been revised many times (necessarily) since it was first rewritten. The two-credit library research class has been rewritten twice, and we continue to rework it (the details of *that* experience will have to wait for another time). Every public service librarian at the UCSB Library is now involved in some way with the instruction program, many of the technical services librarians are also teaching in the program, and our AUL for collections and information services teaches the library skills class once or twice every year. We can truly say we are a teaching library.

I'm no longer in charge of the instruction program, as an assignment as computerized information services coordinator finally beckoned successfully with its siren song. But I still do teach library skills as well as many one-shot composition classes each term because, now, well, I'm hooked.

They didn't warn me about this aspect of instruction way back when I was dragooned into administering the program, about the adrenaline rush that comes with a really good class, about the high that becomes a part of you like breathing. It is an addiction. You, of all people, know exactly what I'm talking about: it's the teaching fever in the blood.

Having regenerated the instruction program and survived the experience, having successfully run that initially much-feared, uncharted broken field of instruction at twilight, ironically, now, I can't give it up. No matter what else I may be doing in my job at the moment, I'm in the library instruction business. To stay.

SCRATCH THAT GLITCH: OR,
THE FINE ART OF GLITCH MANAGEMENT

Dan Ream

[Ed. Note: This presentation relies heavily on clips from videos which cannot be reproduced here. LOEX has a videotaped version of the presentation available to borrow from LOEX Clearinghouse, Eastern Michigan University Library, Ypsilanti, Michigan 48197. Special thanks ar due Scott Eddy, Eastern Michigan University Corporate Education Center, for a glitch-proof presentation.]

Good Evening! It's Friday the 13th....the only Friday the 13th in 1994...and I've got it!

What is a glitch? It's when a tool fails to work properly.

Tonight we'll focus on situations in which our teaching tools fail us—in a very public way. Our glitches might include

- a gopher that refuses to connect during an Internet demonstration; or

- an online catalog that unexpectedly goes down just before—or during—a library instruction session; or

- a burned out projector bulb; or

- perhaps lowest on the hierarchy of glitch sophistication—the last piece of chalk, which crumbles into bits when writing your first word on the board.

Ream is head, instruction and outreach services, James Branch Cabell Library, Virginia Commonwealth University, Richmond.

As these examples illustrate, glitches are *not* a new phenomenon. However, as technology marches on, our glitches do get fancier and managing them gets a little tougher.

Let me begin by asking that everyone here who has ever suffered a glitch in front of an audience please rise or, if wheelchair bound, please raise your hand.

[Approximately 75 percent of the audience stood.]

Well, now this is what I expected. Please remain standing for a minute.

Now, let's take a look at those who remain seated. I believe these folks may be categorized into four types:

- **the babes in the woods**—who haven't taught enough classes to have a glitch yet;

- **the very lucky—so far**—whose guardian angels will, one day, take a day off;

- **the sleeping or daydreaming**—give them a poke if you will; and

- concerning the remaining members of our seated population, let's just say that they illustrate the old 12-step program saying: "Denial *ain't* just a river in Egypt."

Please be seated.

Now, if anyone here tonight would like to explore complex theories of glitch causation or learn detailed technical steps to prevent glitches, I'm afraid you're in the wrong place...or maybe I am.

Instead, upon being offered the coveted LOEX after-dinner speakers' slot, I contacted Tom McNally, whom some of you veteran LOEX-goers may recall as the early and mid-1980s king of the LOEX after-dinner speech. Tom did two LOEX after-dinner talks on the subject of library instruction videos that were tremendously popular and successful. Thanks in part to Tom's sage advice, I bring "Glitch-Light," your LOEX dessert. I hope you enjoy it.

I'd like to start off by showing a videotape I compiled at Virginia Commonwealth University (VCU) Library in Richmond, Virginia, where I work. For the past year in my library, I've had hidden cameras running in one of our library instruction classrooms in the hope that I might catch some glitches. Unfortunately, our equipment, technical support staff, and librarians are so outstanding in their glitch prevention and management that I only have four glitches to show you. However, I think each illustrates some interesting aspects of glitch management.

Our first glitch captured on video features one of our reference librarians introducing a new automated reference product to an audience of deans and department heads.

[First video segment shown—projection of computer screen won't work; audience tries to help, officious technician finally plugs it in.]

I believe that example illustrates the old glitch axiom that the more prestigious your audience, the more likely the glitch—and the more painful it is when it arrives. Second, I think this glitch nicely illustrates that "helpful" audience members sometimes only add to the stress of the moment, making matters worse. Third, this also illustrates that some, and I emphasize the word "some," technicians may have more going for them in the realm of technical knowledge than in social graces.

Our second glitch on video features a librarian trying to introduce the Internet to a freshman class.

[Second video segment shown—network is down; librarian writes endlessly on flip chart while audience zones out.]

Does anyone here recognize these students from your own experience?

Anyway, I think that glitch nicely demonstrates that glitches can be as painful for the audience as for the librarian—that is, if they're paying attention in the first place!

Our third glitch on video features one of our former reference librarians in her last library instruction session with us. She was demonstrating our locally mounted PsycInfo database to one of our psychology classes.

[Third video segment shown—database won't come up on screen; librarian throws keyboard on floor.]

I've seen that video six or seven times now and seeing that keyboard crash to the floor still sends a shiver up my spine. Have any of you ever wanted to do that to a keyboard? If so, I hope you found that video vicariously satisfying.

Our fourth and last glitch on video came about after I had given glitch management training to some of our teaching librarians at VCU. I think you'll see that our librarian handles her glitch quite well.

[Fourth video segment shown—librarian accepts glitches calmly, attempts to take class to another floor; elevator gets stuck with class in it.]

Well, I guess that glitch illustrates what Roseanne Rosannadanna used to say on Saturday Night Live many years ago: "there's always *something*." At this point I guess I'll confess about our hidden cameras: I made that up.

Actually, our librarians in these videos were played by graduate theater students at VCU who, over the past year, also worked at our reference desk. They, along with a number of our library staff, served as our "glitch players"; let's look at the credits.

I would like to turn the next ten minutes over to you. You may have noticed my yellow table-tents scattered about. I'd like persons seated at each table to confer for ten minutes to determine, by consensus, who among you has the most interesting glitch story—whether it be a glitch horror story or a glitch you cleverly sidestepped. Each table's best-glitch-story winner is to receive a sticker to attach to his or her LOEX conference badge for the remainder of the conference. At the end of ten minutes I'll ask each table's winner to stand and be acknowledged.

[ten minutes later]

In case you were wondering, the figure on our stickers tonight is the cartoon character Wile E. Coyote, the perfect symbolic glitch character. Wile E. was famous for buying ACME products with which he could catch the Roadrunner. And each one blew up in his face. I would like to thank Ed Perry of the University of Regina for suggesting Wile E. Coyote as my glitch poster-boy tonight. Could we have our Wile E. Coyote sticker-bearers please rise. Let's have a round of applause for their accumulated wisdom and, in some cases, embarrassment.

Some of you may recall that before the conference I sent out a mailing asking for good glitch stories. I received quite a few interesting stories and bits of advice from about 20 to 25 of you. Thanks. From these stories I have selected two for special awards—although many others were also deserving. For the glitch management advice or anecdote that best illustrates keen glitch management skills I offer this Wile E. Coyote canteen for the following comments:

> My advice to anyone going into a presentation, whatever the topic, is to be armed with as many of the following as possible: a piece of chalk, a flip chart, several felt tip pens, some write-on transparencies (assuming an overhead projector), write-on pens, some good hand-outs. With any or all of the above and if you know your stuff nothing need be lost if technology fails—in fact you may hold the attention of the audience longer than having them sit in a darkened room watching a live demo.

Please come up and accept your award with my thanks, Judith Hesp of the Hahnemann University Library in Philadelphia.

My other award, for the most embarrassing glitch story, is this Wile E. Coyote hand puppet, which may come in handy during our winner's next glitch. Our most embarrassing glitch story goes as follows:

> Dan—Don't we all have horror stories?? I guess the one that sticks most in my mind is the most recent—AND the first public presentation I participated in after arriving here at Regis University. Anything that COULD go wrong seemed to go wrong…Two library faculty colleagues and I teamed up to give a "Faculty Brown Bag" Internet introduction. Since the three of us had varying experience and backgrounds with Internet, we divided up the presentation, rather than "team-teaching" the entire workshop. One of my colleagues volunteered to take the equipment across campus to the presentation room days in advance to test/verify the phone/line connections. (Note: we have an "odd" phone system on this campus; very few analog phone lines for "dialing out." Since the ONE and ONLY analog phone line in the building in question gets pulled from room to room, testing the phone line was of prime importance.) Mistake #1 = ONLY the phone line was tested, NOT dialing out. On the day of the presentation, we all arrived at the workshop from separate points on campus, but NO ONE brought along the laptop, modem, etc. We thought Media staff would bring it along with the overhead projection equipment; Media thought WE

would bring it along. Mistake #2 = NO ONE took explicit responsibility for equipment set-up. Once all the equipment was finally in place, dialing out proved impossible. Frantic calls to the Telecommunications Office (out to lunch; this was during a "Brown Bag" period, after all) and to Academic Computing (also out to lunch) were of no help. Fortunately, the Head of Academic Computing dropped by to listen to the presentation and volunteered to assist. He thought we had something wrong with the telecommunications software, so he spent a good deal of time re-installing the software. By this time, faculty were starting to arrive and the three library faculty presenters were getting a bit tense. So, we quickly regrouped, re-arranged the order of the presentation and led off with background information and non-screen dependent descriptions. I, ever the pessimist, had down-loaded screens and prepared overhead transparencies, just in case. It's not hard to guess that foresight saved my part, somewhat. By now, it's been determined that the problem was not with the computer hardware or software, but rather with the phone line. Mistake #3 = Too many chefs ruin the broth. The real problem is truly amusing in hindsight, but it was not at all amusing at the time; all this time we had been dialing 9 + the phone number, as ALL campus lines (or so we erroneously thought) went through the central switchboard and we HAD to dial 9 before the phone number to get an outside line. Little did we know that there were TWO phone lines on campus with DIRECT outside line access, and this phone line was one of the two. We did NOT have to dial 9, after all. Mistake #4 = See Mistake #1. Well, we obviously got through the presentation. We even got logged on, eventually. And, the faculty didn't seem to mind very much. We were probably much more conscious of each glitch we encountered than they. Moral of the story? Keep a sense of humor, prepare a few contingencies (although you can never anticipate every possibility), never assume anything when dealing with computers or network technology, and TEST EVERYTHING in advance. You weren't planning on giving credit for these stories, were you?"

Well, as a matter of fact I was—Kathleen Lance of Regis University, please step forward and accept this award and my thanks for the best embarrassing glitch story at this year's LOEX Conference.

Now, for the heart of our program, I would like to present "The Four Commandments of Glitch Management." In May 1993, I posted a question on six Internet listservers read by librarians, computer trainers, and A-V professionals, asking for their advice and anecdotes about how to manage glitches. I received 90 answers, some from as far away as Australia.

Many of these offered some wonderful advice and wisdom, which I hope I summarized well on the pink sheets placed at each table here tonight.

Distilling that wisdom down further still, I now offer the "Four Commandments of Glitch Management."

- Our First Commandment is "Always Have a Plan B." Specifically, this might include using screen-capture software and presentation software to a slideshow on diskette.

  Today I'm using Word Perfect Presentations to show these computer-generated slides, including some showing Internet screens that I captured using a tool called HiJaak Pro. These captured screens enable me to show an Internet session even when I suffer connection failures. You can also make such slides illustrating an online catalog search. Many slideshow or presentation software slides can also be made into plain old overhead transparencies, such as these. Last but not least I recommend having a whiteboard or blackboard in case all else fails. In some cases, a collaborative learning exercise may teach as well as or better than a demonstration. For example, Boolean search strategies concocted by small groups can often be instructive.

- The Second Commandment of Glitch Management is to know your equipment before it's too late. One way in which you might do this is to *read the manual*. How many here have used a computer data panel or LCD panel? [About 20 raise hands.] Of you, how many have read the manual about how to operate that equipment? [Only three or four raise hands.] Just as I thought.

  Well, I read *my* manual...last night in my room here at the Radisson. And it was *very* interesting. Another suggestion to advance your equipment knowledge is to try the buttons and switches—before you need them. And, of course, know where your backup equipment is—right now. I know where my extra computer is. It's at 901 Park Avenue, Richmond, Virginia, in my office.

- My Third Commandment of Glitch Management is to know your technicians on a first-name basis. As my slide here says, who would you rather call for help? Someone you know (like our pal Scott Eddy) or the "A-V Guy (or gal)"? "Who's Scott Eddy?," I hear you ask. Scott's the man running our equipment tonight. And as all good glitch

managers do, I've gotten to know Scott quite well. Now, I don't mean to suggest that you'll get any better service by knowing the name of your A-V technician. After all, these folks are professionals and try to serve everyone well. However, knowing them on a first-name basis will help *you* feel more comfortable when you need to call them for help.

Now, here are some suggestions for getting to know your A-V or computer technicians: Get to know their birthdays—Scott's birthday is April 8th, and on Scott's eighth birthday Hank Aaron broke Babe Ruth's home run record. Get to know their hobbies—Scott enjoys bicycling, computing, and he's a big fan of Eric Clapton. Get to know their favorite refreshments—Diet Pepsi, Bud Dry, or Chocolate Milk are Scott's favorites. Thanks to our dining room staff I have some chocolate milk for Scott right here....And get to know the names of their dogs—Freddy and Molly are the names of Scott's dogs.

- Our Fourth Commandment of Glitch Management is to prepare your mind. First and foremost, *expect* the glitch. Don't think *if* a glitch happens; think *when* a glitch happens. One of the most upsetting aspects of glitches is their unpredictability. One good analogy might be the expected versus unexpected traffic jam. Although annoying, the formal never carries the anguish of the latter. Last but not least, be eager to show your equipment knowledge or glitch backup. Once you've invested time in screen captures and presentation software, you may even feel eager for a glitch to show off your preparedness.

Or maybe not.

To conclude I would like to show on videotape two of the most famous and widely seen glitches in modern history. Thanks to the Vanderbilt University Television News Archives, I can present them tonight. The first is from the Ford-Carter presidential debate of September 23, 1976, in Philadelphia. After about one hour of the debate, the sound went dead, leaving the two presidential candidates staring mutely into the camera for 28 minutes. It's interesting to note that Carter was about to criticize the CIA when the sound died. Anyway, I hope you enjoy watching Ford and Carter's reactions, watching Walter Cronkite fill 28 minutes of dead air time, and best of all, watching the analysis from the next evening's newscast.

[First presidential video glitch shown]

Our other famous glitch was so masterfully managed that most observers didn't know about it until after the fact. On the eve of the seventeenth anniversary of the Ford/Carter glitch, President Bill Clinton prepared to address both houses of Congress and a primetime home viewing audience with his first major address on health care reform—perhaps the most important speech of his presidency to date. What then happened is that at some point while acknowledging the crowd's applause, Clinton looked into his tele-prompters (which look like glass plates) and saw the wrong speech—in fact it was his inauguration speech from eight months before. You'll notice that he turns to Al Gore and Gore takes off to get help—and back-stage panic ensues. Anyway, it wasn't until eight minutes into the speech that the right speech was loaded and the text caught up with him. Meaning that for the first eight minutes—Bill Clinton "winged it." Immedi-ately afterwards, you'll see Clinton's own recap of the teleprompter incident in a town meeting televised the next night.

[Second presidential glitch shown]

Well, as you can see, no one is too big to suffer glitches—even presidents. Having now seen Bill Clinton's glitch performance several times, I'm still in awe of it. Regardless of your feelings about Clinton's politics, I think you have to admire his mastery as a public speaker. In this case, Clinton had two back-ups—some notes on paper at the podium and the fact that he'd written the speech himself. Art Buchwald wrote an amusing column several days later speculating about what President Ronald Reagan would have done with the wrong speech in the teleprompter. I'll leave that to your imagination.

Before concluding this amazingly glitch-free presentation, let's have a round of applause for our "A-V Guy," Scott Eddy.

Thanks for your attention and I hope tonight has made you eager for your own next glitch!

INSTRUCTIVE
SESSIONS

USING THE TEACHING PORTFOLIO TO DEFINE AND IMPROVE THE INSTRUCTIONAL ROLE OF THE ACADEMIC LIBRARIAN

Judith M. Arnold and Karen B. Pearson

Introduction: The Teaching Portfolio Concept

Teaching portfolios provide documentation of teaching performance and include such components as statements of teaching responsibilities, strategies and goals, and a teaching philosophy. Support documentation in the form of instructional materials and evaluations of teaching from other faculty and from students are also part of the teaching portfolio.

Teaching portfolios are gaining prominence in academic institutions, particularly as a renewed interest in teaching undergraduates has become a national focus in the quest for accountability demanded by legislators. The portfolio can serve both as a vehicle for teaching improvement and for faculty development, and as a basis for personnel decisions, including promotion and tenure. The portfolio concept has been accepted in the K-12 environment as an alternative method of assessing student achievement, particularly in writing and reading. In the world of higher education, the portfolio concept has been explored for nearly a decade by the Canadian Association of University Teachers[1] and more recently (1990s) in the United States advanced by Peter Seldin[2] and promoted by others such as Edgerton, Hutchings, and Quinlan through the American Association for Higher Education (AAHE)[3] as a method of documenting effective teaching in an effort to counter the emphasis upon research at the expense of teaching

Arnold is public service/reference librarian and coordinator for BI and *Pearson* is public service/reference librarian, Saint Xavier University, Chicago, Illinois.

in higher education. Following Ernest Boyer's redefinition of scholarship to include effective teaching,[4] proponents of the teaching portfolio argue that the portfolio system presents an occasion for faculty to express teaching values and philosophies and to offer evidence of their teaching effectiveness, a document that can provide a balance to the evidence of scholarship represented in the traditional *curriculum vita*. Preparing a portfolio encourages reflection, evaluation, and improvement. Seldin and Annis write:

> It is in the very process of creating the collection of documents and materials that comprise the portfolio that the professor is stimulated to: 1) reconsider personal teaching activities; 2) rethink teaching strategies; 3) rearrange priorities; and 4) plan for the future.[5]

The portfolio encompasses evidence beyond student evaluations, which are typically the only evidence that a faculty member has of teaching performance.

A search of *Library Literature*, LISA, and ERIC revealed a limited amount on the teaching portfolio; selected items from this search are included in the accompanying bibliography (see appendix 1). A look at this list will reveal that little has been written in the library world addressing the use of the teaching portfolio; however, Barbara Wittkopf, in her editorial "Teaching Portfolios: How Are *We* Doing?" in the Summer 1992 issue of *Research Strategies*, offers a perspective for instruction librarians on the applicability of the teaching portfolio:

Even BI librarians who teach course-integrated components or give one-shot lectures can build portfolios that characterize their teaching effective-ness and identify areas for improvement.[6]

For academic librarians, who typically find themselves responsible for reference service and bibliographic instruction, the format of the teaching portfolio can provide the opportunity to articulate the relationship between reference service and BI. This instructive session was designed to define the teaching portfolio as conceptualized in Peter Seldin and Associates' *Successful Use of Teaching Portfolios* and realized in a mentoring process outlined and practiced by Peter Seldin, to provide individual and small-group activities that enabled the participants to begin developing their own teaching portfolios, and to explore interactively how the document can lead to improving instruction and assist in assessing teaching effectiveness. (Refer to appendix #2 for an overview of the session.)

What are the elements of the teaching portfolio and how is the portfolio best accomplished? There has been debate in the literature over the content of the portfolio. Standardized elements make assessment of the portfolio easier; when it is used for promotion and tenure decisions, this uniformity is more crucial.[7] There is general agreement that the materials assembled in the portfolio should selectively reflect your best and most effective teaching efforts. Some have recommended organizing the portfolio around activities associated with teaching, such as 1) planning and preparation; 2) teaching presentation; 3) evaluating and giving feedback to students; and 4) keeping current in the field.[8] The components of the portfolio include three basic categories of materials (material from oneself, material from others, and products of good teaching) that will demonstrate one's teaching performance.[9] Appendix #3 provides examples of the types of documentation that might be included in each of these categories. The individual plan of assembly for the portfolio and the uniqueness of the content reflect the versatility of the portfolio as an individual statement, as demonstrated in figure 1.

The portfolio is best assembled through a mentoring process because it is in the process of discussing the document with a peer that one's clarity of purpose, philosophy of teaching, and evaluation of the relationship between one's philosophy and methods emerge most successfully. Often the eyes of another—particularly one from another discipline—can compel you to clarify for a diverse audience and to examine your role in the mission of the institution. Frequently, too, this mentoring process leads to a

clearer understanding by faculty of the significance of your role in the education of the student.[10] Edgerton et al. have suggested several mentoring arrangements, including 1) a "buddy" system of two faculty members; 2) a mentoring model between senior and junior faculty; and 3) a program of portfolio development set within an academic department.[11]

The Statement of Teaching Philosophy

Writing a statement of one's teaching philosophy establishes the core of the teaching portfolio and the narrative statement, for it is from this statement that the other elements of the document gain their place. A teaching philosophy is not to be a scholarly treatise that discusses abstract philosophical concepts; rather it is a personal reflection about fundamental assumptions, beliefs, and values regarding the role of teaching and learning. Understandably, one's teaching philosophy evolves over time, through experimentation with new methods and strategies, discussion with colleagues, and knowledge of the literature. When we talk about a "statement" of teaching philosophy, we are referring to a set of philosophical assumptions, which may comprise two or more paragraphs; a teaching philosophy does not have to be distilled into just one sentence.

Teaching philosophy may be expressed in varying ways. Looking at the tables of contents from our portfolios (see figure 1), you can see that we outline our statements of teaching philosophy in slightly different ways. For Judith, strategies and philosophy are so intertwined that her mentor suggested that she keep the two joined in one section titled, "Teaching Philosophy and Strategies"; Karen, on the other hand, conceptualizes the two as distinct elements, separating her set of assumptions and beliefs about the role of teaching and learning from the section that articulates the strategies that she has employed in her BI sessions and at the reference desk.

In figure 2 you will see a portion from both of our statements of teaching philosophy. From the examples given, you can see that we share similar ideas about teaching although we express them differently. You will notice that we each address the affective component in our teaching, again in slightly different ways. The organizational differences indicated by the tables of contents and the individuality of expression in the examples given from our portfolios illustrate one of the strengths of the teaching portfolio—its ability to reflect the individual that it represents. Because the document so clearly reflects the individual, it can also be a powerful and more effective method of self-presentation in a job search.

— JUDITH M. ARNOLD AND KAREN B. PEARSON —

Teaching Portfolio
Judith M. Arnold
Public Service/Reference Librarian
Saint Xavier University
1993-1994

TABLE OF CONTENTS

I. Teaching and Reference Responsibilities
II. Teaching and Reference Service: Philosophy and Strategies
III. Instructional Methods
IV. Teaching Effectiveness
V. Teaching Improvement
VI. Goals
VII. Appendices
   A: Teaching and Reference Responsibilities: BI Summary Sheet; Bibliographic Instruction at SXU; Bibliographic Instruction Statistics, 1987-1993
   B: Instructional Materials: Annotations; Course Syllabus/HUM 301: Strategies for Researching Authors and Literary Works; Teaching Overhead; English 158 Worksheet; Transitions Goals and Objectives
   C: Student Evaluations
   D: Student Products
   E: Peer Evaluation
   F: Teaching Improvement: Workshops and Conferences Attended; Transitions Evaluations; Teaching Journal

Teaching Portfolio
Karen Burdick Pearson
Public Service/Reference Librarian
Saint Xavier University
Spring 1994

Table of Contents

I. Statement of Teaching Responsibilities
II. Statement of Teaching Philosophy
III. Statement of Teaching Methods and Strategies
IV. Teaching Improvement Activities
V. Teaching Evaluation Data
VI. Products of Teaching and Bibliographic Instruction
VII. Goals
VIII. Appendices

Figure 1: The Teaching Portfolio as Individual Statement

I believe that students and teachers learn from each other. It is important to me in teaching and providing reference service to relate to the students personally and to encourage their feedback on expectations, learning, and feelings about research and the library.

It is important to me that students come away from a BI session or reference encounter with a sense that library research can be non-threatening and even rewarding, and that they can feel successful in the learning process.

Figure 2: Writing a Philosophy (of Teaching, Reference) Statement

One of the best ways to grasp a concept is to spend time working with it, and this session was designed to provide time for the participants to work on articulating a teaching philosophy using a worksheet. (See appendix 4.) Also included for further development of your portfolio is appendix 5, developed by Peter Seldin for use in his workshops to facilitate writing of the total narrative component of the portfolio.) In keeping with the nature of the *process* of developing a teaching portfolio, which includes a mentoring component, the session also incorporated activities for participants to work in pairs to develop instructional strategies, and in small groups to write objectives and list assessment techniques, all based on the teaching philosophy statement.

Developing Instructional Strategies

A strategy gives an overall, practical focus to one's teaching philosophy. Implementation of this strategy is possible through a variety of methods. Looking back at our statements of teaching philosophy (see figure 2) as examples, a strategy that one might employ would be to help students feel comfortable in the library. Specific methods that implement this strategy could include coming to a BI session early and chatting informally with the students. Additionally, one might ask students to complete the sentence, "Doing library research is like...," and follow it up with a group discussion that focuses upon attitudes towards libraries and research. This strategy will help students realize that they are not alone in their fears about using the library or encountering a research paper, a symptom Mellon addresses in her theory of library anxiety.[12]

A simple strategy at the reference desk to alleviate anxiety is to be sure to smile and find at least one affirming or encouraging thing to say to each student. Explaining the steps you take as you instruct at the terminals or when you locate a reference source is another possible strategy to reduce patrons' fears of the library and help them feel more comfortable.

It is important to make a direct connection between *what you believe* and *what you do*. Having someone else read your statement of philosophy and suggest strategies and methods provides you with a broader perspective and is, to some degree, the beginning of the mentoring process. In a practical sense, participants in this workshop were able not only to articulate their beliefs about the role of teaching and learning but also to gain, from working with others, one or two new strategies to try in their teaching.

The Interrelationship between Teaching Philosophy, Strategies/Methods, Objectives, Assessment, and Documentation

From the statement of philosophy naturally flow the strategies that one employs in the classroom or at the reference desk. If, for example, your statement of philosophy says that you promote critical thinking in your teaching and reference encounters (see figure 3), then from this statement you might extract a specific strategy for advancing critical thinking by stating that in your instruction, whether it be in the classroom or at the reference desk, you will help students learn to evaluate sources. Figure 4 represents the ease of translating philosophy into strategy and measurable objectives. Extracted from this strategy might be several methods for implementing it in library instruction, such as presenting ways of evaluating the relevance and authority of sources through a lecture, or by initiating a small group discussion wherein students examine a bibliography of potential sources or issues of scholarly and popular publications and come to a consensus on ways to determine relevancy and authority; or perhaps you might design a worksheet to be completed individually or in small groups, or a pathfinder. Your method will also be directly related to your teaching philosophy. If you advocate a role as facilitator rather than information-giver, then you might choose the small-group approach over the lecture approach. You might solve the information-giving task by providing a handout that summarizes what students have formulated in their groups, along with any additional points that you may wish to present.

A specific performance objective might be written, such as "Students will list three characteristics that distinguish a scholarly article from a popular article on a given topic." Depending upon the teaching method chosen, ways to assess this success of the objective might include a test following a lecture, small-group consensus, a performance test, success completing a worksheet, or your own observations of the students as they decide upon which source(s) to select. In addition to evaluative measures, products of teaching that might document the success of this objective could include the bibliographies from student papers, annotated working bibliographies, graded worksheets, or tests. Letters from faculty stating that students' papers reflected use of appropriate sources would offer another method of documentation, material from others.

Let's consider another example from your role reference librarian. A student who wants information on current economic conditions in South Africa approaches the reference desk. She needs several quite recent articles. You discover by questioning her that her professor has instructed the class not to use news

The student is a central, if complex, component of bibliographic instruction. I do not believe that students come into an instruction session as "blank slates." They bring with them personalized understandings and misunderstandings of what is involved in using a library, especially an academic library. My role is to help them make sense of the research process. The literature calls this **critical thinking**, and this is the goal which drives my instructional philosophy.

<u>Critical Thinking</u> Activities in the Research Process

--*exploring, analyzing, and narrowing a topic*

--*deciding where to look for information*

--*deciding on appropriate search statements*

--*evaluating sources*

Strategy: Have students learn to distinguish between scholarly and popular sources

Figure 3: Translating Philosophy into Strategy

Concept: critical thinking-----------> **Strategy:** To help students learn to distinguish between scholarly and popular source

Objective: *The student will list three (3) characteristics that distinguish a scholarly article from a popular article.*

Methods: Lecture
Small group work
Worksheet (individual or small group)
Pathfinder

Assessment: Test following lecture
Small group consensus
Performance test
Fill-in worksheet
Observation (obtrusive or participative)

Documentation:
[Products of teaching]

Bibliographies from final paper
Annotated working bibliographies
Graded tests
Graded worksheets

Letters from faculty

Figure 4: Translating Philosophy into Measurable Terms

magazines such as *Time* and *Newsweek*. Before you send her to a more specialized index such as SSI, you decide to send her first to InfoTrac because of the ready availability of most of the journals in your library. The mixture of popular and scholarly sources on InfoTrac also offers the opportunity to help the student learn to differentiate between the two. It is important to you that the student be successful and that she learn the appropriate use of tools as well as their limitations. You believe in incorporating critical thinking at the reference desk as well as in the classroom. How can you use this opportunity to help this student develop the ability to make appropriate choices in sources? When guiding her to InfoTrac, you might wish to steer the student towards the subdivision "research," which will have a higher percentage of scholarly articles cited, as well as the subdivision "economic conditions." Provided that you have the time, you might suggest that she analyze the printout that she receives, perhaps drawing from her some criteria for deciding the suitability of a source (or if you have a printed sheet that provides this information you can hand it to her). Ask her to select articles based upon these criteria, and if she is still in need of more sources, she can return for additional searching help. Assessing the success of this endeavor is admittedly challenging; you might follow up later and observe what she has chosen. You might ask her to report back on the success of her paper. You might even, if she does return, ask for a copy of the paper, providing you with documentation of your teaching involvement.

This combination of articulating philosophy, associated strategies, and chosen methods, and then translating them into a measurable objective that can be documented by the teaching portfolio is another strength of the document. Rather than simply offering evidence of your success through the traditional summation of student evaluation results, the teaching portfolio expands the evidence of teaching performance into a whole picture of you and your role as a reference and instruction librarian. Moreover, it gives you evidence that your *are* or *are not* putting your philosophy into practice, and documentation either evidences your success or your need for improvement. From the perspective of your institution, the teaching portfolio provides an excellent element in an institution-wide outcomes assessment program.

Articulating Objectives, Determining Assessment Tools, and Gathering Documentation

The next activity of the session demonstrated how easily this interrelationship between philosophy, strategy and method, objectives, and assessment flows. Working in small groups of four to six persons using

appendix 4, each group was to extract from the teaching philosophy and corresponding strategy a measurable objective and list methods of accomplishing this objective. Following this task, the group was to list ways of assessing this objective and indicate types of documentation demonstrating the success of the objective. Time was provided for discussion and questions in the group at large following the small group activity.

Summation: Where Do I Go from Here? The Importance of Goals

The teaching portfolio is a dynamic document. The "Goals" section presents the opportunity to express an individual plan for improvement, whether it is in applying an active learning technique in your sessions, or a new way of emphasizing critical thinking in the reference encounter, or plans for professional development. One immediate example of the value of articulating goals is our presence here today. Last year when we developed our teaching portfolios, we listed submitting a proposal to LOEX in the "Goals" section.

Examining your accomplished goals offers an occasion to present evidence of success to yourself and to your evaluators. Examining those goals not met can provoke thought on alternative ways of meeting them or even revising them. The value of articulating and setting goals is enhanced within the context of the teaching portfolio. We can all set goals for ourselves, but within the teaching portfolio, there is a clearly expressed connection between what we want to do (philosophy), what we are doing (strategies, methods, and goals), evidence of how well we are doing it (products of teaching, other documentation), and reflection and goal-setting related to how well we have done and how we might do better. The value of the teaching portfolio is in its ability to provide this unique focus.

The *process* of preparing a teaching portfolio has three tangible outcomes. First, it leads not only to a more thorough and reflective examination of BI and reference service but also to a better *articulation* of such classroom and individual instruction. Second, as one faculty member stated, "a most important outcome of teaching portfolio preparation [is that] assumptions are tested and we can become better teachers as a result."[13] This is directly applicable to our role as instruction librarians, for we must continually assess our strategies and their underlying philosophical bases. Third, better collaboration with library colleagues and classroom faculty is attained through the process of preparing the teaching portfolio.

NOTES

1. Bruce M. Shore, et al., *The Teaching Dossier: A Guide to its Preparation and Uses* (Montreal: Canadian Association of University Teachers, 1986).

2. Peter Seldin, The *Teaching Portfolio: A Practiced Guide to Improved Performance and Promotion/Tenure Decisions* (Bolton, MA: Anker Publishing, 1991).

3. Russell Edgerton, Patricia Hutchings, and Kathleen Quinlan, The *Teaching Portfolio: Capturing the Scholarship in Teaching* (Washington, DC: American Association for Higher Education, 1991).

4. Ernest Boyer, *Scholarship Reconsidered: Priorities of the Professoriate* (Princeton, NJ: Carnegie Foundation for the Advancement of Teaching, 1990).

5. Peter Seldin, "The Teaching Portfolio Concept," in *Successful Use of Teaching Portfolios* ed. by Peter Seldin and Associates (Bolton, MA: Anker Publishing, 1993), 9.

6. Barbara Wittkopf, "Teaching Portfolios: How Are *We* Doing?" *Research Strategies* 10 (1992): 103.

7. Kenneth Wolf, *Teaching Portfolios: Synthesis of Research and Annotated Bibliography* (San Francisco: Far West Laboratory for Eductional Research and Development, 1991), 8-11. Also available as ED 343 890.

8. The categories were taken from the Stanford Project. Edgerton, Hutchings, and Quinlan suggest ways of documenting these areas (p.10-11).

9. See Seldin, 6-8.

10. See Linda F. Annis, "The Key Role of the Mentor," in *Successful Use of Teaching Portfolios*, ed. by Peter Seldin and Associates (Bolton, MA: Anker Publishing, 1993), 19-25.

11. Edgerton, Hutchings, and Quinlan, 51.

12. Constance A. Mellon, "Library Anxiety: A Grounded Theory and Its Development," *College and Research Libraries* 47 (1986): 160-165.

13. Seldin, *Successful Use,* 16.

Appendix 1:

The Teaching Portfolio:
A Selected Bibliography

Boileau, Don M. *"Scholarship Reconsidered": A Challenge to Use Teaching Portfolios to Document the Scholarship of Teaching*. ERIC, 1993. ED 361 752.

Centra, John A. *Use of the Teaching Portfolio and Student Evaluations for Summative Evaluation*. ERIC, 1993. ED 358 133.

Edgerton, Russell, Patricia Hutchings, and Kathleen Quinlan. *The Teaching Portfolio: Capturing the Scholarship in Teaching*. Washington, DC: American Association for Higher Education, 1991.

Eison, James A. "Setting the Stage: Introducing the Teaching Portfolio Concept to One's Campus." *The Journal of Staff, Program & Organization Development* 11 (1993): 115-121.

O'Neil, Carol. *Recording Teaching Accomplishment: A Dalhousie Guide to the Teaching Dossier*. Halifax, NS: Dalhousie University, 1993.

Pacanowsky, Michael. "Current State of Blindness." *Communication Education* 42 (October 1993): 317-323.

Robinson, Jack. *Faculty Orientations toward Teaching and the Use of Teaching Portfolios for Evaluating and Improving University-Level Instruction*. ERIC, 1993. ED 358 149.

Seldin, Peter, and Associates. *Successful Use of Teaching Portfolios*. Bolton, MA: Anker Publishing, 1993.

Seldin, Peter. *The Teaching Portfolio: A Practical Guide to Improved Performance and Promotion/Tenure Decisions*. Bolton, MA: Anker Publishing, 1991.

Shore, Bruce M., et al. *The Teaching Dossier: A Guide to Its Preparation and Uses*. Montreal: Canadian Association of University Teachers, 1986.

Urbach, Floyd. "Developing a Teaching Portfolio." *College Teaching* 40 (1992): 71-74.

Wittkopf, Barbara. "Teaching Portfolios: How Are *We* Doing?" *Research* 10 (1992): 102-103.

Wolf, Kenneth P. *Teaching Portfolios: Synthesis of Research and Annotated Bibliography*. ERIC, 1991. ED 343 890.

Appendix 2:

USING THE TEACHING PORTFOLIO
TO DEFINE AND IMPROVE
THE INSTRUCTIONAL ROLE OF THE
ACADEMIC LIBRARIAN

LOEX, May 1994
Ypsilanti, Michigan

Presenters: **Judith M. Arnold, Saint Xavier University, Chicago, IL**
Karen B. Pearson, Saint Xavier University, Chicago, IL

I.   Mini-lecture: Introduction to the Teaching Portfolio Concept   [5 minutes]

II.   Writing a Philosophy of Teaching Statement   [10 minutes]
         (individual participation)

III.   Developing Instructional Strategies   [5 minutes]
         (individual participation)

IV.   Mini-lecture: Example of the Interrelationship Between the
         Teaching Philosophy Statement, Strategies/Methods,
         Objectives, Assessment, and Documentation   [10 minutes]

V.   Articulating Objectives, Determining Assessment Tools, and
         Gathering Documentation   [10 minutes]
         (group participation)

VI.   Summation   [5 minutes]

The Teaching Portfolio

The following is <u>not</u> an inclusive list of <u>all</u> of the items that might be included in a teaching portfolio. Rather, it is a sampling of the types of items to consider including.

Products of Good Teaching

* Student pre/post scores before and after a course

* Student essays, creative work, field-work reports

* Statements by alumni on the quality of instruction

* Student publications or conference presentations on course-related work

* Examples of graded student essays along with the professor's comments as to why they were so graded

Material From Oneself

* Statement of teaching responsibilities

* A reflective statement by the professor describing personal teaching philosophy, strategies, and objectives

* Representative course syllabi

* Description of curricular revisions, including new course projects, materials, and class assignments

* Steps taken to evaluate or improve one's teaching

Material From Others

* Statements from colleagues who have observed the professor in the classroom

* Statements from colleagues who have reviewed the professor's classroom materials, syllabi, and assignments

* Student course and teaching evaluation data

* Invitations to present a paper at a conference on teaching one's discipline or on teaching in general

* Distinguished teaching awards or other recognition

© Peter Seldin
(used with permission)

Beginning Your Teaching Portfolio

1. What is your teaching philosophy?

2. List the strategies or methods that you would employ, based upon this statement of philosophy.

3. From the statement of philosophy and list of strategies, focus on one strategy that implements the philosophy and write a measurable objective for this strategy.

4. A. Write 1-2 ways that you might assess or evaluate this objective.

   B. List 1-2 types of documentation that would demonstrate the success of this objective.

Appendix 5:

Getting Started on Your Teaching Portfolio

This form has been designed to help you get started on the important narrative section of your teaching portfolio. Please appropriate, to further illustrate your responses.

1. Please describe your teaching responsibilities.

2. Please describe your teaching methods and explain <u>why</u> you teach as you do. (Particular attention should be given to strategy and implementation.) Give examples.

3. Please describe course projects, class assignments or other activities that help you integrate your subject matter with your students' outside experiences.

4. If you overheard your students talking about you and your teaching in the cafeteria, what would they likely be saying? What would you like them to say? Why is that important to you?

5. Give examples and explain specific ways that you motivate your students to help them achieve better performance.

6. Please describe your efforts to develop your teaching effectiveness.

    a) **Teaching Workshops Attended**—for each workshop indicate who conducted it, the topic, and what the impact was upon your teaching.

    b) **Informal Research Conducted on your Own Teaching**. (Describe the course(s) involved and how the research results influenced your teaching.)

    c) **Describe Your Seminars, Presentations or Publications on Teaching.**

7. How do you stay current in your discipline? How do you translate this new knowledge into your classes?

©Peter Seldin
(used with permission)

INTERNET INSTRUCTION: PLANNING AND DESIGNING FACULTY WORKSHOPS

Abbie Basile

Summary

This presentation will explore the issues, options, and tasks involved in planning and designing Internet instruction, from the beginning stages where user needs are identified and a timeline is drafted, to the final stages where the format and content of the workshops are decided upon. Discussion topics will include staff training, equipment needs, and options for course structure and content.

In addition to the verbal presentation, several handouts have been distributed, including

- an outline of the major issues and options addressed in the presentation (divided into two sections: "Planning a Program" and "Planning a Session");

- an equipment "wish list";

- a sample planning timeline for Internet workshops;

- a substantial list of pertinent Internet resources for instructors;

- a glossary geared toward Internet instructors;

- a selective bibliography of Internet-related readings for instructors; and

- a list of Internet teaching tips.

Basile is electronic services instruction librarian, Miami University Libraries, Oxford, Ohio.

PLANNING A PROGRAM

>>>>>>>>>>>>>>>>

Internet Instruction: Planning and Designing Faculty Workshops
Abbie J. Basile, 5/94

1.   What equipment and staff resources are available?

- ideal v. reality   (see last page)

- size of classroom (several classes necessary?)

- type of connection to the Internet (wired v. dial-up)

- hands-on activity possible?

- need for instructor training?

2.   How will the program be structured?

Some possibilities:

- one-shot class (length?)

- series of classes (novice, advanced, bi-weekly)

- incorporated into general instruction (enough time?)

- subject-based classes

- credit courses

- part of pre-scheduled meetings (ex: dept'l meetings)

— ABBIE BASILE —

PLANNING A PROGRAM
>>>>>>>>>>>>>>>>>

Internet Instruction: Planning and Designing Faculty Workshops
Abbie J. Basile, 5/94

3.   Publicity

- flyers, posters, mailings

- table displays, news articles

- electronic forums

- a great name or theme helps

- make the net relevant in publicity (give examples)

- include registration details

4.   Staff training

Factors to consider:

- level of teaching experience

- level of Internet experience/knowledge

- subject content knowledge

- creation of training materials   (coursepack, session outline)

- net expert/subject expert/teaching expert

PLANNING A PROGRAM

>>>>>>>>>>>>>>>>>

5a.   Use a timeline

A detailed, dated plan of the various tasks involved with:

- staff training

- producing course materials

- scheduling of classes and rooms

- publicity

5b.   Benefits of using a timeline :

- can see interdependency of tasks

- makes omissions less likely

- reminds you what deserves emphasis

- puts deadlines in place and makes them visible

PLANNING A SESSION

> > > > > > > > > > > > > > > > > > >

Internet Instruction: Planning and Designing Faculty Workshops
Abbie J. Basile, 5/94

1a. Class Structure

   <u>Series of Short Classes</u>

   - how many classes in the series

   - length of time (one, two, three or more hours?)

   - hands-on section possible

   - how many tools to teach

1b. Class Structure

   <u>Series of Short Classes</u>

   One hour session:

   w/hands-on: 1 tool

   no hands-on: 2 tools

   Longer sessions:

   grouped tools: 2 - 3 tools

PLANNING A SESSION

> > > > > > > > > > > > > > >

Internet Instruction: Planning and Designing Faculty Workshops
Abbie J. Basile, 5/94

2a. Course Content

Possibilities for Grouping Tools

Novice tools:

- Telnet

- Freenets

- Gopher/Veronica

- Electronic communication
  (E-mail, Listservs, Usenet News, Netfind)

2b. Course Content

Grouping Novice tools:

- Telnet, Gopher (incl. Veronica)

or

- Telnet, Gopher (incl. Veronica), WWW

or

- E-mail, Telnet, Gopher (incl. Veronica), WWW

or

- E-mail, Netfind, Listservs and Usenet News

PLANNING A SESSION

> > > > > > > > > > > > > > > >

2c. Course Content

Grouping Advanced Tools:

- E-mail address finding tools

- FTP

- Archie

- WAIS

2d. Course Content

Introductory Internet Information:

- History of the Internet

- Problems involved with using the Internet

- How to access the Internet
  (specific local network info)

PLANNING A SESSION
> > > > > > > > > > > > > > > >

2e. Course Content

Possible Course Materials:

- Glossary

- Reading List

- Exercise sheets/ scavenger hunts

- Step by step info on using tools (screen captures?)

- List of pertinent addresses and resources

2f. Course Content

General Design Issues:

- format: hands-on / lecture / demonstration?

- what's a reasonable amount of time for a session?

- how many instructors? helpers?

- hands-on at end or throughout?

BEYOND THE CLASSROOM

Other Internet Instructional Materials:

- Internet readings on reserve for easy access

- mini-sessions for Library staff to keep them updated

- produce Internet pathfinders on specific subjects

AN EQUIPMENT WISH LIST

EACH particpant:

- workstation with direct connection
- at least one printer per two students

Instructor:

- workstation connected directly to the net   (NOT dial-up!)

- overhead projector

- rearview or Ceiling-mounted projection

- large writing surface NOT blocked by projection screen

- switch to control power to students' monitors

- note-taking lights, dimmer switches

—Sample—
INTERNET CLASS TIMELINE

MID–NOVEMBER

- "coming soon" publicity blurbs for new net class offerings
  (incl: campus papers, library newsletter, academic dept. flyers)

- begin creating coursepack (handouts/user guides, outline, backup overheads) for other librarians to use in net sessions.

- prepare outline of "teach the teacher" sessions for librarians

- schedule "teach the teacher" sessions, reserve room for sessions

EARLY DECEMBER

- release longer publicity announcements which include brief Internet definition, examples of how useful it is, classes TBA. Possible publicity outlets/forums:

    campus papers, library newsletter, library and campus listservs, dept'l liaisons, library branches/campuses, Chairs, Deans, posters/signs, table tents, OPAC announcement/news screen, general campus mailing

- settle upon class registration process (class size, drop-in or pre-register, how to register, are accounts required, etc.)

- finish handouts for sessions, have packets collated and prepared

MID DECEMBER

- train library instructors who'll be doing general net sessions for campus community.

- schedule campus-wide training session dates/times for Spring term.

- announce and schedule general informational sessions for library staff so they don't feel left out of the "loop."

JANUARY

- announce specific dates/times of classes for campus community

- have practice sessions for net instructors

- visit workshop locations if they are unfamiliar classrooms

ON THE NET
>>>>>>>>>>>>
A Selected List of Information and Instructional Support Resources

Internet Instruction: Planning and Designing Faculty Workshops
Abbie J. Basile, 5/94

Contents:

A) Electronic discussion lists
B) Internet Guides
C) Lists of Information Resources
D) FAQs (lists of frequently-asked questions with their answers)
E) Self-guided tutorials and classes
F) Miscellaneous (but not to be overlooked!)

A) ELECTRONIC DISCUSSION LISTS

1. net-happenings@is.internic.net

This list is an excellent source for one-stop Internet-related announcements. A good deal of relevant and useful announcements are posted here by the moderator, Gleason Sackman, from other discussion lists. To quote its introductory message:

The purpose of the list is to distribute to the community announcements of interest to network staffers and end users. This includes conference announcements, call for papers, publications, newsletters, network tools updates, and network resources. Net-happenings is a moderated, announcements-only mailing list which gathers announcements from many Internet sources and concentrates them onto one list. Traffic is about 8-12 messages a day.

To Subscribe:
Send the following e-mail message to listserv@is.internic.net: (do not use a subject line!)

 subscribe net-happenings your name

To Unsubscribe:
Send the following e-mail message to listserv@is.internic.net: (do not use a subject line!)

signoff net-happenings

2. nettrain@ubvm.cc.buffalo.edu

This listserv is devoted to issues and questions dealing with Internet training. This is an excellent source for practical information on Internet instruction. This list does have heavy traffic and sends out about 8-12 messages a day.

To Subscribe:
Send the following e-mail message to listserv@ubvm.cc.buffalo.edu: (leave subject blank!)

 subscribe nettrain your name

To Unsubscribe:
Send the following e-mail message to listserv@ubvm.cc.buffalo.edu: (leave subject blank!)

signoff nettrain

3. publib-net@nysernet.org   (Public libraries and the Internet info)
   publib@nysernet.org   (General public libraries info, incl. the Internet)

PUBLIB-NET is a focused discussion list concerned with the use of the Internet in public libraries. All discussions on PUBLIB-NET will also be posted to PUBLIB , which is now a general issue public library discussion list that includes net related topics. [Please introduce yourself to the list after you receive the welcome message back from the listserv.]

To Subscribe:
Send the following e-mail message to listserv@nysernet.org: (do not use a subject line!)

 subscribe publib-net your name

To Unsubscribe:
Send the following e-mail message to listserv@nysernet.org: (do not use a subject line!)

signoff publib-net

4. kidsnet@vms.cis.pitt.edu or kidsnet@pittvms.bitnet

This is a mailing list formed to provide a global network for the use of children and teachers in grades K-12. It is intended to provide a focus for technological development and for resolving the problems of language, standards, etc. that inevitably arise in international communications.

All requests to be added to or deleted from this list, along with other questions and problems, should be sent to <u>one</u> of the following addresses. Messages do not have to follow any specific form, but should be brief.

KIDSNET-REQUEST@VMS.CIS.PITT.EDU or JOINKIDS@PITTVMS.BITNET

5. go4lib-l@ucsbvm.ucsb.edu

This is the Library Gopher List. It is an excellent information source for librarians involved in maintaining a Gopher server. Topics includes announcements of new

Internet sources, new Library-run Gophers and questions related to Gopher administration.

<u>To Subscribe</u>:
Send the following e-mail message to listserv@ucsbvm.ucsb.edu:
 subscribe go4lib-l your name

<u>To Unsubscribe</u>:
Send the following e-mail message to listserv@ucsbvm.ucsb.edu:
signoff go4lib-l

6. CWIS-L@WUVMD.BITNET   listserv@wuvmd.wustl.edu

This is a mailing list for discussing the creation and implementation of campus-wide information systems. The term CWIS includes systems which make information and services publicly available on campus via kiosks, interactive computing systems and/or campus networks. Services routinely include directory information, calendars, bulletin boards, databases and library information.

<u>To Subscribe</u>:
Send the following e-mail message to listserv@wuvmd.wustl.edu:
 subscribe cwis-l your name

<u>To Unsubscribe</u>:
Send the following e-mail message to listserv@wuvmd.wustl.edu:
signoff cwis-l

7. bi-l@bingvmb.cc.binghamton.edu

This is the Bibliographic Instruction discussion list. It is an excellent source for practical information relating to instruction. Discussions also take place on such topics as the philosophy of instruction and theoretical approaches to teaching.

To Subscribe:
Send the following e-mail message to listserv@bingvmb.bitnet: (do not use a subject line!)

 subscribe bi-l your name

To Unsubscribe:
Send the following e-mail message to listserv@bingvmb.bitnet: (do not use a subject line!)

signoff bi-l

8. pacs-l@uhupvm1.bitnet

This is the premier electronic discussion list for libraries. Its focus is the use of technology in libraries and though it is moderated, it still has very heavy traffic (10-15 messages a day.)

To Subscribe:
Send the following e-mail message to listserv@uhupvm1.bitnet: (leave subject blank!)

 subscribe pacs-l your name

To Unsubscribe:
Send the following e-mail message to listserv@uhupvm1.bitnet: (leave subject blank!)

signoff pacs-l

9. libref-L@kentvm.kent.edu

 (from the welcoming message:)

This list focuses on the changing environment of library reference services and activities. Topics include traditional reference services, patron expectations, staff training, as well the impact of CD-ROM and online searching on reference service. This forum will serve as a professional networking and information source. We will share ideas, solutions and experiences.

To Subscribe:
Send the following e-mail message to listserv@kentvm.kent.edu: (leave subject blank!)

  subscribe libref-l your name

To Unsubscribe:
Send the following e-mail message to listserv@kentvm.kent.edu: (leave subject blank!)

signoff libref-l

10. **web4lib-l@library.berkeley.edu**

This is an electronic discussion for library-based World-Wide Web developers and managers. Below are excerpts from the welcome message that describe the list.

PURPOSE

The Web4Lib electronic discussion exists to foster discussion of issues relating to the creation and management of library-based World-Wide Web servers and clients. Particulary appropriate issues for discussion include, but are not limited to:

  * web resource selection and information mounting in relation to existing acquisition
    and collection development procedures
  * cataloging issues regarding web information
  * in-house patron access to web servers (e.g., Mosaic on patron-accessible computers)
  * using the web ISMAP feature to provide library information keyed to a building
    floorplan

To Subscribe:
Send the following e-mail message to listserv@library.berkeley.edu: (leave subject blank!)

  subscribe Web4Lib your name

To Unsubscribe:
Send the following e-mail message to listserv@library.berkeley.edu: (leave subject blank!)

signoff Web4Lib

B) COLLECTIONS OF INTERNET GUIDES

1. CNI (Coalition for Networked Information)

Buckets o'guides! This is a great collection of Internet guides, from the thorough
EARN and NSFNet guides to ascii versions of Zen and the Art to Rinaldi's Netiquette
guide. You may want to browse the list on the CNI gopher before accessing the
ftp archive. There's plenty to choose from!

FTP: ftp.cni.org
Directory: /pub/net-guides

Gopher: UMinn list of Gophers/USA/All/Coalition for Networked Information/

              Coaltion FTP Archives/Publicly accessible documents/Guides to network use

2. NYSERNet (New York State Education and Research Network)

The NYSERNet Guide includes information on 52 Internet resources, using telnet, ftp and
e-mail. The guide describes each service and gives detailed instructions on accessing the
service. (As of Nov. 1993, version 2.2 is the most current.) Several other helpful
resources are listed on NYSERNet's Gopher under the "Special Collections: Internet Help"
section. These resources are <u>not</u> necessarily produced by NYSERNet but, they're
conveniently located in one handy place.

FTP: nysernet.org
Directory: /pub/guides   (note: NYSERNet guide file =new.user.guide.v2.2.txt)

Gopher: UMinn list of Gophers/New York/New York State Educ. and Research
              Network/Special Collections: Internet Help

3. Network Training Materials Gopher (Trainmat)

This Gopher was set up to promote and encourage network training. Though the
primary training materials available are those in the UK-based Network Training Pack,
there are also many other good guides and training resources here.

FTP: tuda.ncl.ac.uk
Directory: /pub/network-training   (for Network Training Pack)
Gopher: UMinn list of Gophers/Europe/UK/Networking Training Materials

4. Merit Network Information Resources

Merit Network, Inc., oversees the maintenance of the National Science Foundation Network (NSFNet) backbone. Merit has made available several valuable files in the "Introducing the Internet" section on their Gopher. The Merit Guide may be accessed using anonymous FTP, or Gopher.

FTP: nic.merit.edu
Directory: /introducing.the.internet

Gopher: UMinn list of Gophers/Michigan/Merit Network

4. University of Michigan Library Clearinghouse of Subject-Oriented Internet Resource Guides

The Clearinghouse for Subject-Oriented Internet Resource Guides is a joint effort of the University of Michigan's University Library and the School of Information and Library Studies (SILS). Its goal is to collect and make widely available guides to Internet resources which are subject- oriented. These guides are produced by members of the Internet community, and by SILS students who participate in the Internet Resource Discovery project.

FTP: una.hh.lib.umich.edu
Directory: /inetdirsstacks

Gopher: UMinn list of Gophers/Michigan/Univ. of Michigan Libraries/What's New

C) LISTS OF INFORMATION RESOURCES

1. Information Sources: The Internet and Computer-Mediated Communication (CMC).

The purpose of this project is to list pointers to information describing the Internet, computer networks, and issues related to computer-mediated communication (CMC). Topics include the technical, social, cognitive, and psychological aspects of computer networking and applications of CMC.

FTP: ftp.rpi.edu
Directory: /pub/communications/internet-cmc.txt   (plain ascii file, 80-columns)

2. Special Internet Connections (aka the Yanoff List)

This is one of the most popular and heavily-used list of Internet resources. Maintained by Scott Yanoff, of the Univ. of Wisconsin, it is updated on a bi-weekly basis and includes information on over 100 valuable Internet resources.

FTP: csd4.csd.uwm.edu
Directory: /pub   (note: filename = inet.services.txt)

3. Directory of Scholarly Electronic Conferences

Maintained by Diane Kovacs, of Kent State Univ. Libraries, this is an extensive list covering BITNET, as well as Internet sources. Accessible via ftp and e-mail.

FTP: ksuvxa.kent.edu
Directory: library

E-mail to: listserv@kentvm.kent.edu   (leave subject line blank!)
message: get acadlist readme

D) FAQs (frequently-asked questions)

1. The FAQ archive at MIT

FAQs are lists of frequently-asked questions, with their answers, on internet-related topics. The goal of a FAQ is to eliminate the duplication of basic questions being asked and answered on USENET newsgroups and other electronic discussion lists. FAQs deal with basic information and are often a good starting point for new Internet users and instructors. The MIT archive contains FAQs from many of the USENET newsgroups, as well as those on more general net topics.

FTP: rtfm.mit.edu
Directory: /pub/usenet/news.answers/internet.services

2. Quartz Text Archive

One of the largest collections of FAQ archives organized by subject. Check out the guides and FAQs in the "Internet" section!

FTP: quartz.rutgers.edu
Directory: /pub/internet

Gopher: UMinn list of Gophers/New Jersey/Rutgers Quartz Text Archive

E)   Self-guided Tutorials and Classes

1. Merit Internet Cruise

Based on a comparison of the Internet to the ocean, this nicely done instructional program takes you on an interactive tour of the Internet.

FTP: nic.merit.edu
Directory: /internet/resources   **Don't forget to ftp the readme files too!**

The Macintosh version requires:
     -Mac II or higher
     - a color monitor
     - a high-density disk drive

Cruise - Macintosh requirements (cont'd)

     - system 6.07 or higher
     - approximately 2MB or disk space
     - 4MB of RAM.

The Windows version requires:
     - An IBM-DOS or DOS-compatible computer
     - XGA or XGA-compatible adapter set to display 256 colors at 640 x 480
     - Microsoft Windows(TM) version 3.1
     - Approximately 1.5 MB of disk space
     - 2 MB RAM minimum

*Note: this file will have a .hqx extension, which means it is in a binhex format and requires either BinHex 4.0, Compact Pro, or the StuffIt software programs to "unbinhex" the file and make it usable.

2. InfoPop

This is a hypertext guide to the Internet available for IBM-compatible PCs. It provides information on various net resources, including how to access them via their addresses and how to use them. As of 11/93, the most recent version is 1.12. The file is compressed and will need to be "unzipped" with PKUnZip. You can ftp the InfoPop and PKUnZip programs from the directory below.

FTP: ftp.gmu.edu
Directory: pub/library   (filename = ipwin112.exe)

3. **Navigate the Internet** and **Let's Go Gophern**

These two classes were offered over the Internet by Richard Smith. The course contents and lessons were distributed over several weeks and arrived in the students' electronic mailboxes. "Navigate" covers information and how-to general Internet resources and tools. "Gophern" covers information on the use, structure and overall wonders of Gopher systems. Key Gopher resources were highlighted, along with a section on Gopher subject arrangements.

Navigate files   (note: filenames with a -v are for VMS users)

FTP: ubvmsb.cc.buffalo.edu
Directory: .internet.navigate

Gophern files

FTP: ubvmsb.cc.buffalo.edu
Directory: .internet.gophern

Gopher: UMinn list of Gophers/California/U South. Calif./Free Gopher Course

F) MISCELLANEOUS

1. **Special Issue of Current Cites**

The March 1994, vol. 5 (3), issue of the electronic journal, <u>Current Cites,</u> was devoted to recent articles on Internet training. Special Issue: Internet Training. VERY USEFUL!

FTP: ftp.lib.berkeley.edu
Directory: /pub/Current.Cites

2. Internet Hunts

Rick Gates' ever popular Internet scavenger hunts. Great for testing your knowledge, refreshing your skills and for creating Internet class exercise sheets!

FTP: ftp.cni.org
Directory: /pub/net-guides/internet.hunt

Gopher: UMinn list of Gophers/USA/All/Coalition for Networked Information

3. Gopher Jewels

This is a collection of all the Gopher subject sections. For instance, when you access GopherJewels and select "Education" from the menu, a list will be displayed of the various Gopher servers which have an Education section listed. A good reference source for creating Internet subject - based exercises and especially handy if you are building or maintaining a Gopher yourself.

Gopher: UMinn list of Gophers/California/U South. Calif./Other Gophers and
              Information Resources/Gopher-Jewels

GLOSSARY
>>>>>>>>>>

Internet Instruction: Planning and Designing Faculty Workshops
Abbie J. Basile, 5/94

Archie - System which allows you to search indexes of file archives which are publicly available on the Internet. In other words, it allows you to do a keyword search of anonymous ftp sites.

BITNET - **b**ecause **i**t's **t**ime **net**work. An international academic computer network which supports e-mail, mailing lists, and file transfer.   Does <u>not</u> support remote login (aka telnet).

Client/Server software - The model used for many of the popular Internet tools, such as Gopher, WWW, Archie and WAIS.

> The **server** is the software on the host computer which provides services to other computers. Server also may refer to the computer which has the server software loaded on it. A client asks a server to display a file. The server will then "serve up" the data to the client.

> The **client** software makes requests of the server.   Locally mounted clients allow your session to look like your local environment.   They also give the user access to additional features which usually are not available with a vt100 client. For example, if you are using Gopher with a local client, your Gopher session will be Mac-based, with the use of icons, the mouse, clicking on menus, etc. In this way, client/server computing allows users to work in their familiar computing environments.

CNI - Coalition for Networked Information.   A joint project of ARL, CAUSE and EDUCOM which promotes access to information resources in networked environments. CNI maintains a Gopher server, several CNI-related listservs, as well as an ftp site of various networking-related documents. CNI has recently added a BRS search feature for their ftp archives.

CWIS - Campus Wide Information Systems. Provide electronic access, via Gopher or other software, to campus information such as course schedules, telephone numbers, publications.

Domain name - a structured, alphabetic-based unique name for a computer on a network. Such names are counterparts to the computers IP name. Either name can be used. Ex: 128.04.12.62 or abc.lib.uma.edu

Electronic Journals (e-journals) - full-text journal publications which are available only in electronic form. Like print journals, they cover a wide variety of subjects.

FAQ (pronounced fak) - a list of **f**requently **a**sked **q**uestions and their answers. Many USENET news groups, along with other lists, maintain such a list so that folks won't waste time asking and answering the same questions over and over again.

Fetch - A public domain, FTP program for the Macintosh environment.

Freenet - Community-based bulletin board systems with e-mail, information resources and conferencing capabilities. Based on the public television/public radio model of community access and support.

FTP - file transfer protocol. A software program which allows you to transfer files from one computer to another. Facilitates the movement of large files very quickly over the Internet.

Gopher - Menu-based software which allows you to navigate across the Internet to access resources. This is public domain, client/server based software.

Internet (aka the net) - A world-wide network of heterogeneous computer networks that provides access to electronic mail, remote login, file transfer and other services. It connects over 10, 000 different networks and over 2 million computers!

IP (internet protocol) name - a structured, numeric-based unique name for a computer on a network. The number includes four sections separated by periods.
Ex: 128.04.12.62 or abc.lib.uma.edu

Listserv - Subject-oriented electronic mailing list to which anyone on the Internet with electronic mail access may subscribe. A message posted to a listserv is received by all other subscribers to the list. Listserv also refers to the software that runs some mailing lists. (**Note**: Not all electronic mailing lists use Listserv software, so user commands will vary.)

Remote host - The computer or computer network which has resources which can be accessed by another computer on the Internet. These hosts are usually accessed via telnet. Ex: when you telnet to another library's online catalog, the remote host is the computer on the other end which supports that catalog.

TCP/IP - transmission control protocol/internet protocol. The sets of standards on which the Internet is based. Most importantly, they allow data to pass between the variety of networks which make up the Internet.

Telnet - Software program which allows you to log in to remote computer systems on the Internet. The systems you log in to are often referred to as remote hosts.
(Note: it is important to remember that when you telnet to another computer, you are using computing resources on the other end, and, thus, you will be affected by any slow time or down time that remote system is experiencing.)

UNIX - Computer operating system which played a key role in the development of the Internet. Unix is case-sensitive and since many machines on the Internet run Unix as their operating system, users often have to be careful about typing their login commands exactly as directed in instructions.

Usenet (aka netnews) - This is an informal group of electronic systems which uses subject-specific groups, referred to as newsgroups, to exchange news and information on a vast array of topics. There are currently over 4,000 Usenet newsgroups.

Veronica - very easy rodent-oriented net-wide index to computerized archives. Performs a keyword search of gopher menus and titles. Search results are displayed via a newly created gopher based on your Veronica search.

vt100 - A standard protocol for terminal emulation. This is the most common protocol used when telnetting to a remote host. Many telnet connections require vt100 emulation. It is a bare-bones, lowest common denominator terminal emulation which does not usually allow for commands and features which are available with a workstation-based client. (see client/server)

WAIS - Wide-area information servers. Powerful public domain software which allows you to do a keyword search of more than one Internet database at a time.

WWW (aka the web or W3) - World-Wide Web. A global hypermedia-based system which allows access to the universe of Internet resources, ie users can access text, audio, graphics and moving image files from the Internet. This is public domain, client/server based software.

IN PRINT
>>>>>>>>>
A Selection of Introductory Readings for Internet Instructors

Internet Instruction: Planning and Designing Faculty Workshops
Abbie J. Basile, 5/94

ACRL Bibliographic Instruction Section Emerging Technologies Committee. (July/August 1991). "Teaching Methods for End-User Searching: a Checklist for Planning." College and Research News. 52: 431-436.

Comer, Douglas E. (1991). Internetworking With TCP/IP: Principles, Protocols, and Architecture. 2nd ed. Englewood Cliffs, NJ: Prentice Hall, Inc.,

Delfino, Erik. (1993). "The Internet Toolkit: File Compression and Archive Utilities." Online 17(6): 90-92.

Dern, Daniel P. (1994) The Internet Guide for New Users. New York: McGraw-Hill.

Kehoe, Brendan P. (1993) Zen and the Art of the Internet: a Beginner's Guide. 2nd ed. Englewood Cliffs, NJ: Prentice Hall.

Krol, Ed. (1994) The Whole Internet User's Guide and Catalog. 2nd ed. Sebastopol, CA: O'Reilly & Assoc., Inc.

Lane, Elizabeth S. & Summerhill, Craig. (1993). Internet Primer for Information Professionals: Basic Guide to Internet Networking Technology. Westport, CT: Meckler.

LaQuey, Tracy with Jeanne C. Ryer. (1992). The Internet Companion: A Beginner's Guide to Global Networking. Addison-Wesley: Reading, MA.

Lynch, Clifford & Preston, Cecilia. (1990). "Internet Access to Information Resources." Annual Review of Information Science and Technology. 26: 263-312.

Polly, Jean Armour. (June 1992). "Surfing the Internet: An Introduction." Wilson Library Bulletin. 66(10): 38-42.

Scientific American. (1991). Special issue: Communications, Computers and Networks. 265(3).

Simmonds, Curtis. (1993). "Painless File Extraction: The A(rc) - Z(oo) of Internet Archive Formats." Online 17(6): 60-65.

Tennant, Roy, Ober, J., & Lipow, A. G. (1993). Crossing the Internet Threshold: An Instructional Handbook. Berkeley, CA: Library Solutions Press.

TOP 10 INTERNET INSTRUCTION TIPS
>>>>>>>>>>>>>>>>>
(plus a few extra)

Internet Instruction: Planning and Designing Faculty Workshops
Abbie J. Basile, 5/94

1. For hands-on sessions, have at least one helper for every 8-10 participants.

2. Be prepared for all levels of questions, from modem access to ftp'ing compressed files.

3. Have referral information ready, if necessary, for answers to questions.
   (ex: phone numbers for the campus computing help desk and the reference desk)

4. Stress the dynamic nature of the net so everyone will be prepared for problems.

5. Show your enthusiasm! :-)   Acknowledge the problems that will occur with Internet use but don't focus on them. This is fun stuff!

6. Know the appropriate break keys for telnet sessions and pass this information on before hands-on time begins.

7. Remember, no one knows everything about the Internet. People will be grateful for the information you pass along.

8. Know how participants access the net, so you're prepared for related questions and familiar with commands and process.

9. Have a back-up ready for equipment/connection trouble. (ex: overheads, boards, handouts with screen captures, software with dummy" online session, etc.)

10. Be aware of heavy net traffic times and plan your demonstrations accordingly! (hint: California sleeps while we're awake.)

11. Stress the need for people to look at the text files which accompany the library catalogs telnet session. These files contain important login/logout command instructions which may not be displayed once they're in the catalog.

12. Double check any internet addresses you use in handouts and demos.

13. Know your room, its equipment and how you will access the Internet. Preparation plays a key role in an instructor's confidence.

Scholarship, Propaganda, or Mediocre Research: How Can Librarians Help Students Tell the Difference?

Sonia Bodi

Introduction

Whether we are in a small college or a large university library, many of us have observed the increasing independence of students in doing research, primarily by using CD-ROMs and online catalogs. While we are gratified to know that students may become lifelong learners because of library technology, some of us are also troubled by their seeming indiscriminate use of journals and books. How can we assist students in judging the value and significance of the sources they find through all of the accessing tools available to them?

In our college of about 900 undergraduates, we stress critical thinking skills in our first-year bibliographic instruction taken by all students in their required English composition course. Our goal is for them to begin to judge the significance of books and articles by finding the expertise and qualifications of the authors, reading book reviews, and examining the viewpoint of journals. The students write partially annotated bibliographies on their research topics for this assignment. Students actually do begin to learn how to assess the expertise of an author, read a book review and find the viewpoint of a journal, and to decide whether or not a source will be relevant and of value to their work. But how do they judge the text? While

Bodi is professor of bibliography, head reference librarian, North Park College, Chicago, Illinois.

we encourage them to use bibliographies compiled by other scholars as a means to finding sources of value, they are still unlikely to know how to judge the text for themselves. After their first-year instruction, many find their own books and articles with little or no assistance from the librarians. We continue to emphasize the importance of judging the value of resources in other course-related instruction, but many students have this instruction only one or two more times.

Student evaluations of first-year bibliographic instruction show high marks of an 85 to 90 percent and above positive response to questions such as the following about the instruction:

- Do you think learning the basic search strategy will be helpful to you in the future when you are required to write a research paper?

- How confident do you feel in your ability to use the library compared to your level of confidence before you took the instruction?

- As you think over what you've learned about using the library, how useful do you think it was for your research paper?

- As you think over what you've learned about using the library, how useful do you think this instruction will be for your future research and information needs?

One question, however, has a consistently lower positive response of 75 percent:

- Do you think you have some understanding of how to evaluate the significance and value of books and journal articles as a result of doing this instruction?

While we have been delighted with the overall evaluation, we have been troubled by the students' perception that they are not learning critical assessment, particularly since the primary focus of our instruction is just that. We wondered how we could address this issue more directly and concretely.

Most librarians and teaching faculty would agree that while knowledge is moved forward by research of excellent quality, there are numerous books and articles published of dubious quality, if not questionable logic, inaccurate data, and contrived conclusions. Some texts proffer propaganda and others proffer merely mediocre research. We like to think the top-ranked journals in a discipline and the first-rate publishing houses will publish the best, but how do undergraduates know how to identify the "best"?

We have tried to think of ways to assist students in their critical assessment of the text and to reinforce their professors' objectives in critical analysis. In this paper I will discuss some characteristics of propaganda and mediocre research and provide a list of indicators that might assist students in judging the difference between genuine scholarship and what passes for scholarship. Finally, I will give a practical example of a class in which we used these indicators as a guide to help students better assess a text.

PROPAGANDA

As librarians, we are providers of information. Jacques Ellul, a French ethicist who has written several books on the ethical implications of a technological society, one of them primarily on propaganda, argues that our contemporary world worships "facts" as ultimate reality because facts provide evidence and proof and we tend to subordinate values to them. Because a fact is the sole criterion, we think it must be good. Propaganda operates with many different kinds of truth: half-truth, limited truth, truth out of context; in other words, propaganda is not all lies. However, propaganda provides the interpretation to the fact and that is the real realm of the lie. We sometimes think that all propaganda is false and that obviously we can tell the difference between falsehood and truth; we become susceptible to propaganda

because we assume when propaganda does tell the "truth" it is no longer propaganda.[1]

Another distinction between propaganda and scholarship is that scholarship is even-handed in addressing a diversity of points of view on an issue while propaganda tends to present one point of view as the only point of view. Propaganda, like the term "critical thinking," has numerous definitions. A colleague has suggested a distinction between scholarship and propaganda that I have found more useful than others:

Scholarship is a fair-minded attempt to represent a point of view while propaganda is a deliberate attempt to mislead.[2]

Propaganda, to be successful, must result in changed attitudes and/or motivation to action. Ellul argues that we live in a mass society with inadequate resources to cope with the multiple conflicts in our personal and corporate world. We feel isolated, lonely, and ineffective; propaganda provides us with an opportunity for personal involvement and participation in important events by giving us explanations that allow us to have opinions or take a position. Just as information is necessary for awareness, propaganda is necessary to prevent this awareness from being desperate. Propaganda enables us to feel we have mastery over our chaotic world and provides us with solutions to problems.[3] The problem for our undergraduates is that propaganda provides them with ready-made answers and causes them to stereotype, which encourages them to avoid thinking, taking personal stands, or forming their own opinions.[4] The more we read of a particular point of view the more we believe we have an informed opinion.

In a recent article on deniers of the Holocaust in *The Chronicle of Higher Education*, Deborah Lipstadt argues that many students find it impossible to recognize when a movement has no scholarly validity. They cannot say that something is nonsense and has nothing to do with ideas.[5] I would agree. I think undergraduates, not to mention graduate students, not to mention adults in general, have a great deal of difficulty knowing when something is a prejudice or a piece of propaganda and is not an idea or viewpoint or opinion.

How do students distinguish if an author has a bias, is a propagandist, or has a point of view? Eileen Gambrill, a professor of social work, may be helpful. Those who are biased try to persuade others but may be unaware they are doing so. They may use propaganda techniques and faulty reasoning in an effort to get an uncritical or emotional acceptance of a biased position. Those who are propagandists are aware of their interests and usually intentionally disguise these. Their messages are couched in a way to get uncritical acceptance. Finally, those who have points of view are aware of their interests but their sources are described and propaganda devices and faulty reasoning are avoided. Statements are made in a manner that encourages critical review, and their views can be examined because they are clearly stated.[6] Obviously, there is a fine line among these.

In another of Ellul's works, *Humiliation of the Word*, he argues that our contemporary world usually thinks in images. We need the stimulus of an image, and the bare information in an article or in a book no longer has an effect on us.[7] Sometimes we overtly, sometimes inadvertently, encourage students to be impressed with charts, graphs, and so forth as signs of bona fide research. However, this data can also be manipulated, and research findings, facts, statistics, explanations, and analyses can eliminate our own judgment and critical thought and drown us rather than enlighten us.

Finally, Ellul argues that educated people are most vulnerable to propaganda because we absorb the largest amount of secondhand, unverifiable information and have a compelling need to have an opinion on every topic and easily succumb to opinions offered us by propaganda. Furthermore, we consider ourselves capable of judging "for ourselves." My concern is that in our instruction program, we may be giving students an inflated sense of their ability to judge the value of resources "for themselves."

I have purposely avoided giving examples of propaganda used by different disciplines, because to mention a few would imply only those disciplines employ propaganda and others do not. Not using examples may be a weakness of this study. However, I also wish to make the point that, while we may identify propaganda in our own fields and in areas of particular interest for us, I would suggest that most of us could not identify propaganda in areas about which we know little. How much more difficult, then, for undergraduates who have very little in-depth knowledge about any discipline to be able to distinguish between scholarship and propaganda.

MEDIOCRE RESEARCH

Distinguishing between propaganda and scholarship is difficult for undergraduates. However, judging the scholarly value of books and articles is further complicated by sloppy research with which we are all familiar. It is not so easy for undergraduates to identify research that is mediocre or worse. How are students able to judge the expertise and qualifications of an author? What do students know about the publishing practices in the disciplines? How do students know the differences between the top-ranked journals in a field, the reporting and digest journals in a field, and the journals that publish with little discrimination. How do students know when reading a book if the theories promoted are no longer acceptable? How do they know if the research is of high quality?

There are two primary purposes for publishing; one is to communicate findings and to advance knowledge, and the other is to achieve academic credit, which usually depends more on quantity than on quality. In a recent study, Herbert White challenges the premise that peer review is fair and unbiased in determining what is worthwhile and what should be published. He argues that most scholarly communities are small and authors are known to reviewers, if not through the text, then through the references cited. A 1987 study found, though, that some publishers publish inferior material to fill issues and to keep an article written by a well-known person from going to another journal.[8] However, a study done by sociologists examining the articles published and rejected in the *American Sociological Review* between 1977 and 1981 found that the relative status of a scholar has no perceptible influence on the evaluation of a manuscript. They did find that the prestige of an institution has a consistent, direct effect on publication. The reasons may be less of the author than that a prestigious institution recruits and retains older faculty with established records of scholarly publication and younger faculty with promise. These institutions are also most likely to provide environments that offer more resources for scholarly work, encourage publication, and provide more released time—all of which factors contribute to higher quality manuscripts.[9]

An author's prestige or background may make us think he or she knows the truth, but has the person actually investigated the issue, does the person have a sound reason for making an assertion? We stress to students the importance of citing sources; students think, then, if they have an answer to the question, "What is your source?" that they are dealing with accurate information and with truth. This is not enough. Eileen Gambrill, professor of social work at The University of California at Berkeley, gives rules of thumb for assessing an authority:

- An authority in one area is not necessarily an authority in others.

- An authority's opinion should not necessarily be accepted when experts disagree or there is little known in a field.

- Evidence, reasons, and arguments should be examined when experts disagree.

• The track record of an expert should be reviewed.[10]

We can make some generalizations about publishing in various disciplines, which may be helpful to students as they try to assess a text. Humanities journals reject the greatest number of submissions, social sciences the next largest, and sciences the least. There is great variation, however. For example, the most selective science journal may reject most of the submissions it receives, although rejected articles are likely to be published elsewhere.[11] Humanists are more concerned with interpretation than with unearthing facts,[12] and humanities journals would rather risk rejecting worthy manuscripts than publishing a worthless one.[13] The sciences publish much of what is received for several reasons. There are many more journals in the sciences than in other fields, but there is also a great need to publish anything that has the slightest chance of contributing to knowledge.[14] In the sciences, many scientists depend on their colleagues and the grapevine to inform them of particularly significant articles or breakthroughs in their field. However, verbal communication is limited because it excludes many people, such as undergraduates, and it lacks the permanence of written communication.[15]

Undergraduates understand scientific articles and books to be written by impartial scientists. However, scientific literature is also written by specialists who have commercial interests, by specialists not broadly enough trained to speak with adequate perspective, by people on the fringe of science, and by charlatans unqualified in science but accepted by the public as scientists. Furthermore, journalistic reports in the sciences tend to focus on results rather than processes and emphasize spectacular claims more than cautious qualified reports. Demands for brevity may eliminate important information and leave the wrong impression.[16]

Finally, the sciences, the health fields, and to some extent the social sciences are highly competitive disciplines in terms of government and foundation funding, attracting young people into research and teaching careers, popularizing particular developments, and shaping public policy. These priorities influence the kind of research that is done and the nature of the manuscripts written and accepted for publication.

How, then, do we as librarians assist undergraduates with all of these complexities in publication?

IMPLICATIONS FOR BIBLIOGRAPHIC INSTRUCTION

Our library has had a teaching library philosophy for over a decade. We have a library instruction program for first-year students mentioned in the introduction to this paper, which is complemented by other upper-division level instruction sessions. We decided to try our idea for helping students distinguish between propaganda and scholarship in an English composition class after students had completed the first-year library instruction.

First-year students are enrolled in one semester of English composition which is a course comprised of two parts. The first half of the course focuses on general writing skills at the college level and the second half focuses on writing within the context of a particular topic. One of these courses had as its topic propaganda, an especially appropriate class for our instructional program. The students read *War Without Mercy* by John Dower[17] as the primary text to introduce them to propaganda. *War Without Mercy* is a splendid example of a well-balanced work of scholarship, which examines the use of propaganda by both the Americans and the Japanese during World War II. We compiled about 20 different articles from the bibliography of this book; some of the articles were examples of propaganda and some were examples of scholarship.[18] All of the students read one article in common, and all read their individual article as well.[19] The articles were distributed prior to our coming to class.

We distributed the following "Indicators of Scholarship" and "Indicators of Propaganda" for the students to use as they read and assessed the articles. These indicators were designed by Eileen Gambrill, who has researched the use of propaganda in her own field of social work.[20] They are as follows:

Indicators of Scholarship

• Describes limits of data,

• Presents accurate description of alternative views,

• Presents data that do not favor preferred views as well as data that support these,

• Encourages debate/discussion/criticism,

• Makes use of special methods for discovering bias (e.g., repetition of experiments; clear accurate description of sources of data),

• Settles disputes by use of generally accepted criteria for evaluating data,

• Looks for counter-examples,

• Uses language in agreed-upon ways,

- Updates information,

- Admits own ignorance,

- Attempts to discuss general laws/principles,

- Finds own field/area of investigation difficult and full of holes, and

- Relies on critical thinking skills.

Indicators of Propaganda

- Excessive claims of certainty (We have "the way"; "the view"),

- Personal attacks/ridicule,

- Appeals to emotions,

- Distorts data unfavorable to preferred views,

- Suppresses contradictory views,

- Suppresses contradictory facts,

- Appeals to popular prejudices,

- Relies on suggestion (e.g., negative innuendo),

- Devalues thought/critical appraisal,

- Transforms words to suit aims,

- Magnifies or minimizes problems/suggested remedies, and

- Presents information/views out of context.

Put another way, the requisite virtues of scholarship in the search for truth include intellectual modesty, openness, self-awareness, teachability, justice, fair-mindedness, coherency, and a moderate, reasonable tone.

Our presentation to the class began with a brief lecture on propaganda and on some of the differences between propaganda and scholarship. We then discussed the article read in common. Interestingly, we had chosen an article that we thought represented scholarship but that the students thought represented propaganda. We had not anticipated that the students would read the article from a contemporary viewpoint, which made the article appear to be quite racist. When we talked about the culture of the 1940s, however, the students understood the article quite differently. It was a brief

but effective lesson on reading primary sources. We then divided the class into groups of four, which were determined by the common subject matter of their articles. For example, one group of articles covered the psychology of the war, another the actual fighting, another the issue of color, and another the Japanese perspective. After discussing the articles using the indicators, one group spokesperson summarized the findings. The articles were from news magazines, scholarly journals, and popular magazines of the time.

The professor of the course had the students work in groups of four to research and produce a literature review of ten pages on one aspect of propaganda. The students chose topics such as "The Media in the Vietnam War: What Effects Did the Media Have on the Peace Movement at Home?"; "Propaganda and Racism: How Much Does Propaganda Depend on Racial Prejudice for Its Success?" and "The Process of Defining an Enemy: What Common Characteristics Do Enemies Have?" After working collaboratively on a group research project, the students each took one aspect of their group projects, such as "Race in the Propaganda Films of Frank Capra: How Much Was the Films' Motivation to Fight Based on Racial Stereotypes of the Japanese?" and "Propaganda and the Nightly News: Does the Nightly News Portray Crime in Racist Terms?" and wrote 15-page research papers as their final assignment for the course.

CONCLUSION

The problem of helping students assess the value of resources remains. We might assume that faculty help students assess texts as they progress in their major courses. We would expect that in a senior seminar or in some other senior course, students would be taught by their professors to distinguish between first-rate scholarship and either mediocre research or propaganda. However, many students are not instructed in the analysis of texts. The problem also remains of determining the most effective and appropriate time to introduce students to the distinction between propaganda and scholarship. While it may be appropriate to introduce students during their first year in college to the problems of mediocre scholarship and propaganda, William Perry's levels of cognitive development may indicate that the third and fourth years are more appropriate times.[21] Finally, it is arguable that librarians are not responsible for educating students to assess resources; our responsiblity is to provide them. I would argue, however, that we do have a responsibility to educate students to know that resources are not uniformly valuable or relevant, and that the students need to maintain skepticism and to suspend judgment until they have assessed the text. If we can do that effectively, we will have contributed in some measure to the independent, lifelong learning of our students.

NOTES

1. Jacques Ellul, *Propaganda: The Formation of Men's Attitudes* (New York: Alfred B. Knopf, 1969), xv, 52-53, 57.

2. Nancy Arnesen, associate professor of English, North Park College, Chicago, IL.

3. Ellul, *Propaganda*, v-vi, 140, 147, 159.

4. Ellul, *Propaganda*, 112-114, 162-169.

5. Deborah E. Lipstadt, "Academe Must Not Legitimate Denials of the Holocaust," *The Chronicle of Higher Education* 39 (28 July 1993): B3.

6. Eileen Gambrill, *Critical Thinking in Clinical Practice: Improving the Accuracy of Judgments and Decisions About Clients* (San Francisco: Jossey-Bass, 1990), 95.

7. Jacques Ellul, *The Humiliation of the Word* (Grand Rapids, MI: Eeerdman's, 1985), viii, 210-211.

8. Herbert White, "Scholarly Publication, Academic Libraries, and the Assumption That These Processes Are Under Management Control," *College & Research Libraries* 54 (July 1993): 293-301.

9. Von Bakanic, Clark McPhail, Rita J. Simon, "The Manuscript Review and Decision Making Process." *American Sociological Review* 52 (October 1987): 631-642.

10. Gambrill, 95.

11. Mary Biggs, "The Impact of Peer Review on Intellectual Freedom," *Library Trends* 39 (Summer/Fall 1990): 145-167.

12. Biggs.

13. Bakanic, et al., 633.

14. Biggs, 147.

15. Philip H. Abelson, "Scientific Communication," *Science* 209 (4 July 1980): 60-63.

16. Fred Decker, "Scientific Communication Should Be Improved," *Science* 125 (1957): 101-105.

17. John Dower, *War Without Mercy: Race and Power in the Pacific War* (New York: Pantheon, 1987).

18. Following is a list of the articles we used: "Jap Surrenders Are Increasing: Psychological War Proves Effective," *Life* 19 (9 July 1945); Edgar Jones, "Fighting with Words: Psychological Warfare in the Pacific," *Atlantic Monthly* 176 (August 1945): 47-51; Karl Lowith, "The Japanese Mind: A Picture of the Mentality That We Must Understand if We Are to Conquer," *Fortune* 27 (December 1943): 132-135; Judith Silberpfenning, "Psychological Aspects of Current Japanese and German Paradoxa," *Psychoanalytical Review* 32 (January 1945): 73-85; "Murder in Tokyo," *Time* 41 (3 May 1943): 19-20; "How Japs Fight," *Time* 41 (15 February 1943): 24-26; "Bataan: Where Heroes Fell," *Time* 40 (20 April 1942): 18-21; "The Jap as Boss-Man," *Time* 41 (3 May 1943): 26; "Why Americans Hate Japs More Than Nazis," *Science Digest* 17 (March 1945): 5; Charles Bolte, "This Is the Face of War," *The Nation* 160 (3 March 1945): 240-241; Helen Mears, "Why the Japanese Fight," *The New Republic* 108 (29 March 1943): 418-419; Roger Bastide, "Color, Racism and Christianity," *Daedelus* 96 (Spring 1967): 312-327; "Are We Afraid to Do Justice?" *Christian Century* 60 (9 June 1943): 687-688; Hiroshi Wagatsuma, "The Social Perception of Skin Color in Japan," *Daedelus* 96 (Spring 1967): 407-443; "Foreigners, Attitudes Toward," *Kodansha Encyclopedia of Japan* (Tokyo and New York; Kodanshay, 1983); John Embree, "Democracy in Postwar Japan," *American Journal of Sociology* 50 (November 1944): 205-207; Joel Berreman, "Assumptions About America in Japanese War Propaganda to the United States," *American Journal of Sociology* 54 (September 1948): 108-117; "World War II, "*Kodansha Encyclopedia of Japan.*

19. The article the class read in common was Virginius Dabney, "Nearer and Nearer the Precipice," *Atlantic Monthly* (January 1943): 94-100.

20. These indicators were handouts by Eileen Gambrill, professor, School of Social Welfare, University of California at Berkeley, at the Twelfth Annual International Conference on Critical Thinking and Educational Reform, 9-12 August 1992, Sonoma State University.

21. William Perry, Jr., *Forms of Intellectual and Ethical Development in the College Years: A Scheme* (New York: Holt, Rinehart and Winston, 1970).

DANCE RESOURCES:
GROWING BY LEAPS AND BOUNCES!

Mary S. Bopp

Introduction

I want to congratulate all of you for attending this session. When Linda Shirato told me that my presentation had been selected as one of the LOEX subject-sessions this year, she said that they usually like to offer one or two "off-the-wall" sessions, and that this would be one of them! I am flattered to be known as "off-the-wall," and I'm delighted that a few adventure-some spirits are willing to spend an hour learning about dance in the context of libraries.

The Nature of Dance

If I were to *dance* this presentation, instead of *verbalizing* it, this is what a mini version would look like:

(In motion: Open Arms, Shrug Shoulders, Fists Pound, Flicking Fingers, Hands to Heart, Shaking Hands and Leg, Bow)

But as I am here chiefly to verbalize my presentation, not dance it, I will begin with some general thoughts about dance. Dance is many things—a visual art, a performing art, a social endeavor, a cultural expression, a means of communication, a religious ceremonial. There are many forms and styles of dance. Ballet, modern, tap, and jazz are our most visible per-

Bopp is librarian at the undergraduate library, Indiana University, Bloomington, Indiana.

forming arts; social forms include ballroom, contra, hip hop, and swing; dances are as much a part of our cultural heritage as music, sculpture, architecture, and religion.

Dance has also been difficult to document. Some choreographers have resisted documentation; written notation systems have not been universally taught or used; film and video recordings have been inconsistent, volatile, and offer flat representations of a three-dimensional art. Because many dance companies have not had the money, facilities, or staff to adequately record their repertory, many dances have not been documented at all.

Dance has also lacked a universal method of recording. A major mode of passing dances from one generation to the next has traditionally been through a combination oral/demonstration process, which is often impermanent and imprecise. Access to dance materials has traditionally been very poor as well. Hundreds of primary dance materials lay uncataloged in back rooms of archives around the world. Subject headings for dance have also been vague and inaccurate. And a great deal of dance has been lost forever due to the destructive forces of heat and humidity on video tape and film.

Dance and Libraries

So what kinds of dance information do people expect to find in libraries? Why don't we see more dance in libraries? How many standard reference sources can you name off the top of your head for each of the related disciplines: music, theatre, visual and fine arts. Now, how many dance titles can you name from your dance reference collection? Why is it that millions of people attend dance concerts and participate in dance activities each year, but still there is comparatively little dance in our libraries? I asked myself this question about eight years ago as I was sitting in a literature of the humanities class during my last semester in Indiana University's School of Library and Information Science.

Professor Nancy Lair had passed out an extensive, annotated bibliography of the major reference sources in the performing arts. I quickly turned to the page on dance and was shocked to find perhaps five or six sources. Having looked at page after page of dictionaries, encyclopedias, and guides for literature, religion, drama, music, philosophy, and history, I began to formulate questions about the documentation and bibliographic control of dance. Why was it so poorly represented? Are there any librarians who are addressing the gaps in dance bibliography? Within a few days I realized what many of the problems were, knew what steps had to be taken, and saw a future for myself as an instruction librarian who dabbled in dance.

But enough about the past; my purpose (fists together) today is to first let you know that there are indeed people in libraries who are deeply concerned about the problems I just mentioned. And we are committed to rectifying those problems in an organized manner. I also want to make you aware of some of the projects being developed and new products that are available. But first, a brief overview of the depth and breadth of scholarship and research in dance.

Areas of Dance Study (flicking fingers)

- See appendix 1.

- Other disciplines that look at dance: music, anthropology, folklore, theatre, comparative literature, visual arts, kinesiology/physical education, semiotics, American studies, women's studies, philosophy, psychology.

Dance in Print (Hands to Heart)

- BIBLIOGRAPHY—See appendix 2.

- Reference books just out: *International Dictionary of Ballet* (St. James).

- Essential publications: *The Dance Handbook*, the *Biographical Dictionary of Dance*, the *Dance Film and Video Guide*, *Research in Dance III* and *IV*,

Completed Research in Health, Physical Education, Recreation and Dance.

- *A must for all college/university libraries: *Index to Dance Periodicals*.

- Watch for on the horizon, and go into the red to purchase: *The International Encyclopedia of Dance*. (forthcoming).

- Useful sources outside the mainstream: *Attitudes and Arabesques, Dance Abstracts and Index*, Conference proceedings from Congress On Research in Dance, Society of Dance History Scholars, National Dance Association, Dance Critics Association, American Dance Guild, Cross-Cultural Dance Resources, Dance Notation Bureau.

SOURCES THAT ARE NOT ON THE HANDOUT...MAKE A NOTE OF THESE:

Sources for librarians wanting to bone up on specifics about dance librarianship: *The Humanities and the Library* (Couch and Allen) section on dance; new book to watch for: *Managing Performing Arts Collections* (Carolyn Sheehy, ed.)

Electronic Sources (Shaking hands, leg extends)

- *Dance On Disc* demonstration: *Dance On Disc* is the complete catalog of the New York Public Library dance collection, the largest repository of dance materials in the world. It is an annual cumulation, distributed by G.K. Hall. While much of the collection does not circulate, the CD is nevertheless useful for identifying items that can then be located and borrowed from ones' own institution or through interlibrary loan from another institution.

Sample searches:

1. "About this Disk."

2. Free text searching: hip hop, jerome robbins, nureyev video.

3. Boolean operator: "and"
   labanotation and hutchinson and 1992
   set design and benois
   jerome robbins and photos

4. Boolean operator: "and not"
   baryshnikov and not articles
   baryshnikov and not books
   baryshnikov and not american ballet theatre

— MARY S. BOPP —

5. Nesting:
   (tap or jazz) and instruction
   (modern or post modern) and tharp
6. Indexes:
   AU denby, edwin
       mcdonagh, don
       de mille, agnes

   TI next week swan lake
       where she danced

   SU a broken twig
       acrobats of god
       folk dancing
       post modern dance
       judson church

   MT prints & drawings and nijinsky

   LA french and folk dance

   NA graham, martha
       tharp, twyla
       waldeen
       ballet suedois

   SO dance magazine and (tap or jazz)
       ballet review
       dance pages
       dance observer

7. Truncation: waltz* (gets all endings)

8. Wild Card: ?
   waltz? waltz?? waltz???

Other Interesting Electronic Sources

- Internet: Can telnet to the NYPL Dance Collection: nyplgate.nypl.org. Password: nypl.

- Dance server at Ohio State University: URL: <HTTP://www.dance.ohio-state.edu>.

Listservs

If you have a reference question, the DLDG-L is a great place to post it. Send questions to me and I will post, or subscribe yourself and post questions.

Address is: listserv@iubvm. In the message type: subscribe dldg-l firstname lastname. Then send. You should receive a confirmation message if you connected successfully.

   Ballroom (Ballroom Dance)
   DLDG-L (Dance Librarians Discussion Group)
   DANCE-HC (Dance Heritage Coalition)
   DANCE-L (International Folk and Traditional Dance)
   MORRIS-L (Morris Dance)
   RENDANCE-L (Renaissance Dance)

Miscellaneous Sources

- Dance Groups to Follow and Ask for Assistance: The Dance Librarians Committee and Dance Librarians Discussion Group of the Arts Section of the Association of College and Research Libraries, and the Dance Heritage Coalition (DHC)—a privately-funded consortium of dance archives in the U.S. The DHC provides a calendar of dance and dance/archives meetings on the Internet, a list of oral histories, and a list of exhibitions of dance materials. DHC is also working with LC to more clearly define cataloging guidelines and standards for dance.

- *Afterimages* (ISSN 1073-2101), the Dance Heritage Coalition newsletter, is an excellent source of information on dance documentation and preservation activities.

- PRESERVE at Jacob's Pillow Dance Festival in Lee, Massachusetts, provides seminars and workshops on the care and preservation of a variety of formats.

Conclusion

Through the dedication and energy of a handful of librarians and dance scholars, the documentation and preservation of dance is finally being addressed. Significant new resources—electronic, print, and video—are appearing with regularity. Projects are developing with cooperation from several constituencies. Librarians now have an ALA-affiliated group to contact for assistance. There is great hope for rescuing the record of dance history from being an endangered species.

Branches of Study in Dance

Branches of Study in Dance

History
periods
countries
cultures
styles
biography

Religion
sacred dance

Science
kinesiology
biomechanics
dance medicine

Psychology
therapy
healing

Folk/Ethnic Dance
dance ethnology
anthropology
folklore
ethnomusicology
ritual
forms:
(by geographic region)
asian, slavic, etc.

Sociology
popular dances
social dance forms
gender

Education
methodology
curriculum
facilities
administration
children's dance
creative movement
improvisation

Visual Arts
painting
sculpture
film/video
photography

Notation
laban
benesh
kineseography
eshkol-wachman
stepanov

Performing Art
technique
criticism
choreography
dance music
theory/philosophy
forms:
ballet
modern
jazz
performance art

Literature
comparative literature
poetry

— MARY S. BOPP —

Appendix 2:

A Core Reference Collection in Dance

Mary Bopp
Indiana University
LOEX Annual Conference, 1994

Encyclopedias, Dictionaries:

GENERAL:

Barba, Eugenio, and Nicola Savarese. A Dictionary of Theatre Anthropology: The Secret Art of the Performer. New York: Centre for Performance Research/Routledge, 1991. ISBN 0415053080

Chujoy, Anatole, and P.W. Manchester. The Dance Encyclopedia. New York: Simon and Schuster, 1967.

Cohen, Selma Jeanne. The International Encyclopedia of Dance.(forthcoming)

Jonas, Gerald. Dancing: The Pleasure, Power, and Art of Movement. New York: Harry Abrams/WNET, 1992. ISBN 0810932121

The JVC Video Anthology of World Music and Dance. 30 videocassettes, 9 books. Fujii Tomoaki, ed. Ichikawa Katsumori, producer. Tokyo: JVC, Victor Company of Japan; distributed by Rounder Records, 1990.

Sachs, Curt. World History of the Dance. New York: Norton, 1965, c1937. ISBN 0-393-00209-8

Handbooks, Guides, Bibliographies:

Adamczyk, Alice J. Black Dance: An Annotated Bibliography. Garland Reference Library of the Humanities, vol. 558. New York: Garland, 1989. ISBN 0-8240-8808-5

Beaumont, Cyril. A Bibliography of Dancing. New York: Arno, 1978 (reprint).

Bopp, Mary S. Research in Dance: A Guide to Resources. New York: G.K. Hall, 1993. ISBN 0-8161-9065-8

Dance Films Association. Towers, Diedre, comp. The Dance Film and Video Guide. Princeton, NJ: Dance Horizons/Princeton Book Co., 1991. ISBN 0-87127-171-0

Forbes, Fred R. Dance: An Annotated Bibliography, 1965-1982. Garland Reference Library of the Humanities, vol. 606. New York: Garland, 1986. ISBN 0824086767

Gray, Judith, ed. Research in Dance IV: 1900-1990. Reston, VA: National Dance Association, 1992. ISBN 0-88314-528-6.

Harris, Jane A. Dance A While: A Handbook for Folk, Square, Contra, and Social Dance. 7th Ed. New York: MacMillan, 1994. ISBN 0-0235-0581-8

Jacob, Ellen. <u>Dancing: The All-in-One Guide for Dancers, Teachers, and Parents</u>.
    Revised Edition. New York: Variety Arts, 1993. ISBN 0-937180-10-6

Magriel, Paul David. <u>A Bibliography of Dancing: A List of Books and Articles on the
    Dance and Related Subjects</u>. New York: B. Blom, 1966.

Overby, Lynette Y., and James H. Humphrey, eds. <u>Dance: Current Selected Research</u>.
    New York: AMS, 1989- . ISSN 0894-4849

Robertson, Allen, and Donald Hutera. <u>The Dance Handbook</u>. New York: G.K. Hall,
    1990. ISBN 0-8161-9095-X

Biographical:

Getz, Leslie. <u>Dancers and Choreographers: A Selected Bibliography</u>. (forthcoming)

Cohen-Stratyner, Barbara. <u>Biographical Dictionary of Dance</u>. New York: Schirmer
    Books, 1982. ISBN 0028702603

Mapp, Edward. <u>Directory of Blacks in the Performing Arts</u>. 2d ed. Metuchen, NJ:
    Scarecrow, 1990. ISBN 0-8108-2222-9

Directories of Organizations:

<u>Stern's Performing Arts Directory</u>. New York: Dance Magazine, Inc., 1989- .

<u>Dance Magazine College Guide, 1992-93</u>. New York: Dance Magazine, Inc., 1992.
    ISBN 0-930036-21-2

<u>Scholars Directory, 1993</u>. Brockport, New York: Congress On Research in Dance, 1993.

Indexes to Periodical Literature:

POPULAR:

InfoTrac: Academic and Magazine Index, National Newspaper Index
Wilson: Readers' Guide to Periodical Literature
NewsBank: Performing Arts Index

SCHOLARLY:

<u>Index to Dance Periodicals</u> <u>Dance Abstracts and Index</u>
<u>Dance On Disc: The Complete Catalog of the NYPL Dance Collection</u>

<u>Humanities Index</u>	<u>MLA International Bibliography</u>
<u>Art Index</u>	<u>Music Index</u>
<u>Abstracts in Anthropology</u>	<u>Sport Discus</u>
<u>ERIC</u>	<u>RILA</u>
<u>RILM</u>	<u>Social Sciences Index</u> <u>Sociofile</u>

Periodical Subscriptions:

American Journal of Dance Therapy

Ballet Review   Ballroom Dance Magazine

Choreography and Dance: An International Journal

Choreography and Dance Studies   Contact Quarterly: A Vehicle for Moving Ideas

Dance Chronicle: Studies in Dance and the Related Arts

Dance Magazine   Dance Research(London)

Dance Research Journal   Dance Teacher Now

Impulse: The International Journal of Dance Science, Medicine, and Education

Kinesiology and Medicine for Dance   National Squares   The New Dance Review

Studies in Dance History   UCLA Journal of Dance Ethnology

Specialized Resources:

Aesthetics:

Fraleigh, Sondra Horton.   Dance and the Lived Body: A Descriptive Aesthetics.
    Pittsburgh, PA: University of Pittsburgh Press, 1987. ISBN 0-8229-3548-1

Anthropology:

Royce, Anya Peterson. The Anthropology of Dance. Bloomington: Indiana University
    Press, 1977. ISBN 0-25330752X

Ballet:

Koegler, Horst. Concise Oxford Dictionary of Ballet. 2d. ed. New York: Oxford
    University Press, 1982. Updated, 1987. ISBN 0-19-311300-9
Bremser, Martha, ed. International Dictionary of Ballet. Detroit: St. James Press, 1993.
    ISBN 1-558620842
Studwell, William E., and David A. Hamilton. Ballet Plot Index: A Guide to Locating
    Plots and Descriptions of Ballets and Associated Material. New York: Garland,
    1987. ISBN 0-824083857

Black Dance:

Emery, Lynne Fauley. Black Dance in the United States from 1619 to Today. 2d, rev.
     ed. Forward by Katherine Dunham. Princeton, NJ: Princeton Book Co., 1988.
     ISBN 0-916622614
Long, Richard A. The Black Tradition in American Dance. New York: Rizzoli, 1989.
     ISBN 0-847810925

Caribbean:

Thompson, Donald. Music and Dance in Puerto Rico From the Age of Columbus to
     Modern Times: An Annotated Bibliography. Metuchen, NJ: Scarecrow Press,
     1991. ISBN 0810825155

Indian:

Menon, K.P.S. A Dictionary of Kathakali. New Delhi: Longman, 1979.
Kendadamath, G. C. Indian Music and Dance: A Select Bibliography. Varanasi, India:
     Indian Bibliographic Centre, 1986. ISBN 0-8364-0903-5

Jazz:

Giordano, Gus. Anthology of American Jazz Dance. 2d ed. Evanston, IL: Orion
     Publishing House, 1978.
LaPointe-Crump, Janice. Discovering Jazz Dance: America's Energy and Soul.
     Madison, WI: WCB Brown and Benchmark, 1992. ISBN

Medicine:

Ryan, Allan J., and Robert E. Stephens, eds. Dance Medicine: A Comprehensive Guide.
     Chicago: Pluribus, 1987. ISBN 0-931028-92-2

Modern:

Livet, Ann. Contemporary Dance. New York: Abbeville Press, 1978.
     ISBN 0896590070
McDonagh, Don. The Rise and Fall and Rise of Modern Dance. New York: Popular
     Library, 1977. ISBN 0-445-08623-8

Native American:

Native American Dance: Ceremonies and Social Traditions. Charlotte Heth, general ed.
     Washington, DC: National Museum of the American Indian, Smithsonian
     Institution, with Starwood Publishers, 1992. ISBN 1563730200

Sweet, Jill. <u>Dances of the Tewa Pueblo Indians: Expressions of New Life</u>. Santa Fe, NM: School of American Research Press, 1985. ISBN 093345211X

<u>Notation</u>:

Guest, Ann Hutchinson. <u>Choreo-graphics: A Comparison of Dance Notation Systems from the Fifteenth Century to the Present</u>. New York: Gordon and Breach, 1989. ISBN 2-88124-714-8

Knust, Albrecht. <u>Dictionary of Kinetography Laban</u>. 2 vols. Plymouth, England: MacDonald and Evans, 1979. ISBN 0-7121-0416-X

<u>Sacred Dance</u>:

Troxell, Kay, ed. <u>Resources in Sacred Dance</u>. Rev. Ed. Peterborough, NH: Sacred Dance Guild, 1991. ISBN 0-9623137-1-8

<u>Social</u>:

Franks, A.H. <u>Social Dance, A Short History</u>. London: Routledge and K. Paul, 1963.

Malnig, Julie. <u>Dancing Till Dawn: A Century of Exhibition Ballroom Dance</u>. New York: Greenwood Press, 1992. ISBN 0-313276471

Ray, Ollie M. <u>Encyclopedia of Lines Dances: The Steps that Came and Stayed</u>. Reston, VA: National Dance Association, 1992. ISBN 0-88314-500-6

<u>South American</u>:

Castro, Donald S. <u>The Argentine Tango As Social History, 1880-1955: The Soul of the People</u>. Lewiston, NY: E. Mellen Press, 1991. ISBN 0773499237

<u>Spanish</u>:

Matteo (Vittucci, Matteo Marcellus). <u>The Language of Spanish Dance</u>. Norman: University of Oklahoma Press, 1990. ISBN 0-8061-2257-9

<u>Square Dance</u>:

Goss, Gordon, ed. <u>National Square Dance Directory</u>. Jackson, MS: National Square Dance Directory, 1990. ISBN 0-944351-03-4

<u>Tap</u>:

Marion, Sheila. <u>Tap Dance: A Dictionary of Steps in Labanotation</u>. New York: Cook, 1986. ISBN 0-9602002-9-0

Therapy:

Payne, Helen, ed. <u>Handbook of Inquiry in the Arts Therapies: One River, Many Currents.</u> Philadelphia: J. Kingsley, 1993. ISBN 1-85302-153-9

Tools for Collection Development:

<u>Attitudes and Arabesques</u>   <u>Dance Research Journal</u>   <u>Ballet Review</u>

Resources on the Internet:

Listserves:

Ballroom@ATHENA.MIT.EDU (Ballroom Dance)
DLDG-L@IUBVM.BITNET (Dance Librarians Discussion Group)
Rendance-L@MORGAN.UCS.MUN.CA (Renaissance Dance)
Morris-L@SUVM.BITNET (Morris Dance)
Dance-HC@CUNYVM.CUNY.EDU (Dance Heritage Coalition)
Dance-L@HEARN.BITNET (International Folk and Traditional Dance)

Telnet address to NYPL Dance Collection: nyplgate.nypl.org   Password: nypl

Gopher to college catalogs/dance information

Dance server at Ohio State University-

URL address: HTTP://www.dance.ohio-state.edu

Conference Proceedings from Scholarly Societies:

American Dance Guild
American Dance Therapy Association
Congress On Research in Dance
Cross-Cultural Dance Resources
Dance Critic's Association
European Association of Dance Historians(Paris)
Historical Dance Foundation
National Dance Association
Society for Dance Research(London)
Society of Dance History Scholars
World Dance Alliance(UNESCO)

REFERENCE OR RESEARCH EDUCATION? THE REQUIRED CONSULTATION AS AN INTERVENTION/ASSESSMENT TOOL

Linnea M. Dudley, Michael J. Kruzich, and Sally Weston

The Interrelationship of Reference and Instruction

The historical connection between reference and library instruction is as unmistakable as it is multi-faceted: administratively, most instruction librarians are, also or primarily, reference librarians. New information technologies are vastly increasing the instructional aspects of reference work. In educational terms, the reference environment is the laboratory where research skills, presented theoretically in the library classroom, are practiced "hands-on." Research education would further strengthen this connection.

"Research education" is a term coined by the information services librarians of the University of Michigan-Dearborn. It was adopted first by the Southeast Michigan League of Libraries Committee on Research Education (formerly the Committee on Bibliographic Instruction), and then by several academic libraries in the southeast Michigan area. It is not simply another way of saying "bibliographic instruction." Research education is an active, holistic, process-based approach to developing students as information-literate critical thinkers and lifelong learners. Research education seeks to integrate not only the goals and practices of classroom learning and research, but library instruction and reference service as well.

Dudley is reference librarian, Marygrove College Library, Detroit, Michigan, *Kruzich* is research education coordinator, and *Weston* is information services librarian, The University of Michigan-Dearborn, Mardigian Library, Dearborn, Michigan.

"Research consultation" is an alternative form of reference. Individual, intensive, it addresses all aspects of learning: the affective, the cognitive, and the physical or practical. The *required* research consultation, jointly assigned by a collaborating faculty member and librarian, provides planned intervention/assessment points throughout the student's research experience.

This paper will explore the benefits of the required consultation as it

- alleviates library and computer anxiety,

- emphasizes process-based research,

- encourages critical thinking,

- enhances collaborative teaching and learning, and

- offers an additional approach to learning outcomes assessment.

Finally, as examples of research education in practice, the ongoing development of two classes that now require a research consultation will be presented.

Anxiety

Library anxiety is a common phenomenon that often short-circuits students' attempts to complete research assignments. The research consultation appointment is an effective strategy for relieving library anxiety and for helping students to develop the confidence to proceed.

Forms of Library Anxiety

Library anxiety takes a few different forms. Constance Mellon's description of the phenomenon of library anxiety pinpointed students' fears. These include

- the size and complexity of the academic library,

- the fear that they are the only ones who do not know how to use the library,

- the idea that the instructor thinks they know how to use the library,

- not knowing where to start, and

- feelings of being overwhelmed.[1]

Another variation on library anxiety is what Jane Keefer has described as the "Hungry Rat Syndrome": Students (hungry rats), operating under time constraints and anxiety, experience the need for information in a more than normal or average manner. They become "rattled" and miss ordinary external cues (call numbers, online catalog menu items) which they would not miss if their sense of need were not so acute. They become less capable of thinking through their situation. They have trouble negotiating the "noisy" library system with its hundreds of "details."[2]

There are also some gender differences in the manifestations of library anxiety. According to a study by Frances Jacobson, men experience more library anxiety, while women experience more computer anxiety. The presence of computers in libraries lowers men's library anxiety, but increases women's.[3]

Remedies for Anxiety

Bibliographic instruction classes can and do address library anxiety in a group forum, and, in fact, Mellon recommends describing the phenomenon of library anxiety to students so that they know that their fears are not unusual. Library anxiety may also be addressed, briefly, in the reference desk encounter—which may be enough to assuage the anxiety. Then again, the student may need more time with the librarian in order to feel truly comfortable with the library and the research process.

For many students, the research consultation session is an additional and perhaps even more effective method of dealing with the affective component of

library research. Within the context of a research consultation appointment, the student and the librarian genuinely introduce themselves, establishing a relationship that is significantly different from the anonymous encounters of the traditional reference desk. The environment of the research consultation is also different: quieter, free from interruptions.

The Focusing Period

Many, possibly most, appointments occur at the beginning of the research process, when, according to Mellon, students are most anxious. Because it gives students an opportunity to think "out loud," with guidance and feedback from an information professional, the research consultation is extremely useful in facilitating the focusing experience, the effects of which continue to be felt throughout the information search process. Without a research focus, students will experience anxiety throughout the remainder of the assignment; with the selection or development of a focused topic, students report a sense of relief and a surge of confidence.

Computer Anxiety

Technology has in many ways reinforced and even reinvented the connection between reference and instruction. Many reference librarians now spend much of their professional time training students in the use of CD-ROMs and online databases. The scheduled research consultation provides a framework in which librarians can effectively address library anxiety, computer anxiety, and training concerns. The consultation appointment, which promises privacy as well as the undivided attention of the librarian for a certain period of time, frees students to experiment, make mistakes, and unself-consciously ask as many questions as are needed.

Information Mentoring

While bibliographic instruction and reference assistance make some headway in relieving library anxiety, the one-on-one research consultation, with its emphasis on the concerns of the individual student, is tailor-made for handling the affective aspects of library research. By first considering students' emotional states, the research consultation prepares and empowers beginning researchers to cope with the cognitive and practical challenges of academic library use. The research consultation appointment also allows librarians and students to work together in ways not possible at a busy reference desk, or even in a library classroom. Typically, students who have scheduled appointments in connection with one class or assignment continue to do so in others. Librarians who have the opportunity to work closely with students in the context of a private consultation are better able to recognize individual students and recall their assignments or projects; in this way ongoing working relationships are fostered.

Process and Sequencing

Students benefit from the sequencing of required research consultation appointments at different points in the research process. The steps of this basic or generic process model are adapted from the work of Carol C. Kuhlthau:

- selection of a general topic,

- preliminary exploration of background/information sources,

- selection and development of a focused topic,

- systematic search for relevant/appropriate sources,

- assessment of gathered information (contents and sources),

- presentation of results, and

- final assessment of project.[4]

Kuhlthau's recent work identifies "zones of intervention" with implications/opportunities for both reference and instruction.[5]

Dangerous Intersections

Depending on the subject area and factors such as educational level or academic preparedness, research consultation appointments may be appropriate at different points in the research process. According to Lynda Jerit, of the Oakton Community College Critical Literacy Project, "dangerous intersections" are those difficult, critical points in a course, or assignment, where, without support, students may not continue to progress. There are parallel dangerous intersections in the library research process. The faculty member and the librarian can decide what those points might be for a given course or library assignment, and agree to require research consultation appointments for students at those critical junctures.

For example, in the early stages of the process, the librarian can serve both as a sounding board and as an advisor: she or he can give advice on the feasibility of researching a particular topic in a particular library or suggest alternatives. The librarian can also recommend appropriate exploration sources or guide a student through the focusing process using cognitive mapping techniques. Throughout the information-gathering stage, librarians can help students examine the "artifacts" of their research (i.e., bib cards, printouts) to ensure thorough and efficient use of appropriate tools. At the "assessment of contents and sources" stage, the research consultation appointment can be used to teach or reinforce the critical thinking skills needed to evaluate information sources. At the "final assessment," the librarian can coach the student in reviewing the strategy, methods, and time management aspects of his or her project.

The research process, in practice, is not usually as orderly as the framework presented above. Stages may overlap, there is backtracking, some stages are not fully executed or blur into others. Sequenced required research consultations serve as opportunities for feedback and guidance along the way.

Cognitive/Critical Thinking Advantages

Beyond working to lessen library anxiety, the research consultation provides an environment for productive cognitive development and for learning to use critical thinking skills in the context of research activities.

Critical thinking has been defined in many different ways by those in the fields of philosophy, psychology, and education. While the "critical thinking movement" includes such distinguished scholars and educators as Robert Ennis, John McPeck, and Robert Sternberg, this application to library instruction draws especially on the work of the Oakton Community College Critical Literacy Project. For this purpose, critical thinking is defined as the activity of intellectual inquiry, which requires the use of higher order thinking skills. For example:

- analysis in the process of research topic formulation,

- evaluating sources of information based on the criteria of scholarship, authority, and discipline standards,

- questioning deeply the positions, assertions, arguments, evidence, and conclusions of the texts one reads, and

- clarifying and supporting one's own position based on evidence rather than on opinion and emotional biases.

In *Developing Critical Thinkers*, Stephen Brookfield notes that critical thinking comprises two interrelated processes: identifying and challenging assumptions, and imagining and exploring alternatives.[6] This is the heart of the research consultation process. Engaging students in a thoughtful exploration of research activities is beyond the scope and logistics of both the traditional reference desk and overview or introductory library instruction classes. Individual instruction by appointment, however, provides a meaningful context for teaching both critical thinking skills and the library research process.

Librarians experienced in this practice have discovered that students are not only receptive to making appointments, but are also more successful in using research strategies and information sources. As an intervention strategy, the required research consultation reinforces and enhances student learning, particularly when librarians are working in collaboration with classroom faculty who, in the language of Brookfield, adopt critical thinking as their "rationale for teaching."[7]

Collaboration

Collaboration as a preferred teaching/learning strategy becomes possible when classroom and library faculty have as their shared goal not simply the mastery of course content or the acquisition of library skills but the development of the whole person. Research education, which also merges instruction and reference, promotes the development of intellectual inquiry as the basis of "learning to learn."

Some of the hallmarks of collaborative teaching relationships are

- co-responsibility for planning learning outcomes, sequencing of research activities, and assessment,

- sharing expertise and resources, and

- coordination of feedback and providing check points throughout the process.

Beyond the obvious practical advantages, collaboration between librarians and classroom faculty also results in deeper and more synergistic learning. Research consultation appointments can model collaborative learning as well as collaborative teaching. Where appropriate, small groups of three to five students working on a project may be required to make consultation appointments with a librarian. The librarian, acting as a resource person and facilitator, is able to coach students in "real world" applications of collaborative information seeking and problem solving.

Two Cases

Marygrove College is a small, urban, liberal arts college. The library's philosophy of bibliographic instruction, now "research education," is rooted in the concept of process, and for several years its reference services have included research consultation by appointment.

Recently, two upper-level classes elected to require a research consultation as a possible solution to different problems in the administration and design of their library instruction components. These examples offer working models of the collaboration/communication between library and classroom, which makes the required consultation so effective an intervention in student research.

Planning/Problem Solving

BUS 440/Current Issues in Business and Management—A long history exists of thoughtful and active collaboration between the library and the business department, in connection with a required senior-level research project. Over a period of years, bibliographic instruction for this seminar course took on a number of different configurations—one library session, two library sessions, two formal and one informal sessions—but because business seniors included both four-year students (with a fair amount of library experience) and transfer students (some with almost no library experience), none of these arrangements was completely satisfactory. Inevitably some students were bored while others were left behind. In Fall '93, the second library session was made optional, with the frustrating but predictable result that very few students actually attended, whether they needed the additional instruction or not.

In planning for Winter '94, the course instructor and the reference/instruction librarian selected the required consultation as a way of tailoring bibliographic instruction to the special needs of this mixed group of students. There remained an initial class presentation, which reviewed basic research methods and search strategies in the content areas of business and management. In addition, however, each student was required to make an appointment with the reference librarian.

The course instructor developed a form for observations and comments, which was to be dated and signed by the librarian and which explicitly stated the materials the students were to bring to the reference interview (i.e., all bibliography and note cards completed as of that time). When the appointments were made, either by telephone or in person, the librarian added printouts to the list of research artifacts that would be examined/assessed. The consultation form was due to the instructor four weeks from the date of the library presentation.

ENG 312/Advanced Writing and Oral Communication—A newly required course, English 312, posed similar problems for bibliographic instruction. The "advanced" research assignment (including written and oral presentations) is intended to prepare students for writing intensive and seminar courses within their major programs. The two Winter '94 sections would need to use a number of different search strategies, with enrolled students from business, child development, English, human ecology, language arts, mathematics, political science, psychology, social studies and social work. As a further complication, the oral communication component put class time at an even higher premium than is usually the case.

The course instructor, who is also the director of the writing program and an advocate of information literacy, and the instruction librarian decided together on a single library presentation that would 1) review the process approach to basic library research and 2) discuss the need for discipline-specific adaptations of the information search process. Students would then be required to make appointments with the reference librarian for in-depth counselling and tutoring in the specialized strategies and tools of their different disciplines.

The instructor-designed English 312 form (see appendix 3) was somewhat more detailed than the one provided for the business seminar: it asked the students to recognize which stage of the research process they were currently engaged in; it asked for titles of books and articles already read; it asked the librarian to list in sequence recommended indexes and other resources. It was due two weeks after the library presentation.

Implementation

BUS 440—The consultations lasted anywhere from ten to 15 minutes (for students who were able to demonstrate strong research progress) to two hours for some students who required extensive coaching. The extended sessions usually involved a diagnostic overview, hands-on instruction in one or more indexes or databases, and an "exit" exchange indicating the next step or steps in the process. Careful referral to alternate academic or research libraries was also a part of most consultations. Several students chose to schedule multiple appointments.

Students were encouraged to think out loud for problem-solving purposes. Time was spent defining/discussing subject headings and other subject-specific terminology (printouts that included subject headings or key words were invaluable for trouble shooting). Additional time was spent applying critical reading techniques to the interpretation of on-screen instructions and the evaluation of potential sources. Some students were advised to slow down: to spend more time reading and taking notes on materials already located before going on to using additional indexes.

There was only one practical problem connected with the consultations for Business 440: most of the 21 students waited to schedule their reference appointments until the week before the due date. The anticipated problem of at least some student resentment at being required to see a librarian simply did not materialize, even though many expressed surprise at the amount of time and attention that was given to their research projects by the reference librarian. In fact, of the 12 students who commented in writing on the "most useful aspects" of the consultation, four mentioned being referred to specific reference books, indexes, or databases; four listed cognitive or critical thinking elements such as help with focusing or source evaluation; and four indicated that they found the affective component (nurturing, encouragement) to have been the most valuable part of the experience.

ENG 312—In addition to each student's major and preliminary topic choice, the instructor provided the date of the student's last Marygrove research instruction and/or experience. (This was extremely advantageous for the librarian, being alerted in advance to the more "at risk" researchers.) A typical consultation took between 30 and 45 minutes and discussed exploration sources and focusing, search strategy and source evaluation. In almost all cases time was also spent teaching at least one new index or database, for example, Psychological Abstracts or ERIC. A number of students chose to schedule multiple appointments.

Having learned from the administrative problems of Business 440, the English 312 appointments were handled more efficiently; however, a very small percentage of the writing students were irresponsible about keeping, cancelling, or rescheduling their consultations.

Sequencing

The objectives of a research consultation depend upon its timing and relationship to the process overall. The senior business students' appointments coincided with the assessment stage, by which time many had successfully completed a significant portion of their library work. Most of the junior-level writing students met with the librarian just as they were beginning to systematically collect information on their focused topics. This was essential for both discipline-based research planning and instruction in unfamiliar information tools. However, for at least some of the English 312 students, a second consultation would probably have been helpful, one which, like Business 440, included assessment of bib cards, printouts, note cards, and other research documents. (In Fall '94, a follow-up appointment will be required at the discretion of either the librarian or the instructor.)

Communication

In addition to using the consultation forms, the librarian and both instructors communicated in writing, by telephone, and in person throughout the remainder of the semester, clarifying educational objectives and sharing concerns for individual students' special problems or circumstances.

Faculty Response

Both instructors were extremely pleased with the results of these experiments. The instructor of the business seminar commented in writing that she had never received so many "excellent papers and presentations." The writing instructor, differentiating between research and writing skills, said in a meeting at the end of the semester that never had so many of her students done such, "solid research." She also relayed her students' comments regarding the helpfulness of the library consultations.

Librarian's Response

For the academic reference or instruction librarian, there can be few opportunities as illuminating as this: to be able to spend a significant amount of time with individual students all engaged in the same process, pursuing the same purpose or product. It was often alarming, occasionally shocking, to sit beside a student as she or he struggled to interpret the information presented on the computer screen. It was also tremendously rewarding to witness the breakthroughs, the moments when new concepts, facts, or terminology suddenly connected in meaningful relationships and patterns.

As an Intervention for Student Success

Through the required consultation, these students received feedback on a number of research elements (focus, strategy, procedural knowledge of specific tools, critical reading/critical thinking, source evaluation) from both instructor and librarian in an especially timely and meaningful manner. The course instructors, the librarian, and the students themselves believed that the required research consultation made a significant contribution to the successful completion of these research assignments. One Business 440 student wrote, "The librarian made me feel as if all the time put in the research of my paper was really paying off."

Outcomes Assessment

As an ongoing element in a system for measuring effectiveness and improving the quality of bibliographic instruction, the required consultation can be extremely useful, to the course instructor (and/or department or program) as well as the librarian (and library). The research consultation will always provide useful insights into the research habits and learning processes of individual students. According to some initial data at Marygrove, the *optional* consultation tends to attract the better and/or the poorer students, but when everyone in a specific class is required to participate, a clearer picture emerges of the range of student information competencies and problems within that class or group of students. This information can be used in planning or modifying

- individual research assignments,

- research across the curriculum programs,

- teaching relationships between instructors and librarians,

- research education/bibliographic instruction practices,

- reference services and practices, and

• assessment tools or methods.

Librarians who combine the process approach to research with the research consultation are uniquely positioned to study the thinking and learning activities of student researchers: to better understand how students think about information, how they integrate new ideas, and where and how the inevitable crises occur in the complex experience of locating, evaluating, synthesizing, and employing information. The *required* consultation, which unites affective, cognitive, and practical support for students, also provides librarians with the opportunity to intervene at anticipated critical moments and thus ensure the greater academic success of student researchers.

NOTES

1. Constance Mellon, "Library Anxiety: A Grounded Theory and Its Development," *College & Research Libraries* 47 (March 1986): 162.

2. Jane A. Keefer, "The Hungry Rats Syndrome: Library Anxiety, Information Literacy and the Academic Reference Process," *RQ* 32 (Spring 1993): 336-337.

3. Frances F. Jacobson, "Gender Differences in Attitudes toward Using Computers in Libraries: An Exploratory Study," *Library and Information Science Research* 13 (July-September 1991): 267-279.

4. Carol Collier Kuhlthau, *Teaching the Library Research Process* (West Nyak, NY: Center for Applied Research in Education, 1985).

5. Carol Collier Kuhlthau, *Seeking Meaning: A Process Approach to Library and Information Services* (Norwood, NJ: Ablex, 1993), 155-162.

6. Steven D. Brookfield, *Developing Critical Thinkers: Challenging Adults to Explore Alternative Ways of Thinking and Acting* (San Francisco: Jossey-Bass, 1987), 15.

7. Steven D. Brookfield, *The Skillful Teacher: On Techniques, Trust, and Responsiveness in the Classroom* (San Francisco: Jossey Bass, 1990), 20.

Marygrove College Library and Information Literary
1993/94 Summary of Programs and Applications:

Across the curriculum:

In 1991/92, the Faculty of Marygrove College adopted information literacy as one of seven necessary "across the curriculum" emphases. In 1992/93, the Library staff began consider information literacy as a faculty development issue, and in 1993/94, the faculty Library Committee continued the process of defining this concept within the framework of a new general education curriculum.

Marygrove's existing bibliographic instruction program provides the initial stages for a sequence of developmental library or research experiences culminating in information literacy/competencies at the senior level.

Library goals and objectives:

In collaboration with classroom faculty, course specific goals and objectives have been developed around the principle that we educate/serve the *whole person*; therefore, library instruction includes not only the intellectual aspects of research and information management, but the emotional and practical as well.

Marygrove 102:

Marygrove's required first year seminar includes one library orientation (as opposed to instructional) session.

    Library goal: Provide a "warmth seminar" to alleviate "library anxiety."

    Objectives: Introduce information literacy (reading/discussion from the ALA *Information Literacy Report*); academic (as opposed to other type) libraries; the Marygrove Library's staff, services and collections; information technology (the example used is *The Multimedia Encyclopedia).*

English 107:

Introduction to Writing, required for students who do not test *into* 108, includes one library session (class discussion and hands on activity usually involving reference sources).

     Library goals: Introduce students to a reference librarian; heighten awareness of different information formats.

     Objectives: introduce the information chain theory; concepts of information generation, storage/preservation and access; connect characteristics of information types/formats with effective/appropriate use in "controlled" research paper project.

English 108:

Academic Writing, Marygrove's required introductory composition class, includes three library sessions (5.5 hours).

     Library goals: Introduce students to the *basic* methods and tools of library research.

     Objectives: Introduce students to process based research; to the role of the information professional; to the appropriate use of different types of information sources; enable students to develop a focused research topic; to use the Marygrove public catalog and book collection; to use printed indexes and the Marygrove periodical collections; to use a CD/ROM index; to effectively manage time for research activities; to evaluate individual sources; to evaluate groups of sources; to use the MLA documentation style.

Assessment (library outcomes are measured in 2 ways):

1) There is an information skills and concepts test which is taken by students at the close of the research paper project.

2) Copies of final "works cited" pages are given to the library and reviewed for student use of substantive, timely and authoritative sources.

English 312:

Advanced Writing and Oral Communication, required as of Fall 1993, includes one library session and mandatory research consultation appointments with a reference librarian.

Library goals: Introduce upper level students to discipline specific research methods and tools; prepare students to function successfully in a number of libraries/information environments.

Objectives: introduce discipline specific standard reference works; on-line public access research catalogs; discipline specific print and CD/ROM indexes; reiterate discipline specific evaluative criteria for information sources; enable students to use discipline specific styles of documentation.

Assessment: Copies of final "works cited" pages are given to the library for review.

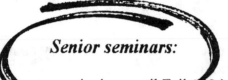

Senior seminars:

Although not required by the new curriculum until Fall 1994, a number of majors have traditionally offered or required a seminar experience which included a library class period, for example, Biology, Business, Child Development, Human Ecology, Social Work, Special Education, etc.

In general these are no longer instructional but consulting sessions.

Library goal: Enable senior researchers to do appropriate, comprehensive/in depth research in a subject area of their discipline/major.

Objectives: Review as necessary all basic research methods/library practices; assist students in formulating effective research strategies; insure student awareness of essential research tools; of library services such as database searching and interlibrary loan.

Special problems:

In the past , there might easily have been a gap of 2 or more years between English 108 and the senior level departmental research project, requiring students to *relearn the basics* before being going on to more advanced research tools/methods. In addition, transfer students who had not taken 108 may have had *no library assignments in any classes*, and therefore no familiarity with either the Marygrove Library or the process approach to research, which we believe to be an important aid to academic success.

Additional courses which have included library instruction:

It is the option of every Marygrove instructor to request one (or more) sessions of library instruction for each class with research or information based assignments. These sessions are tailored in terms of time and content to the goals of the assignment and the needs of the students.

In 1993/94, 28 classes attended specialized library presentations, accounting for almost 40 % of all library instruction so far this year.

Assessment: In 1993/94, 98% of the students who filled out library instruction evaluations agreed that the library session had made them aware of needed resources; 93% indicated that the library session had helped them with project management issues; 95% found the special library handouts developed for their classes had been useful.

For the future:

Information literacy as a "necessary emphasis across the curriculum" suggests that each academic program should

1) identify the advanced information concepts and skills essential to its discipline;
2) determine which course or courses (possibly the "writing intensive" designates) would best extend or reinforce the research competencies which now have a foundation in English 108 and 312;
3) develop the information literacy components and integrate into course syllabi;
4) consider which assessment techniques will best measure information literacies in different disciplines/content areas.

LOEX copies
Reference or Research Education?
L. Dudley/M. Kruzich/S. Weston
1994 Annual Conference, Ypsilanti, MI

Appendix 2:

Marygrove College Library, 1993/94

Report on Assessment of Instruction and Reference Services for Academic Writing Classes (English 108)

Note: English 108 is a required, introductory composition class which includes 3 sessions (6 class periods) of basic library instruction.

Library goals:

Knowledge and use of a process approach to research
Understanding the role of the reference librarian
Appropriate use of reference and other sources
Development of a well focused research topic
Use of the public catalog and Mg book collection
Use of printed indexes and Mg periodical collections
Use of a CD/ROM index
Understanding and practice of time management for research activities
Evaluation of individual sources; of groups of sources
Use of the MLA style manual

(1992-1993) Assessment methods:

1) In-class writing assignment: For the first 10 minutes of the final library session, students write about their library work to-date, relating it to the research process and giving specifics. These "writes" are not graded but are read by the librarian and returned to the students with comments and suggestions; copies of some classes' writings are kept for later reference.

Beginning in 93/94, a record was kept for comparison with other assessments, in which each students' reported research was assessed as being "acceptable", "needing assistance" (review) or "unacceptable".

2) Library skills and concepts test: Upon completion of their research papers, students take a test which is scored by the librarian (80-100% acceptable, 60-79% needs review, 59% or lower unacceptable).

3) Student bibliographies: A copy of each "works cited" page is given to the librarian for evaluation (Is it substantive? Are the sources timely? Does it include authoritative as well as popular sources?): acceptable (3 out of 3), needs review (2 out of 3), unacceptable (1 or none of the above characteristics).

Information for each class and each semester is compiled and kept by the library.

All assessments results are shared with the Academic Dean and the Director of the Writing Program as well as the individual course instructors.

Examples of library use of assessment results:

Tests and *instruction* --

Fall 1993: A majority of students tested could not define or explain "key word" searching.

Winter 1994: Library presentation/class discussion on *InfoTrac* was revised/expanded; a majority of students tested so far are now able to differentiate between "subject" and "key word" searching.

Writings/tests/bibliographies and *reference* --

Fall 1993: The 3 sets of data were compared; generally speaking, students whose in-class writing indicated an understanding and use of the research process did better on all aspects of the test and produced better bibliographies.

Winter 1994: The information was used to encourage all librarians at the reference desk to more carefully identify the 108 researchers and more consciously and actively reinforce the research process in the 'laboratory" setting.

(1994) Additional Assessment tool:

The reference calendar: Marygrove encourages students to schedule research consultation appointments (some instructors now require this for some classes). By including more information in the appointments calendar (class, section, project, stage in process), it was possible to compare the assessment results of those 108 students who made (and kept) consultation appointments with those who did not.

Results: Of the 2 classes assessed so far, students who made research consultation appointments either did very well on the library test-- *or very poorly.*

Tentative interpretation: Two types of Marygrove students may be "self-selecting" in making research consultations appointments: the highly motivated, academically successful, and those who are struggling.

Library use:

Summer and Fall 1994: A greater effort will be made to identify the "at risk" researcher:

Instruction:
Closer collaboration and more timely feedback, both to and from the course instructor, should be developed, with additional assistance offered to the student as appropriate.

At the reference desk:
1) Librarians might try to pay even more attention to the affective aspects of student research: "How do you feel about this project?" etc.
2) Librarians might also try to pay more attention to the physical artifacts of student research: bib cards, print outs, note cards, etc.
3) Students who are recognized as struggling should be encourage to make additional appointments.

Additional observation:

Summer students invariably score higher than those in the Fall or Winter semesters, presumably because they receive more time and individual attention from the librarian...

LOEX copies
Reference or Research Education?
L. Dudley/M. Kruzich/S. Weston
1994 Annual Conference, Ypsilanti, MI

English 312
Consultation with Reference Librarian

Name:_____

Date of Consultation: _____

Topic of Research: _____

(Reminder: a minimum of 10 *library* sources are required for this assignment.)

Research steps completed:

_____
_____
_____
_____
_____
_____

Indexes consulted to date:

_____
_____
_____
_____

Sources read to date:

_____
_____
_____
_____
_____
_____

Indexes to be consulted:

_____
_____
_____
_____
_____

Comments:

_____
_____
_____
_____

Signature of Reference Librarian: _____

Research Conference

Schedule a meeting with the Research Librarian, Ms. Linnea Dudley, during the research period of this course. When you make your appointment, tell her your research topic. When you meet with her, you MUST bring your bibliography cards, and the notes you have already taken.

You must hand in this form on 2/17/194.

YOUR NAME:

RESEARCH LIBRARIAN COMMENTS:

DATE OF RESEARCH CONFERENCE:

Marygrove College
Business 440 (current issues seminar)
Required Research Consultation Checklist

LIBRARY ASSIGNMENTS:
MAKING A GOOD FIRST IMPRESSION

Susan Frey-Ridgway

Many academic reference librarians are faced with the predicament of assisting confused freshmen at the reference desk who must complete library assignments designed to familiarize them with the library. A great majority of these assignments (which are both faculty- and library-created) take the form of short-answer questions. Often, librarians first discover the existence of faculty-created library assignments during the reference interview. Although designed with the genuine intent of motivating students to use the library, these types of introductory assignments are often perceived by novice researchers as pointless scavenger hunts during which they must locate arbitrary sources and record call numbers. Some assignments, created solely by faculty, further antagonize students by referring to defunct sources and services. In the spring of 1993, Professor Sherry Hockemeyer, a faculty member of the School of Business and Management Sciences, and I collaborated in designing a different type of introductory library assignment, which was part of an introduction to business administration course.

The assignment was created to familiarize students with business-related issues, while offering them the opportunity to enhance their information-gathering techniques. Each student was asked to submit a detailed outline of a research paper. Because the assignment focused on the research process itself, rather than a finished product, a completed paper was not required.

Frey-Ridgway is assistant librarian, Walter E. Helmke Library, Indiana University-Purdue University at Fort Wayne.

The resource students used was the library's local area network of six journal indexes on compact disc (ABI, Academic Abstracts, America History & Life, ERIC, PsychLit, Sociofile). Stipulating that records from at least two of the databases had to be obtained to support the outline encouraged students in taking an interdisciplinary approach.

Traditional concerns such as library hours and policy, or location of reference books, were ignored. Instead the assignment, by limiting students to the LAN, concentrated on the creative and analytic aspects of research. Rather than having basic questions about library hours, policy, or reference materials imposed upon them in a library exercise, the assignment motivated students to ask questions related to their specific needs. Thus, they attached greater importance to the answers.

The structure of the assignment encouraged students to view the reference librarians as information counsellors, who could guide them through the creative process of assessing their information needs in relation to the various LAN databases. The assignment helped to create for the student a constructive image of both the librarian and the library. Students remarked repeatedly that they found the assignment stimulating and that they had formed a favorable impression of the library in their minds. Since student reaction to the assignment was so overwhelmingly positive, Professor Hockemeyer has chosen to use the assignment in subsequent semesters. This semester, we plan to distribute a written evaluation of the assignment to the students. We hope to gain additional insight into what motivates students in the library from this data.

Appendix 1:

School of Business and Management Sciences
Indiana University-Purdue University Fort Wayne
BUS X100 Business Administration: An Introduction
Professor: Sherry Hockemeyer

excerpt from Introduction to Business Administration Syllabus:

In today's computer environment, the library has undergone tremendous changes. When you need to gather information and write a paper, you will be way ahead if you know how to access information—that is the purpose of this assignment. In fact, if you write a research paper for another course and the topic can be related to material in this class, you should even be able to combine your research.

The assignment is to prepare a short paper outlining the direction you would take if you were writing a research paper. You need a total of six or more article abstracts from two or more databases. These article summaries will be attached to your assignment and, therefore, must be numbered so you can refer to them easily. Type your assignment with double spacing; it is to be a minimum of two pages in length, a maximum of three pages.

You will write an introduction to the subject and then indicate by a narrative outline what you will write about and how the attached article summaries support your ideas. In order to properly focus on a topic, be specific about the ideas you will develop in the "real" paper. Do not reiterate the material in the article summaries; simply refer to it. You will receive additional information about the library databases prepared by Susan Frey-Ridgway, Information Support Services librarian for business.

Library Guide to Lan Assignment for
Introduction to Business Administration (BUS X100)

The Helmke Library houses many different indexes, catalogs, and databases. In this guide, we will deal with only one aspect of the library, the LAN.

What's the LAN?

On the first floor of the Library you can search a series of databases which are networked to a bank of terminals. These terminals are color-coded orange. At any orange terminal you can search all of the databases in the system, which is called the Local Area Network or LAN.

At each orange terminal you will see a menu listing the databases. Some of the choices do not apply to this particular assignment, so we will not examine them here. The databases useful to this assignment contain summaries of magazine articles. Each database is created by a different publisher and has a different focus. The focus of the database helps you to decide which ones to search.

Examine the menu below. Which option would you choose to find article summaries in the field of Personnel Management? An obvious choice would be option one, the business database. However, there might be times when you would like to search option eight, the psychology database, because psychologists often study people in the workplace.

MENU

1	ABI (Business article summaries)
2	Academic Abstracts (article summaries on many different topics)
3	American History & Life (U.S. History article summaries)
4	(Not used in this assignment)
5	(Not used in this assignment)
6	ERIC (Education article summaries)
7	(Not used in this assignment)
8	PsychLit (Psychology article summaries)
9	(Not used in this assignment)
A	Sociofile (Sociology article summaries)

The Assignment

In this assignment you are required to retrieve article summaries from different databases on the LAN using the same topic(s). Check your course syllabus for additional information.

Accessing Data vs. Evaluating Data

Being able to retrieve article summaries on the topic of "medical malpractice" in a library requires skill. This skill is developed by learning to use your library. Making the distinction between an article summary describing the increase in medical malpractice in the U.S., which appeared in TIME magazine, and a summary on how professional liability for doctors is affecting major U.S. insurers, which appeared in BUSINESS INSURANCE, is yet another skill. Which article would be useful in investigating trends in the insurance industry? Which article would help you write a report on how the rising cost of healthcare is affecting the American family? Both articles deal with "medical malpractice." TIME is geared toward a general audience of readers, while BUSINESS INSURANCE is aimed at the insurance professional with expert knowledge. The skill to evaluate these two articles lies in recognizing the differences in the audiences of these two magazines. If your informational needs are broad enough, you might need both articles. If you were researching a narrower topic, only one might do. TIME is available through option number two, Academic Abstracts. BUSINESS INSURANCE can be found in option number one, ABI.

Where Do I Begin?

There is a big difference between thinking "Hey, how do I get the computer to search for the term MALPRACTICE?" and, "I've no idea what to research; I just don't know where to begin!!!"

Only you can choose your topic(s). Ideas come from many places like conversations, magazine articles, television news, and personal experience. Anxiety in using the library often stems from not having a clear sense of your informational needs. "I need information about medical malpractice" is often enough to start you off. After you research this topic, you can then narrow your search to a more specific concept, such as medical malpractice and AIDS.

HELP!

Service Desk personnel are available to help you practice learning how to use the different databases on the LAN. They can show you how to search, display and print your results. Printed guides on how to use the LAN and its options are also available. If you feel you need more in-depth guidance, make an appointment at the Service Desk to see a librarian. The librarian will help you evaluate your informational needs and construct a meaningful research strategy. Remember, even the most experienced researchers run into snags now and then. Don't be shy about seeking a librarian. Be patient, be committed, and you will find the information to suit your needs.

Example One:

How does a manager deal with a worker who is suspected of abusing alcohol?

ABI - access a FORBES article summary on the increase of drug abuse in the work place
PsychLit - access a JOURNAL OF PSYCHOLOGY article summary on the addictive personality
Sociofile - access a JOURNAL OF SOCIOLOGY article summary of a study conducted on the effects of co-workers' behavior on an addict

Example Two:

How is the European Community affecting the U.S. fashion industry?

ABI - access a FORTUNE article summary on the current state of the U.S. and European fashion industries
Academic Abstracts - access a AMERICAN HISTORY article summary on the history of fashion in the U.S. from 1900 to the present

Prepared for Professor Hockemeyer's BUS X100 class by Susan Frey-Ridgway.

Appendix 3:

BUS X100 Business Administration LAN Assignment Evaluation
Walter E. Helmke Library
School of Business and Management Sciences
Indiana University-Purdue University Fort Wayne

Did you enjoy working on the LAN assignment? Why? Why not?

Is there anything about the assignment you would change? What?

Did the assignment teach you anything? What?

Were you able to use the outline to write a paper for another class? What class?

Did you seek assistance from library staff to complete the assignment? (If no, skip next two questions.)

Did you seek assistance at the Service Desk? Did you make an appointment to see a librarian?

If you did receive assistance in the library, did you get the help you needed? Please explain.

Have you ever worked with a LAN before?

Do you enjoy working in the library? Why? Why not?

Thanks for your time!   SFR/94

FEAR AND LOATHING ON THE INTERNET: TRAINING THE TRAINERS AND TEACHING THE USERS

Esther Grassian

INSTRUCTIONAL CHALLENGE

UCLA has a quite mixed computing environment. It consists of a conglomeration of different local area networks, dialup connections, and hardwired backbone connections. In early 1993, most UCLA librarians knew about the Internet but had not used it much themselves and were quite nervous about teaching it. Yet, the library system wanted to expand on the Biomedical Library's highly popular, intensive Internet classes, begun in January 1993. How were we to accomplish this goal?

MEETING THE CHALLENGE

Training the Trainers

We began by broadening the base of Internet trainers. The Biomedical Library made room for College Library and University Research Library (URL) librarians in their Internet classes, and spent time discussing what to teach and why. At a large group meeting in Summer 1993, everyone agreed that College & URL librarians would begin teaching introductory Internet/Orion Gopher classes in Fall 1993.

Grassian is reference/instruction librarian, UCLA College Library, Los Angeles, California.

Our library administration put together an Internet Training Group (ITG) for this purpose, consisting of the heads of College Library and URL, one line reference librarian from each library, and a backup for each line librarian. The ITG was given the Internet training problem and asked to solve it.

My immediate reaction was panic. I felt that I knew next to nothing about the Internet and gophers. In spite of the classes I had taken and observed, I felt that it just had not sunken in enough to be able to teach it to others. So, I tried to get out of doing it. I carefully explained that I did not know how to use the Internet, did not have a computer on my desk, and needed a lot of practice with it before I could teach it to anyone. But to no avail. I was reassured that once I started using it I would get the hang of it fairly quickly.

At a summer lunch meeting, I realized that it just had to be done, so I plunged in, offered to design an Internet/Orion Gopher class, and to do two rehearsal sessions for library staff. I had two goals in mind in doing rehearsal sessions. First, I hoped to practice in front of library staff members and get their help in improving the sessions. Second, I hoped to show potential Internet trainers that it would be possible for them to teach this sort of class.

So, I designed a basic Internet/Orion Gopher class, and gave two rehearsals to library staff in Fall 1993. We then presented two sessions to end-users in fall quarter, four in winter quarter, and four in spring quarter. We have one set up for the summer, and four more planned for Fall 1994. All of these sessions were free. We experimented with these classes in various ways. In fall and winter we required signups; in spring, we dropped the signup requirement. In fall and winter we tried restricting classes to particular groups (e.g., faculty). In spring, we opened all classes to any students, staff, or faculty who wanted to attend. I taught three of these end-user classes All the other classes were taught by new volunteer librarians.

How did we get them to volunteer? I thought about my initial reactions of panic and concern at the thought of teaching the Internet, and about what would have helped me. It would have helped to

1) watch others teaching an Internet class;
2) have scripts for those classes;
3) have an experienced observer in the room to help answer unexpected questions;
4) have an emergency backup instructor;
5) have Internet drawings and cartoons in the form of overheads to supplement the presentation;
6) talk to other presenters about what went right and what they would change for the next time;
7) have handout originals to copy and/or modify.

This is exactly what we did. Each new presenter observes at least one session before teaching. We also set up a supportive structure with a meeting each quarter for new presenters. The previous quarter's presenters discuss what went well in their sessions and what they would do differently next time. Each new presenter receives a very brief outline of broad areas that need to be covered in the session, and copies of all scripts, which she or he may use as is or adapt. Each new presenter also receives copies of all overheads, originals of evaluation forms for presenter and for audience (to be copied for the class). They also receive originals of other handouts, including step-by-step guides to using the Orion Gopher client in the library and outside the library, as well as a set of sample search demos. An ITG member serves as a backup and observer for each new presenter's session. I have also offered to rehearse with anyone interested. Finally, each presenter gives a brief e-mail report to the ITG following her or his session.

This support structure has been crucial in encouraging librarians to teach the Internet and the Orion Gopher for the first time.

Teaching the Users

To whom have we taught the Internet and our Orion Gopher client? We have taught around 175 faculty, students, and staff since fall quarter; 137

evaluation forms have been returned to us. I will discuss the results shortly.

What have we taught in these classes? Here is a basic outline of the areas we have covered:

1. What is the Internet?
2. What are the three main functions of the Internet?
3. How does the Internet work?
4. What is its value?
5. What sort of help can you get?
   *Archie
   *Veronica
   *Jughead
   *Gopher
   *Subject trees
6. How does the Orion Gopher client work?
7. Demonstration of sample searches using the Orion Gopher client.

PRACTICAL TIPS

* Use overheads of cartoons and drawings to vary the content and to aid visual learners.

* Provide copies of step-by-step searches, so the audience can follow along as you do the demonstration.

* Have some sample searches on overheads to use as backups if necessary.

* Begin your demonstration with a place to go for Help (e.g., "Internet Assistance").

* Include a library catalog among your sample searches.

* Define Archie, Veronica, Jughead, and Gopher simply:

> ARCHIE: Searches for ftp sites.
> VERONICA: Searches for all types of gopher items, including files.
> JUGHEAD: Searches for all types of gopher items, except files.
> GOPHER: Menu-driven software used to search for many Internet resources listed at sites which have installed this software and made these resources freely available.

* Be prepared for off-the-wall questions, such as, "How private is e-mail?"

* Use subject trees in your demonstration, such as University of Southern California's "Gopher Jewels."

— ESTHER GRASSIAN —

* Demonstrate the use of Jughead.

* Use examples that excite you.

* Check and recheck your examples as close to your session as possible, and try to get alternative means of getting to your sample sites.

* Create a bookmark for each example.

* Maintain a positive presentation style and attitude. Remember your own initial anxiety when you teach new users, and be empathetic. Be enthusiastic and supportive of users and your colleagues. They are brave to try something new.

Evaluation and a Look to the Future

How well did it work?

Though we had the feeling that a number of attendees wanted sophisticated sessions, in fact, 86 percent said the workshop was neither too elementary, not too advanced, but just right; 82 percent thought the session length (one and a half hours) was about right; 58 percent rated moving around in the Gopher as the most useful part of the session, followed by how to create a bookmark and how to find resources by subject. Many wanted information about departmental connectivity, especially file transfer protocol (ftp) using their local area network (LAN).

Future Plans

Four new librarian-presenters have already volunteered to teach this basic class in the fall. We are also developing partnerships with various network and departmental computing support coordinators, the "techies" who support networks such as the Humanities Computing Network (HumNet) and the Social Sciences Computing Network (SSCNet). We have already done a subject-specialized Internet session in partnership with HumNet, and others are planned.

The ITG meets next month to brainstorm and plan expanded course offerings, to revise the current course, and to develop more ideas for training trainers. We hope to use an instructional model that is probably familiar to many. We will use the summer to revise existing courses and develop new courses. We will do rehearsals with library staff in the fall, and conduct end-user sessions in late fall, and in winter and spring. The following summer we will again revise and consider the need for new courses. We plan to keep track of evaluations, statistics, and staff and end-user comments and incorporate them into the revision process. And, we hope to learn from our colleagues elsewhere, who are also planning, preparing, and presenting these sorts of classes.

Let me conclude by making three suggestions. First, plan for a constantly evolving process of teaching and training, as technology and user needs evolve. Second, try to keep in mind that it takes time to learn new systems and approaches, and try to accommodate the different learning styles of trainers, as well as end-users. Finally, think back to when we converted from card catalogs to online catalogs. Many of us were scared, nervous, and overwhelmed. It was a major leap, and this is another one. Let us try to bridge this new gap by helping the leapers with as human a chain as possible.

UCLA Library

SAMPLE ORION GOPHER SEARCHES 5/10/94

Note: The following searches may not work at a later date, as the Internet is in a constant state of flux.

A. WHERE TO GET HELP OR GET STARTED
1. Interesting Internet Places to Visit
2. Internet Assistance

B. LIBRARY CATALOGS EXAMPLE (WESLEYAN UNIVERSITY LIBRARY CATALOG)
1. Interesting Internet Places to Visit
2. Internet Assistance
3. Libraries
4. OPACs by Location
5. United States
6. Connecticut
7. Wesleyan University
8. LUCT
9. Press Enter to start the system
[Note: To exit type STOP and press Enter.]

C. SUPREME COURT DECISIONS
1. Interesting Internet Places to Visit
2. Library of Congress MARVEL
3. Government Information
4. Federal Information Resources
5. Information by Agency
6. Judiciary
7. Supreme Court Decisions [   ] Term

D. EARTHQUAKE INFORMATION
1. Other Gopher Servers
2. North America
3. USA
4. California
5. Earthquake Information Gopher
6. Recent Earthquake Info
7. Univ of Washington Information
8. Recent Earthquakes (Univ of WA gopher)

E. RADIO-FREE-EUROPE TRANSCRIPTS
1. Other Gopher Servers
2. Jughead
3. Type **radio free europe** at index prompt screen
5. Directory **Radio Free Europe/Radio Liberty**

F. NAFTA TREATY
1. Other Gopher Servers
2. Jughead
3. Type **NAFTA**
4. "Search the NAFTA treaty.technology.com"
5. Type **environment**
6. NAFTA-PART-NINE-OTHER PROVISIONS/federal/nafta

G. ONLINE CAREER CENTER
1. Interesting Internet Places to visit
2. Online Career Center
3. Company Sponsors and Profiles
4. U.S. Robotics-Skokie, IL.

H. LOW-COST LEAD TESTING
1. Interesting Internet Places to Visit and Things to Do
2. Whole Earth 'Lectric Magazine - The WELL's Gopherspace
3. Environmental Issues and Ideas
4. Low-Cost Lead Testing for Household Water

I. HISTORICAL DOCUMENTS
1. Interesting Internet Places to Visit
2. Internet Assistance
3. Information Organization by Subject (Rice University)
4. History
5. Historical Documents

J. DEAF RESOURCES
1. Interesting Internet Places to Visit
2. Library of Congress MARVEL
3. The Global Electronic Library (by Subject)
4. Social Sciences
5. Area Studies
6. Deaf Studies
7. Deaf Gopher (Michigan State U)
8. Deaf Alert (deaf resources by students)
9. Deafness and the Movie Industry

K. TELEVISION NEWS BROADCASTS (JOURNAL GRAPHICS)
1. Other Gopher Servers
2. North America
3. USA
4. Ohio
5. Cleveland Public Library
6. General Reference Department
7. Telnet Television/Radio News Broadcasts (Journal Graphics)
   (Note: login as user; choose #67 from Main Menu)

8. Type **PAC**
9. Type **5** (i.e., vt100)
10. Type **3** (i.e., Information Databases)
11. Use Quick Word Search--Type **//wsimpsons**
13. Type **d** (to display the list of results)
14. (11 results) Type **8** to display that citation
15. Type **//exit** to quit

L. SHAKESPEARE QUOTE
1. Other Gopher Servers
2. **Jughead**
3. Type **Shakespeare**
4. Telnet Shakespeare Plays (Dartmouth)
5. (3d screen has Shakespeare Plays) Type **Select File Shakespeare Plays**
6. Type **Find Text kill all the lawyers**
7. Type **Display context** to see results: Act 4, Scene 2, line 64 is the answer
(Henry the Sixth, Part II)
*[Note: Type **bye** to quit.]*

M. NATIONAL INSTITUTES OF HEALTH--GRANTS & RESEARCH INFORMATION
1. Other Gopher Servers
2. North America
3. USA
4. Ohio
5. Cleveland Public Library
6. Science & Technology Dept.
7. National Institutes of Health
8. Grants and Research Information

Alternate Means of Getting to the Same Resource:
1. Interesting InterNet places to visit
2. Library of Congress MARVEL
3. The Global Electronic Library (by Subject)
4. Natural Science
5. Biology
6. NIH National Institutes of Health Gopher System
7. Related Databases and the rest of Gopherville
8. NIH Gopher site
9. Grants and Research Information

N. PREAMBLE TO THE U.S. CONSTITUTION; TEXT OF JULIUS CAESAR (Shakespeare play)
1. Go to Gopher Server of Your Choice
2. Type **Info. Rutgers. Edu**
3. Libraries, information resources, reference materials, publications
4. Online dictionary and other reference material

5. U.S. Government: Constitution, etc.
6. Constitution, Bill of Rights, Amendments
7. Preamble
8. (F3 to) Online dictionaries and other reference materials
9. Electronic Texts
10. Text of "Julius Caesar"
11. Directory Act I
12. Display text

O. NIELSEN RATINGS
1. Other Gopher Servers
2. North America
3. USA
4. Ohio
5. Cleveland Public Library
6. General Reference Department
7. Nielsen Ratings

P. INTERVIEW--NOBEL PRIZE WINNER: RIGOBERTA MENCHU TUM
1. Other Gopher Servers
2. Europe
3. European National Entry Points
4. United Kingdom
5. Oxford University, Radcliffe Science Library
6. Anthropology and Archaeology Corner
7. Anthropology and culture
8. Interview with Nobel Prize winner Menchu Tum

Q. HOLOCAUST ARCHIVES
1. Other Gopher Servers
2. Middle East
3. Jerusalem One Network
4. Electronic Jewish Library
5. Special! Holocaust and
      Holocaust Denial Archives

5/94eg

Appendix 2:

UCLA Library
Internet/ORION Gopher Intro: Presenter's Evaluation

Date of presentation: _____ Number of Attendees: _____

Presenter: _____

This session was: ___ *Faculty only* ___ *Grad Students only* ___ *All students & faculty*

1. Please rank the audence's level of knowledge of electronic sources/resources and access skills, based on their questions and comments:

___ *Novice* ___ *Intermediate* ___ *Advanced* ___ *Mixed*

2. Did you use transparencies or other aids? If so, which ones did you use and would you use them again? Why or why not?

3. What other sort of equipment did you use? Were there any problems with the equipment? If so, please explain.

4. Were you able to cover everything you had planned? If not, please explain what you did not cover and why (e.g., ran out of time, people didn't seem to follow you, technical difficulties, etc.).

5. What went especially well?

6. What would you do differently next time?

7. What ideas do you have for other types of Internet training sessions?

8. Other comments or suggestions?

12/20/93eg

Appendix 3:

UCLA LIBRARY INTERNET/ORION GOPHER WORKSHOP 5/10/94

Please help us improve future sessions by providing your opinions & comments below. Thank you.

____Faculty   ____Graduate Student   ____Undergraduate Student   ____Staff

Department: _____

How did you find out about this workshop? _____

1. This workshop was
____ too elementary   ____ about right   ____ too advanced

2. The presentation was
____ too fast   ____ about right   ____ too slow

3. The content was
____ poorly organized   ____ somewhat organized   ____ well organized

4. The speaker was
____ poorly prepared   ____ adequately prepared   ____ well prepared

5. The presentation style was
____ too simplistic   ____ about right   ____ too advanced

6. The handouts were
____ not useful   ____ helpful   ____ very useful

7. The session length was
____ too long   ____ about right   ____ too short

8. Please rank the following parts of this session from (1) not useful to (4) very useful.

	not useful			very useful
What the Internet is..........................	1	2	3	4
How the Internet works	1	2	3	4
What is a gopher	1	2	3	4
What is the ORION Gopher	1	2	3	4
Moving around in the Gopher	1	2	3	4
How to view items	1	2	3	4
How to copy files	1	2	3	4
How to use a bookmark	1	2	3	4
How to find resources by subject.........	1	2	3	4

9. What additional topics would you like to have covered?

10. Additional comments? (Use back of sheet.)

UCSD 12/92rg; rev. UCLA 11/93eg

TURNING FRUSTRATION INTO LEARNING FOR NURSING STUDENTS

Phyllis S. Lansing and Patricia G. Hinegardner

The University of Maryland at Baltimore is called the Campus of the Professions in that it includes the schools of nursing, medicine, pharmacy, dentistry, and social work. The reference and information management services staff shares three basic duties: staffing the reference desk, performing mediated searches, and, as individuals, serving as liaisons to one of the above schools. Liaisons are responsible for collection development, class-related instruction, consultations, and working with faculty. Other instruction includes one-to-one consultations and seminars on searching various databases, file management, and journal article publication.

A new class for undergraduate nurses, "Technology in Nursing," was introduced in 1991/92. An avalanche of more than 100 students hit the reference desk with an assignment to photocopy a page from the *Cumulative Index to Nursing and Allied Health Literature*, on which they were to mark three citations. Next, they were to search the Nursing and Allied Health Literature (CINAHL) database to retrieve the marked citations, printing the search strategy and the three citations. Many students had never searched the database before and they were confused by the assignment. Reference librarians were overwhelmed by the number of questions about the assignment and how to manage every aspect of the search—from the search terminology through Boolean operators to printing!

Lansing is education coordinator and *Hinegardner* is mediated search services coordinator, Health Sciences Library, University of Maryland at Baltimore, Baltimore, Maryland.

Long lines formed behind the eight workstations in the reference area. Frustration abounded for students and librarians alike, in that there was no way to provide enough assistance for everyone.

Before the next semester the liaison talked with the professor about the students' confusion, asking for clarification on the assignment's purpose. The professor thought the assignment reinforced the similarities and differences between the index and database; the liaison was concerned that the key role of subject headings had been overlooked completely. The liaison requested that class time be provided to highlight the importance of subject headings and subheadings and to prepare students for searching the database. The professor said that no more than 30 minutes of class time could be spared, which effectively limited the librarian's presentation to large group lecture with no exercise. By the time the students arrived at the library they still were uncertain about how to use the database to find the three citations and printing was again a mystery. Reference librarians were again run ragged. Although the microlab was available for overflow searching, there was no one available in that location to help students with search strategy or mechanics. The primary advantage of the half-hour class session was that the professor learned some search techniques that were helpful in her research. The liaison continued to assist her with research and course-related needs. As the professor's searching skills improved, she realized the value of repeated hands-on experience.

The next phase in this instructional process came the third semester when the professor called to ask for the same large-group lecture. The librarian suggested that students would benefit most if time could be provided for small groups of students to hear the lecture in the microcomputer lab with an immediate opportunity to work through the assignment. The professor agreed to discuss that plan with the other section instructors. A few days later the liaison was asked to arrange six hour-long sessions in the library microlab to accommodate the students. The microlab has 16 student workstations and a teaching workstation complete with a videolink, which allows projection of the teaching station screen to all monitors for easy visibility. The videolink also helps focus student attention since student keyboards can be disabled until time for the hands-on exercises.

The sessions were the second half of a two-hour class. Some of the section instructors did not adequately prepare the students for the library instruction. The liaison needed to clarify the purpose of the assignment and assure students that they could complete the assignment during the session. This hands-on instruction relieved a lot of congestion and frustration in the reference area. Some students, however, thought they would save time by trying the assignment on their own, so some reference interaction was still needed.

The objectives for the one-hour session were that participants would be able to list advantages of using subject headings for retrieving health sciences literature and to plan strategies for tailoring database search results.

The role of controlled vocabulary or subject headings for retrieving information in health sciences databases was defined and illustrated. Advantages of controlled vocabulary include the following:

1. It retrieves consistently by concept rather than by author's terminology.

2. It indicates greater relevancy.

3. It brings related concepts together by inverting subject heading word order (example: arrhythmias or pneumonias).

4. It allows exploded retrieval by searching more specific headings with a general heading.

5. It searches subheadings—specific aspects of subject headings (e.g., diagnosis, various forms of therapy).

6. It provides links to preferred subject headings (see references).

7. It is used in printed indexes and databases.

After the short lecture a demonstration of a sample assignment was transmitted to the monitors at each workstation with students being asked questions to help them participate in the strategy development and execution. Indexes were placed beside each workstation so students could select topics of interest to use for the assignment. After selecting the three citations they wanted to retrieve, they were encouraged to use the appended worksheet (see appendix 1) to aid them in narrowing their retrieval. (If it is not possible to teach in a microcomputer lab, the worksheet sample included here can be used by individuals or pairs of students in a classroom setting.) Most of them quickly completed the assignment. Although students were free to leave as soon as they finished the assignment, some used their new skills and the remaining time to explore topics for other class assignments.

Providing librarian support in an instructional setting rather than as multiple reference interactions met the needs of the professors, students, and librarians. By scheduling class time for library research instruction, the faculty endorsed information-retrieval as necessary for student performance and professional development. They also found the students had fewer problems with the assignment. The sessions helped reduce student frustration. Students appreciated having reserved workstations available, they realized the exercise focused on skills they would need for later projects, and they received immediate assistance from the librarians during the hands-on session. The librarians were able to focus on the students' questions without other reference desk interruptions. The response from the professors and students was so positive that we plan to follow the same pattern next semester.

— Phyllis S. Lansing and Patricia G. Hinegardner —

Appendix 1:

LOEX NAHL Worksheet
University of Maryland at Baltimore Health Sciences Library

This exercise is planned to help you gain experience and skill in searching for relevant citations in the Nursing and Allied Health Literature database. Each citation record is made up of many fields. Searching by field allows you to narrow a broad search or to search for specific citations. Combining search statements with AND will narrow retrieval. (Ex: #1 and #2)

ASSIGNMENT: Select three citations on the attached page from the Cumulative Index to Nursing & Allied Health Literature. Search the NAHL database to retrieve those three citations. Print your strategy and the three citations.

<u>You enter</u>

Most searches begin with the **DE**scriptor or subject heading field

F9 (function key 9) - At prompt type subject heading
Follow screen instructions.

Limit **DE**scriptor with **SH** (subheading)

Relevant subheadings (topical, age group, or geographic) will display.
Select all or relevant subheadings.

Limit by **PY** (publication year) or by range of years

PY = 1992   or
      PY = 1991-1993

Search by **AU** (author)

F5 (function key 5) - At prompt type author's last name and initial(s).
Ex: **Johnson S** - Highlight desired names; press **F** to search them.

Search by significant words from article **TI** (title).

EX: lumbar **in TI** and chemotherapy **in TI**

Search by **SO** (source or journal name) Can't search by volume or page.

F5 (function key 5) - Type journal name abbreviation exactly as seen in CINAHL. (Ex: Prof Nurse)

Search by **DT** (document type)

Ex: **Review in DT** or you can type
Ex: **DT = Research**

Write below your proposed search strategy for retrieving the three citations as it would appear on the NAHL search screen.

```
SilverPlatter 3.1        CINAHL (R) 1983 - 2/94      F10=Commands F1=Help

   ┌──────────────────────────────────────────────────────────────────┐
   │ No.     Records   Request                                          │
   │                                                                    │
   │                                                                    │
   │                                                                    │
   │                                                                    │
   │                                                                    │
   │                                                                    │
   │                                                                    │
   │                                                                    │
   │                                                                    │
   │                                                                    │
   │                                                                    │
   │                                                                    │
   └──────────────────────────────────────────────────────────────────┘
  FIND:

  Type search then Enter (◄─┘). To see records use Show (F4). To Print use (F6).
```

MAXIMIZING BIBLIOGRAPHIC INSTRUCTION, MINIMIZING REFERENCE

Sara J. Penhale

INTRODUCTION

Common goals of both bibliographic instruction and reference service in an undergraduate setting are to enable students to identify, locate, and evaluate information needed for the completion of course projects; and to help students become independent learners. In effect, these two library services are mirror images: bibliographic instruction is an efficient way of providing reference assistance to groups of individuals, and reference service is a way of providing personalized instruction to specific individuals. Since staff, time, and energy are always limited, it is important for us to look for ways to provide both of these services efficiently and effectively. One way to accomplish this is to incorporate personalized reference assistance into the bibliographic instruction session itself.

At Earlham College, faculty and librarians have developed course assignments that lend themselves to this approach. An examination of a number of these assignments reveals that there are several techniques used in common. Some of these techniques will look familiar since they are methods many librarians already use in their efforts to provide good library use instruction. But re-conceptualizing these techniques as ways to make our reference work more efficient might lead us to fine-tune or improve what we're doing, or give us the motivation and impetus to put something into place that we've had in the back of our minds anyway.

Examining these assignments also reveals the critical role of the faculty member. An understanding of what motivates faculty will help as we make further attempts to maximize our bibliographic instruction in order to minimize reference assistance.

Penhale is science librarian at Earlham College, Richmond, Indiana.

DESCRIPTION OF ASSIGNMENTS

Genetics and Evolution

The first assignment is from "Genetics and Evolution," one of the four introductory biology courses in the Earlham curriculum. In each of these four courses, students write papers based on primary scientific literature. These are challenging assignments that might be expected to result in a flood of questions at the reference desk from the 50 to 175 students enrolled in each course.

But in Earlham College's branch science library, there is no reference desk! The library is staffed during daytime hours by one professional librarian and a secretary; it is kept open evenings and weekends by undergraduate student workers. This means that during the times when students typically like to work, no professional help is available. In fact, it was reflecting on this situation that led me to think about my work in the science library as "maximizing bibliographic instruction, minimizing reference." One might even say that my goal is to have no reference.

The genetics and evolution course is a class for about 75 first- and second-year students. It is team-taught by three faculty members—in 1993, Dr. Amy Mulnix, Dr. Brent Smith, and Dr. Jerome Woolpy—each of whom meets with a laboratory group of about 25 students. The library assignment is to write a five-page paper on a topic in contemporary genetics, based on reading the scientific journal literature. Students are given a list of topics from which to select, such as the use of DNA fingerprinting in forensic cases or the possibility of gene therapy for cystic fibrosis. The students familiarize themselves with their chosen topics by reading two or three popular articles that the faculty have put on reserve in the library.

Prior to receiving any library instruction, the students write one-paragraph summaries of their topics based on these popular articles. Then, each faculty member and his or her laboratory group meets in the library for bibliographic instruction during the three-hour time slot that is reserved on other weeks for course laboratory work. During this lab session, the librarian, the faculty member, and the undergraduate teaching assistant for the course provide hands-on instruction in the use of three different periodical indexes. Students complete a worksheet as they are learning these tools, then spend the rest of the lab session looking for articles on their own topics. They must identify and locate two relevant articles before leaving class. One week later, the students turn in bibliographies for their papers. They turn in the completed papers at the end of the second week.

AMERICAN POLITICS

American politics, with 40 students, is also a relatively large introductory level course. For the library assignment in this course, the students use government documents to prepare 12-page papers analyzing the process by which a particular bill became an act. The emphasis is not on the content of the bill, but on the principal players and the twists and turns of the legislative process. In effect, the students are learning how the government works at the same time that they are learning how to find and use the written traces of that work in government documents.

The assignment begins with a joint presentation in the classroom by the instructor, Dr. Robert Johnstone, and the librarian, Nancy Taylor. They provide an overview of the legislative process and government documents. From a list of legislative acts provided by Johnstone and Taylor, the students choose which acts they will investigate for this assignment. The documents associated with each act on the list have been checked against our selective depository holdings to make sure that we have enough of them to complete the project. Easily misplaced documents, such as those on microfiche, have been placed on reserve in the library.

The next week, Johnstone and Taylor schedule small group meetings of five to eight students in the library. In these meetings, which take place outside of class time, the students are given hands-on instruction for each of the sources they will use in this assignment.

During subsequent weeks, students work on their bills. As the paper deadline nears, Johnstone will occasionally make himself available in the reference area of the library. On the last few nights, student teaching assistants who have completed the assignment in previous years hold evening help sessions. Often one

can observe an intense group of students discussing how to extract the most useful information from the documents they have located, and how to put that information together into a coherent analysis.

INTRODUCTION TO PSYCHOLOGICAL PERSPECTIVES

The goal of Dr. Katharine Milar, who teaches introduction to psychological perspectives to non-majors, is to introduce students to the scholarly literature of the discipline. Their assignment is to support or refute the validity of old saws or common clichés such as, "You can't teach an old dog new tricks" or "Absence makes the heart grow fonder." Working in groups of two or three, students do this by synthesizing the evidence provided in three journal articles which present experiments relevant to the cliché.

In order to guide students through this assignment, the students must first complete a worksheet, which will be checked by upper-class psychology majors who serve as teaching assistants for the course. On this worksheet, the students "translate" the clichés into psychological terminology: "You can't teach an old dog new tricks" becomes "Aging impairs information processing." To do so, students locate encyclopedia entries on the subject. They also identify the three articles they intend to use, and answer questions about the experiments described in the articles. When this worksheet has been satisfactorily completed, the students write papers describing the articles and synthesizing the findings into conclusions of their own.

Nancy Taylor provides a one-hour bibliographic instruction session in the library with the whole class, the course instructor, and the teaching assistants in attendance. Taylor introduces the students to the psychological encyclopedias and demonstrates the CD-ROM version of PsychLit. Each student is then given time to select a cliché from a list the faculty member supplies, and they begin work on the assignment.

Because the size of the class restricts each individual's access to the CD-ROM database, students need to complete most of their research later on. On several evenings close to the due date, the teaching assistants schedule help sessions in the library. They typically spend most of their time helping the students decide which articles will work best for the assignment and helping them understand the articles.

Human Development/Social Relations Senior Seminar

This course, taught by Dr. Nelson Bingham, is the culmination of an interdisciplinary major, which combines psychology, sociology/anthropology, philosophy, education, and biology. The major emphasizes analyzing social problems from the perspectives of these disciplines, obtaining practical experience, and ascertaining the place of values in the educational curriculum.

As part of the comprehensive examination for this major, the seniors are asked to identify a social problem and to propose a strategy for action. The students need to use the literature from a variety of disciplines as they define a problem, provide empirical data illustrating it, present the theoretical issues underpinning that issue, and design a plan of intervention. Their completed work takes the form of a one-hour oral presentation.

The librarian conducts two brief bibliographic instruction sessions for this course. Nancy Taylor comes to the class early in the term to review briefly library sources that the seniors might use as they explore potential topics. Since the students have had library instruction in numerous earlier courses, this time is brief.

Later each student hands in a one-page summary of his or her proposed problem topic. Bingham reviews these for suitability before passing them on to the librarian. Taylor jots down notes on each topic sheet, suggesting specialized sources or research ideas for that topic. She visits the class again, returning the topic sheets and making comments relevant to the work of each group. Students then continue their work over the course of the rest of the term.

Equilibrium and Analysis

Dr. Wilmer Stratton teaches this upper-level chemistry course on the properties and behavior of ionic compounds in aqueous solutions. Laboratory work is a major part of the course. After being introduced to a variety of methods for quantitative chemical analysis, students design projects in which they measure the levels of particular compounds in various solutions. For instance, they measure the level of caffeine in soft drinks or lead in drinking water. The students design their projects based on the methods described in journal articles written by chemists who have conducted similar analyses.

Online searching of Analytical Abstracts, a bibliographic database indexing articles from scientific journals, is ideal for this project. The abstracts of the articles often provide enough detail so that students may not need to read the article itself. In addition, searching for relevant literature is quite straightforward. The basic search strategy is to ask for the substance to be measured, the type of solution under investigation, and the analytical method or methods preferred. Instantly, a list of articles meeting these criteria is presented to the student. In fact, the major library challenge for the students is deciding which articles are the best and the most useful for their purposes.

The class of approximately 25 students is divided into two laboratory sections meeting on different days. Pairs of students in each lab section team up and decide what they would like to analyze. After topics have been chosen, each lab section comes to the library's computer room for an online search session. Each pair of students sits at a terminal together and follows my directions as I guide them through a hands-on sample search of Analytical Abstracts on Dialog. Then the students work on their own projects as Stratton and I circulate around the room offering advice on the mechanics or strategy of online searching. Stratton also assists the students in understanding the abstracts they retrieve and in deciding which methods can be used most successfully with the chemistry department's facilities and equipment. It takes a little over one hour for the class to complete a successful search of the literature. The process repeats itself with the second lab section.

Techniques Used to Minimize Reference

The course assignments just described utilize a number of common techniques, which result in the reduction of reference work on the part of the librarian.

Limiting Topic Choice and Checking Topics Beforehand

The three introductory courses—genetics, politics, and psychology—all limit topic choice. This makes sense from the professor's point of view because formulating a good topic is a hard, yet essential, step for beginning students. Providing a list of topics moves the student beyond that confusing initial stage. It also spares the reference librarian the proverbial problem of responding to the student who claims his or her research topic for a five-page paper is World War II.

Also, the librarian can check topics ahead of time. This ensures that when students search the periodical indexes for a given topic, they will find relevant primary literature and, further, that those journals are in the library's collection. This minimizes the number of frustrated declarations: "I can't find anything in our library!" It has the additional benefit for the library of reducing interlibrary loan.

The bibliographic instruction librarian may not have to be the one to check the topics. For the American politics assignment, for instance, the government documents librarian determined which bills were sufficiently covered by materials in our collection. Student library workers helped screen the genetics topics, and the teaching assistants for the psychology course verified that there was enough journal literature in our library to support each of the cliché choices.

There are drawbacks, of course, to limiting topic choice. Some students may want to investigate topics not on the list. If so, a student might be accommodated by a quick check on the topic and then granting an exception if it seems workable.

Also, limiting topics may mean that several students will need the same library resources. Several steps can be taken to solve this problem. Putting easily lost materials on reserve for the American politics assignment smoothes one of the difficulties encountered in an earlier version of that assignment. For the introductory biology courses, a "no check-out policy" is instituted for books falling within a certain range of call numbers. Thus, students can share these resources since the books remain in the library.

ALLOWING TIME TO WORK ON ASSIGNMENTS DURING BIBLIOGRAPHIC INSTRUCTION

Another technique is to create an opportunity for students to begin their library research during the bibliographic instruction session. In the genetics class and the psychology class, students had time to begin work during the instruction session. The genetics students had a substantial amount of work time since instruction took place during a three-hour laboratory session.

This technique minimizes reference because students utilize their newly acquired research skills before they forget them and find it necessary to ask the librarian to repeat the lesson. Beginning their work during class time also puts students within reach of help during the initial stages of research when roadblocks frequently occur.

The chemistry course provides a special example of working on an assignment during bibliographic instruction. In this case, students completed all of their research during that time. We took advantage of Dialog's Classroom Instruction Program, which offers reduced rates for students learning how to conduct their own online searches. Working with six pairs of students on each day was a manageable undertaking for the librarian and the faculty member. When one compares

these group sessions with individual search appointments with a reference librarian, one can see the time savings was considerable: the group work required a little over two hours; working with pairs separately would have required more than 12 hours.

STRUCTURING AND STAGING THE ASSIGNMENT AND THE BIBLIOGRAPHIC INSTRUCTION

Bibliographic instruction librarians have long recognized the importance of providing library instruction at the time students are ready to begin work on course projects. Students are rarely interested in learning library research techniques just for the sake of acquiring new skills. Students are motivated to learn when they need to use the library to fulfill their professors' assignments.

At a minimum, it helps when students have thought about possible topics prior to their arrival for instruction. They are more ready to listen to instructions and only in this way are students able to begin work during the instruction session, if this is part of the plan.

A further refinement of this is to require students to complete an assignment prior to arriving for instruction. For instance, students in the genetics and evolution class read popular articles and wrote paragraphs on their topics prior to the library session. Subsequently they arrived with a basic knowledge of their topics and were ready for the next step: finding journal articles. Thus, these students were ready for a more advanced level of work during class time.

An alternate approach can be used when students have not selected topics ahead of time. This approach is to schedule only a brief library instruction session and to limit the presentation to suggestions on how to search for a topic. This was used to good effect in the human development/social relation course where senior students could choose any topic from the entire spectrum of human social problems. Since these senior students had considerable prior library experience, the librarian saved time by preparing only an abbreviated handout of sources that would be useful in this exploration stage.

Only when the students were ready to begin in-depth work did the librarian spend time directing them to more sophisticated sources. Each student turned in a topic summary and the librarian wrote comments on each one, noting the library sources to consult next. The advantage of this approach is that "reference" is given at the librarian's convenience. The librarian prepares her written responses to the students' topic summaries at moments in the work day when she has time, rather than responding instantaneously to the unpredictable arrival of students at the reference desk. Further, because she provides a written response for each topic, everyone gets personalized reference attention, even those who wouldn't have asked on their own.

There are other examples of how structuring and staging student work can minimize reference work. Simply requiring students to complete a brief assignment during the instruction session reduces the temptation for students to drift away rather than use the skills they've just learned to buckle down and work while everyone is there to help. Students in the genetics class were required to find three primary sources on their topics; one each from the three periodical indexes they had just learned to use.

The psychology library project was even more highly structured. Students began a worksheet assignment during the instruction session. They were asked to cite the encyclopedia article that allowed them to translate their clichés into psychological terms, and to list three articles and answer questions about the experimental design in those articles. Upon completion, these worksheets were checked by a teaching assistant before the students proceeded with their work.

This interim assignment helped by clarifying what the students needed to accomplish as they worked toward fulfilling the assignment. Further, it inserted the teaching assistants into the research process rather than simply the reference librarian. The assistance offered was considerable: since the teaching assistants had completed the assignment before, they knew the type of journal articles that the students needed to find, they could help the students understand the articles, and they could show them how to use that information in completing the assignment.

INVOLVING OTHERS IN BIBLIOGRAPHIC INSTRUCTION AND REFERENCE

The benefits of involving faculty members and teaching assistants in providing instruction and reference extend beyond the mere addition of more helpful hands. These individuals contribute expertise beyond what the librarian would typically be able to provide.

The continued presence of faculty members allows them to provide additional clarification on what is expected for the assignment. Beginning students, for instance, have a tendency to rely on the types of materials that they used in high school. Not only do they need to be instructed in what constitutes the primary literature of a discipline, but the lesson needs to be reinforced as students encounter the literature for the first time. In both the psychology and the genetics classes, the faculty members instructed students in ways

to judge, from article titles and from the names of the journals, which articles are likely to be primary sources. Then, as students used CD-ROM periodical indexes, the faculty helped them decide which were primary research articles and which were not.

In addition, the faculty member's knowledge of the subject area makes him or her the ideal person to help students select the best and most relevant materials. A clear example of this is the assistance provided by the chemistry professor during the online search sessions. The professor advised the students as they scanned lists of article titles looking for the most promising ones. Then when the students viewed the abstracts of those articles, the professor helped them assess whether or not the analytical methods described could be duplicated in the college's laboratory setting.

The undergraduate teaching assistants also have a special contribution to make. They have knowledge of the subject and the particulars of the assignment, which they can put to good use in assisting their peers. Some played this role in checking the psychology assignment worksheet; other teaching assistants aided the politics students who came to the library for help on the final few evenings before the assignment due date. Also, undergraduate student teaching assistants have a special credibility with their peers because they have previously completed the assignment themselves. This type of student interaction is particularly desirable in an educational climate that increasingly emphasizes collaborative learning and peer teaching.

In summary, note that the various techniques described are applicable in particular settings. For instance, some were drawn from experiences in large introductory classes requiring a major piece of work, which might have resulted in many questions of the reference librarian. Other circumstances might not warrant the use of the techniques. For instance, ordinary reference service at the desk might be manageable for smaller classes, or for less ambitious assignments. Upper-level students with previous library experience may not need the intense instruction, and limiting topic choice may not be appropriate for more advanced work.

THE FACULTY ROLE

As we saw in these assignments, faculty members structure their assignments in particular ways, devote considerable class time for library instruction, or participate in providing the instruction. Why are they willing to put this much time, thought, and energy into developing their assignments? Interviews with faculty members provides some insights. I asked three of the professors why they developed their assignments as they did, and how much work it took on their part. Their responses follow.

Dr. Robert Johnstone, American Politics

"I am willing to put a lot of effort into this assignment because of the variety of important payoffs. It is a project that causes the students to write an original piece of research, modest though it is. Nevertheless, it is a piece of research, and these are students in an introductory class. They get into sophisticated reference materials and data-accessing methods in a way that provides them with a basis for later courses. It causes them to be self-starters in the enterprise. There is, therefore, a tremendous educational payoff. The students find that they are more involved in the subject matter of American politics when they are actually doing this sort of hands-on work, when they can actually make discoveries of their own about the legislative process.

"It took a lot of effort initially. In fact, I had to learn about the government documents myself. In my own research I had only used a narrow portion of primary materials. So when I started to do this assignment, in a way I had to go back to school with the students. I was familiar with the classification system of government documents. I knew generally the uses of such things as the Congressional Record and Committee Hearings, but I had to familiarize myself with a lot of other sources. Fortunately, I had the help of a library staff who kept me fully informed, particularly about new indexing, abstracting, and reference services as they came into being. They would apprise me of these things, and then I would sneak over to the library in the dead of night and look at them. I gradually recognized how very valuable they could be for students in an undergraduate setting. But it did take a good deal of effort in the beginning. Even now, I still have to periodically re-tool myself because new things come online all the time.

"I have been using this assignment now for about 16 to 18 years. The initial bugs were worked out pretty quickly, but we have revised it from time to time, adding a bit here, dropping a bit there. I refine the list of bills they work on, of course, every two years or so as new legislation comes into being. We have found that some bills work well, and that some sources are less successful than others. So we just tinker with it a little bit along the way. Still, it is essentially the same project that we began 18 years ago."

Dr. Amy Mulnix, Genetics and Evolution

"One of the reasons that we spend a lot of time and energy in the introductory courses for biology majors is that the curriculum really builds on the student experience gained in that instruction. So we invest time in teaching students not just how to access the literature, but also how to read and analyze it. We have the students use that experience to do more sophisticated work later in their careers. For instance, our senior seminars are almost completely based on primary literature.

"Also, my fields, which include cell biology, molecular biology, and developmental biology, are moving really fast. Pedagogically, I believe that is more important for me to teach my students how to be current in the field than giving them information out of the textbook, which is likely to be old even if the textbook is published in the year that I am teaching the class. I am willing to give up class time to do instruction and to do library work because it is going to be beneficial for the students in the future.

"I think one of the biggest things that working on this assignment takes is patience. It is very chaotic when you do library instruction in a class of 20 or 30 at the same time. Even with the librarian and a couple of teaching assistants present, you have people who need you 'right now!' So it takes a lot of patience.

"It also takes a fair amount of preparation time. We re-work the assignments nearly every year trying to make them better, using information from what didn't work so well the previous year. Initially, it took me some time just to familiarize myself with a new assignment. This is only my third year here and I was a very poor bibliographic literature user when I finished graduate school. I remember getting ready to teach *Science Citation Index* and Sara saying, 'Do you remember how to use this?' I was too embarrassed to say, 'No, nobody ever taught me to use this!' Sara handled that situation really well because she said, 'Let me remind you about some of its special features.' Then I could make my way through teaching *Science Citation Index*.

"It also requires, in addition to the patience and the preparation, the willingness to give up control of your class, in part to the librarian who is really the person doing the instruction. And as I said, the class is very chaotic and initially I felt very uncomfortable not having control of what the students were doing, and what they were finding, and how they were going about it. It takes a while to learn to live with that."

Dr. Katharine Milar, Introduction to Psychological Perspectives

"I was faced with an introductory psychology class in which the majority of the students were never going to take another psychology course. I knew I needed to design an assignment for people who might be consumers of psychological information, but not necessarily those who were going to need to go on in psychology. So I wanted to design an assignment that would enable them to take something in a popular vein, like the clichés, and translate them in a way that would allow them to find primary literature that spoke to that particular psychological function.

"It is a challenging assignment because for the most part the students are first-year students and I am asking them to read primary literature. The psychological literature is accessible enough that students can find enough that they can understand at some level. They may not understand all of the results section and the detailed statistics, but they can at least get the gist of the articles and that is really what I am most concerned with.

"I was really worried about this assignment because I was afraid it would be too difficult for the students and I was also afraid it would take a long time. Some of my fears were realized. The way I discovered that was that I actually worked through the assignment completely, including translating each cliché, looking up the sources, tracking them down, and writing the report. I include that sample assignment with the handout that the students get.

"I tinker with the assignment yearly, ever since the first time I assigned it. I have added the worksheet assignment. Also, I'm now doing more instruction with my teaching assistants so that when the students bring them articles they have located, the teaching assistants are better able to detect what is likely to be a good article and what is likely not to be good."

Lessons from These Interviews

What can we learn from these brief interviews? First, it is clear that these faculty members are putting considerable time and effort into making their assignments successful. Initially, they had to learn themselves how to use the library research tools, and they have to retrain as new sources come into existence. They train their assistants and provide library instruction to the class as a whole. And it appears that each faculty member finds something about the assignment to work on each year, some bit of "tinkering" to do.

The most important point to emerge is that the faculty members are willing to do this because they are motivated by the quality of work that their students are consequently able to do. When students use the original literature of the discipline, they become independent learners with positive educational outcomes: students become more engaged with the subject matter of the course and they are not limited to knowledge provided in the classroom. As Johnstone has written, "a working

familiarity with the use of the library can serve to achieve one of the most basic purposes of a liberal arts college—it can truly 'liberate' the student to be a self-starter. Bibliographical instruction, when it is accomplished in the context of a substantive academic program and is done with practical rather than with mere formal ends in mind, really frees the student by awakening her or him to the possibilities of the scholarly task. The feeling of achievement when one comes across a gem of information obtained only because one knew where to look is in a very real sense its own reward."[1]

Major efforts with introductory classes have additional payoffs in later courses. These students can be expected to work with even greater independence, exploring topics outside the realm of the faculty member's expertise and finding information more current than would be provided by either teachers or texts.

These professors are all dedicated and demanding teachers. It is important to them to push their students to produce significant work. In their efforts to design and implement successful assignments, the faculty demand a lot of themselves as well.

The professors are also willing to let go of some control: they do this when they place themselves in the role of learner rather than teacher as they perfect their own research skills; then again, when they hand over class time to a librarian or give their student assistants a larger teaching role; and finally, as a bibliographic instruction period moves into the chaotic stage when students go in all different directions and begin their own research.

This suggests that these faculty have a level of self-confidence that allows them to take some risks: the risk, for instance, of showing their ignorance about how to begin library research from the ground level. This lack of prior training isn't something that surprises librarians, but we saw that both a newer faculty member and an experienced one were a bit sheepish when they admitted to it. Also, faculty were willing to take the risk of trying something new. One faculty member noted she went ahead with her project, even though she had some worries about its potential success.

Initiating Change

As we attempt to makes changes in bibliographic instruction that will lead to a reduction in the amount of reference assistance that we should provide, our beginning point must be the faculty. Obviously they play a critical role in shaping assignments that minimize reference and in helping with reference assistance themselves. They are motivated to do so because it serves their own goal of providing a good educational experience for their students. Since the role of a librarian in an undergraduate setting is to help the faculty fulfill this goal, we should look for assignments where the teaching/learning process might be improved through restructuring bibliographic instruction.

Further, we should consider the temperaments of the faculty offering those assignments. Faculty members who have high expectations of their students and of themselves as teachers are likely to be receptive to the idea of altering an assignment in order to make it possible for students to do better work. Faculty who are self-confident about their teaching might be receptive to taking the risks that accompany change.

Librarians are probably already aware of which course assignments at their institutions create reference requests that would be minimized. Courses with large enrollments can generate considerable work at the reference desk. This is especially true if the assignment in such a course is a major one requiring the use of sophisticated research tools. Assignments that don't clearly articulate the faculty member's expectations can result in questions which grow out of the students' basic confusion about what they are required to do.

In responding to such questions at the reference desk, the librarian may be the one to discover an opportunity for improvement. For instance, the tendency for government documents on fiche to become lost was evident to the librarian working with students in the politics class. On the other hand, a faculty member might see the need for change. The psychology professor was the one who realized that her students were finding it difficult to translate the clichés into appropriate psychological terminology.

Once such problems are identified, the librarian and faculty member need to alert each other so that remedies can be sought. The librarian may need to take the initiative, however, in seeking feedback from faculty. It may not occur to faculty that there are ways for librarians to help. The techniques described in this article can be adapted to suit the needs of a variety of assignments. The goals of the assignment, the size of the class, and the prior library experience of the students should all be taken into account.

Also, we should recognize that improving an assignment and minimizing reference do not necessarily require large changes, or many of them, either on our part or on that of the faculty member. One change alone, restricting and checking topics, may lead to considerable improvement. The faculty member's contribution in such a case can be limited to providing a list of potential topics, which the librarian will then check. And even the work of the librarian can be minimized if we ask others, like library student workers, to help.

Finally, flexibility and patience will stand us in good stead. Even the best plans may need minor adjustments during the course of an assignment. Further, the changing nature of academic disciplines, as well as their literature and the access tools, will dictate that changes be made periodically.

SUMMARY

All bibliographic instruction librarians are interested in making changes that will increase the effectiveness of their instruction; my experience shows that it's possible to do that and at the same time reduce the number of requests for assistance at the reference desk. This means that the librarian is working more efficiently, and that the students are becoming better and more independent library users.

There are a number of techniques that can have this effect: structuring and staging a course assignment and its accompanying bibliographic instruction; limiting topic choices; providing time during instruction for students to begin work on an assignment; and enlisting the assistance of faculty and/or students in providing instruction and reference help. Undoubtedly, there must be other techniques besides those I've described.

Whatever technique is employed, it seems to me that an essential element is forming a partnership with the classroom teacher offering the course. That faculty member must be willing to alter the assignment, probably to devote extra class time for library instruction, or to help in assisting students in the library as they begin work on their assignments. If faculty members believe that doing any of this will lead to an improved educational experience for their students, including making them more independent learners, they should be willing to cooperate.

Since the librarian's goal is also to improve the teaching/learning process, we should look for, and perhaps help to create, those opportunities that lead to "maximizing bibliographic instruction, minimizing reference."

NOTE

1. Robert Johnstone, in the newsletter of the Earlham College Teaching and Learning Committee, *A Learned Journal* 1 (29 March 1976): 3.

— SARA J. PENHALE —

Genetics and Evolution

Dr. Amy Mulnix, Biology Department, Earlham College

POPULAR SCIENCE FRONTIERS
Using Popular Literature as a Point of Departure in a Scientific Quest

---

In lab the week of April 11-15, we will initiate a library project that has several goals.

First, it will be an opportunity for you to delve into an interesting topic in genetics in depth.

Second, by researching the literature, you will discover that these topics cover very active fields of scientific inquiry; though you may or may not choose to pursue these fields vocationally, you will gain an appreciation for the excitement inherent in a rapidly changing discipline.

Third, by reading scientific literature you will be exposed to the concise, elegant modes by which scientists communicate with each other and how scientific knowledge builds on itself.

Finally you will acquire skills in accessing scientific information that will be useful now and in the future.

A list of topics, and one or more questions pertaining to them, has been provided by your instructor. Each topic is introduced by one or more short news articles (on reserve in Wildman Science Library under the course name and the name of your instructor) that report some recent discovery in a subfield of genetics. Using these articles as a starting point, you will learn more about the topic by first finding and then using primary scientific literature.

This assignment has four parts.

1. Choose one of the topics from your instructor's list that seems interesting. Read all the articles on reserve for that topic. Gain further background knowledge from the relevant sections of your textbook. Use the following dictionaries, if necessary, to help define terms.
    Dictionary of Genetics and Cell Biology. Sci/Ref/QH/427/M3.3/1987
    A Dictionary of Genetics. Sci/Ref/QH/427/K5.5/1985.

    Write one paragraph describing your topic. Then create a bibliography of all the articles from the reserve folder. List each article using the format for references described on the next three pages. This assignment should not exceed one typed page, and should include your name and drawer number, your instructor's name and your lab day.

DUE IN CLASS ON MONDAY, APRIL 11

2. In lab during the week of April 11-15, your instructor, TA, and the librarian will help you begin to work on your topic by conducting a review of our computerized indexes to scientific literature and then allowing time for individual work. Each person will have time to find at least two sources on their topic and turn these in to the instructor before the end of the period.

TO BE COMPLETED IN YOUR LAB THE WEEK OF APRIL 11-15

3. At the beginning of your lab during the week of April 18-22, you will turn in a typed list of five primary references and one or two secondary references (if the latter exist) that are important and relevant to your topic. In addition, you will turn in a concise one-page summary of the subject. In this summary you should cite all of the references you list. The proper format for the in-text citation style and the Literature Cited list are shown on the next three pages.

DUE IN YOUR LAB THE WEEK OF APRIL 18-22

4. The final, and major, part of the assignment will be an expansion of your work, culminating in a 5-page typed paper summarizing and assessing the scientific issues raised in your topic, with a Literature Cited section containing at least 10 references, of which 7 must be primary articles (you may use as many abstracts as you wish in addition to these 7 articles). All of the references in the Literature Cited section must be cited in your paper. Your written response to the questions raised by the instructor in the list of topics is to be an "answer" in some respects, but most scientific problems do not lend themselves to clear cut, discrete solutions. Your approach, therefore, should be to synthesize the information, theories and interpretations that you find, and provide your own evaluative interpretation.

DUE 9:00 WEDNESDAY, APRIL 27 FOR ALL LAB SECTIONS

SAMPLE QUESTIONS FOR GENETICS AND EVOLUTION

1. DNA Fingerprinting: DNA fingerprinting is a relatively new technique in molecular genetics that has wide applicability, including new capabilities (1) to solve crimes, (2) to rescue endangered species, and (3) to study the inheritance of behavior in animals. Find out what DNA fingerprinting is, and investigate one of the following applications of this technology:

    a. Research the application of DNA fingerprinting in criminal investigations. Evaluate the usefulness and limitations of this technique for providing incontrovertible evidence. Articles: Economist 311:81; Science News 128:390-391; Bioscience 39:6-9

    b. How can DNA fingerprinting be used to study relatedness, preserve genetic variability, and plan favorable matings for endangered species? Article: Scientific American (June 1988):32

    c. How can DNA fingerprinting be used to study animal behavior and explain it on the basis of relatedness: Article: Science News 131:344

2. Sex Determination: Sex is determined in different ways among various groups vertebrates. Choose one of the following two topics:

    a. In mammals, including humans, it is the presence of a Y chromosome that determines maleness. In the article listed below, the author reviews research through 1986 on the genetic control of maleness. Various reports since 1987 claim that they have found the gene for maleness, but these claims have been controversial. Check out the topic of genetic sex determination in humans. Article: Science 234:1076-1077

    b. In some reptiles, an individual's sex is determined by the temperature at which eggs are incubated! Find out more about temperature dependent sex determination in the primary literature. How widespread is it in reptiles? How might such a mechanism have evolved? Article: Discover (Oct. 1986):9

3.   Mitochondrial Eve: Researchers who have studied the make-up of the DNA in the mitochondrion of humans (mtDNA) have made the rather startling statement that all humans share as a common ancestor a single human female (dubbed "Eve") who lived between 140,000 and 240,000 years ago in Africa. You can read about this in a news article published in Time magazine (Jan. 26, 1987, p. 66). This is an example of using what is called a "molecular clock" to infer evolutionary lineages. An article in Science News (131:74-75) describes molecular clocks and some of their problems. Very recently the mitochondrial Eve hypothesis has been debunked (Science 255:686-687). Trace the development of the Eve hypothesis in the primary literature, and describe the evidence and criticisms. In general, find out in the primary literature what some of the pitfalls of molecular clock are.

GENETICS AND EVOLUTION WORKSHEET
(To be completed by pairs of students working together)

Instructor's Name: _____ Lab Day: _____

Partners' Names: _____ and _____

SCIENCE CITATION INDEX ON CD-ROM (1990-1993)

Look for an article which cites the following article:

   Willett, W. 1989. The search for the causes of breast and colon cancer. Nature 338:389-394.

Print out the short record (the author, title, year, journal name, volume and page numbers) of one article you found.

BIOLOGICAL ABSTRACTS ON CD-ROM (1991-PRESENT)

Imagine that you have located the following citation in a bibliography.

   Brennan, M.B. and N. Avdalovic. 1991. Periodicum Biologorum 93(4):583-590.

Since we do not have the journal in our library, locate an abstract of the article. Print out the citation and the abstract for the article.

GENERAL SCIENCE INDEX ON CD-ROM (1984-PRESENT)

Each partner should use this index to find articles on his/her own subject.

Print out the citation to one of the articles. Determine if it is a primary or secondary article, then list it on the back of this sheet.

Use ANY of these sources to find TWO articles (one secondary and one primary) on your topics. Partners should help each other in locating the articles. For each partner, note the topic, then write the author, title, year, journal name, volume number and pages for each article in the correct citation style as shown below.

Author(s). Year. Title of article with only first word capitalized. Name of journal followed by volume number:page numbers.

Taylor, P.D. and M.G. Balmer. 1980. Local mate competition and the sex ratio. Journal of Theoretical Biology 86:409-419.

Name: Topic:

SECONDARY SOURCE

Index used:

Complete citation to article:

PRIMARY SOURCE

Index used:

Complete citation to article (follow above format):

Name: Topic:

SECONDARY SOURCE

Index used:

Complete citation to article (follow above format):

PRIMARY SOURCE

Index used:

Complete citation to article:

American Politics

Dr. Robert Johnstone, Politics Department, Earlham College

TERM PROJECT

I. PURPOSES

1. This project is designed to develop an understanding of the process of government in the United States through direct research in the primary documents of that government. You will examine in detail the development of a bill from its inception in Congress or the Executive, through its legislative career in both Houses of Congress. This study will be accompanied, of course, by the normal classroom lectures and by the reading of assigned texts.

    The final term paper will be a narrative (@12 pages) that analyzes the particular aspects of the process that had significance in the outcome of your bill. The study should provide you with a more intimate, almost "first hand", knowledge of and feel for the processes of government than could be achieved from the secondary sources alone.

2. The principal resources for this project will be government documents. Our library is an official government depository, which means that we receive automatically a significant amount of the material published by the U.S. Government Printing Office. The government produces an awesome amount of material that is of great potential use to us as students of American politics, but this material is often not fully used or even understood by many who are unaware of the extent of information available or who are turned away by their unfamiliarity with the methods of using government documents.

    Knowledge of the skills of information retrieval in these valuable sources can, and should, be a major tool for research in politics. A second purpose of this project, therefore, is to develop these skills in the discovery and use of government documents, as well as the relevant reference, abstracting, and indexing materials in the library.

II. PROCEDURES

1. You will choose a piece of legislation (from a list provided), a bill that meets certain basic criteria for the study (i.e., the legislation must have been of sufficient importance and controversy to have produced committee hearings and floor debates, and these materials must have been sent to Lilly Library as a selective government depository).

2. One class session will be devoted to an introduction to library bibliographical instruction, basic search techniques, and the use of government documents. This instruction, provided jointly by a librarian and me, will cover basic reference materials, and the nature of basic congressional and executive branch documents.

3. The best place to begin the project is by consulting two reference works: Congressional Quarterly Almanac and Congressional Information Service (CIS) (consult the year of your bill's final passage). These publications contain their own "legislative histories" of your bill, plus much valuable information with which to begin your research. Study these works to become familiar with the general nature and subject matter of your bill. It will help later on.

4. The final narrative account that you are to produce (the deadline is listed in your course syllabus) should concentrate upon an analysis of the process of legislation rather than upon the detailed substance of your bill, although some of the latter will be necessary in order to accomplish the former.

(You might wish to include a summary of the bill's contents as an appendix to your paper, but it will be impossible to do a detailed analysis of what may well be a long and complicated statute.)

You should present a chronological and/or topical analysis of the significant steps in the process, noting, for example, such factors as the clash of organized interest groups, the effects of particular procedures (filibuster, Rules committee action, parliamentary maneuvers, etc.), the influence of key individuals or groups, such as the role of president, of the party leadership in Congress, the committee and subcommittee chairpersons, or key bureaucrats.

One of your difficulties will be that of synthesizing a sizable amount of raw data (committee hearings, floor debates, presidential messages and press conferences, etc.). CQ and CIS will be of some help in indicating the major points of significance; you can use them as guides to important testimony or to crucial procedures along the way. Yet they are no substitute for the primary documents themselves; and it is a test of composition to produce a short (12-page) account from a wealth of available information.

5.   The librarians and I will be available to provide assistance. Call on us; we are pleased to help. Additional information will be provided in class and in the library sessions.

6.   To illustrate the sort of final paper that is expected, I have placed a copy of a fine paper from an earlier year on RESERVE at Lilly Circulation Desk.

NOTE: YOU ARE STRONGLY URGED TO BEGIN THIS PROJECT EARLY AND TO WORK ON IT STEADILY OVER THE TERM. THE PROJECT CANNOT BE ACCOMPLISHED EFFECTIVELY IF IT IS DONE IN HASTE AND UNDER THE PRESSURE OF A LAST-MINUTE DEADLINE. A WORD TO THE WISE SHOULD BE SUFFICIENT, BUT I CANNOT STRESS THIS POINT TOO STRONGLY!!

AMERICAN POLITICS ACT OPTIONS
(Rank your choices: 1st, 2nd, 3rd)

Goldwater-Nichols Defense Reorganization Act of 1986

Immigration Reform and Control Act of 1986

Anti-Drug Abuse Act of 1986

Firearm Owners Protection Act of 1986

Omnibus Diplomatic Security and Anti-Terrorism Act of 1986

Comprehensive Anti-Apartheid Act of 1986

Water Quality Act of 1987

Health Omnibus Programs Extension (Title II: AIDS Amendment) of 1988

Omnibus Trade and Competitiveness Act of 1988

Medicare Catastrophic Coverage Act of 1988

Fair Labor Standards (Minimum Wage) Amendments of 1989

Market Reform Act 1990

Americans With Disabilities Act of 1990

Immigration Act of 1990

Civil Rights Act of 1991

Appendix 3:

Introduction to Psychological Perspectives

Dr. Katharine Milar, Psychology Department, Earlham College

TRUE OR FALSE?
Library Assignment for Psychology 15

The purpose of this assignment is to engage you in finding, reading, analyzing, and synthesizing primary literature in psychology. On the attached sheet, you will find a list of clichés and other statements generally accepted as factual. If you haven't heard all of them, you have certainly heard most of them. This is your assignment to be conducted with one partner:

1. Select one of the statements on the list (or you may propose one of your own for my approval) and translate it into psychological terms. For example, "You can't teach an old dog new tricks" might be translated as, "Learning is impaired in the aged." (Some of the statements are followed by helpful hints for translation.)

   HAVE YOUR TRANSLATION AND PROBABLE SEARCH TERMS CHECKED BY YOUR TA OR ME

2. Consult a psychological encyclopedia or dictionary to help you establish a general picture of the issues raised by the statement you select. For example, the encyclopedia may tell you that some types of learning are affected by age while other types are unaffected.

   FILL IN THE APPROPRIATE BLANKS ON THE WORKSHEET. USE THE SAMPLE ASSIGNMENT FOR HELP WITH CORRECT CITATION FORMAT (APA STYLE)

3. Use the terms that the encyclopedia has helped you identify and locate three articles in psychology journals that support or do not support the statement you selected.

   FILL IN THE APPROPRIATE BLANKS ON THE WORKSHEET. CHECK THE WORKSHEET WITH YOUR TA BEFORE PROCEEDING

4. Using the guidelines you have been given on "How to read journal articles," prepare a brief summary of each article. Include in your summary a statement of the problem investigated by the authors, the independent and dependent variables, what the authors found, and what they conclude. Be sure to give the complete citation in APA style.

5. After you have summarized the three articles, in 1-2 paragraphs tell me whether or not the statement you selected is true and what evidence leads you to your conclusion. For example, you may learn that normal aged subjects have difficulty learning new motor skills, but that verbal learning is not influenced by age. You conclude that old dogs can't learn some new tricks, but that other new tricks are no problem.

PSYCHOLOGY CLICHÉS

Birds of a feather flock together. (attraction & similarity)

Spare the rod and spoil the child. (punishment)

A rose by any other name would smell as sweet. (labeling and stereotype)

IQ tests are culturally biased.

The child is the father of the man. (personality development/longitudinal studies)

Nothing ventured, nothing gained. (risk-taking & gain or success or reward)

Violent pornography is an outlet for sexual aggression.

Right-handed people are smarter than left-handed people.

Boys are better at math than girls. (sex differences and..)

Girls are less aggressive than boys.

Women are more empathetic than men.

Out of sight, out of mind. (object permanence)

If you can't beat 'em, join 'em. (cognitive dissonance)

PSYCHOLOGY LIBRARY ASSIGNMENT WORKSHEET

Name_____ EC Drawer #_____

Cliché chosen: _____

Translation: _____

Citation (in APA style) for the encyclopedia entry: (See handout example or Publication Manual of the American Psychological Association Ref/BF/76.7/.P8.3/1983 pp. 119 ff.)

One-two sentence description of information in this entry that is helpful for your assignment:

Citation for first primary source in Earlham Library (Lilly or Wildman):

Is this an experiment?
What is/are the independent variable(s)?

What is/are the dependent variable(s)?

Is this a correlational study? List the variables.

Give a one-two sentence description of this study.

Citation for second primary source in Earlham Library:

Is this an experiment?
What is/are the independent variable(s)?

What is/are the dependent variable(s)?

Is this a correlational study? List the variables.

Give a one-two sentence description of this study.

Citation for third primary source in Earlham Library:

Is this an experiment?
What is/are the independent variable(s)?

What is/are the dependent variable(s)?

Is this a correlational study? List the variables.

Give a one-two sentence description of this study.

TA's EVALUATION: This evaluation is meant to help you identify and correct any problems with your research before writing the final paper. Areas needing improvement are checked below.

_____Citation format is not in APA style for

_____encyclopedia

_____primary source(s)

_____Sources identified as primary are not.

_____Sources do not appear relevant to chosen topic.

_____Sources are not in an Earlham Library.

_____Classification of study as experimental or correlational seems problematic.

_____Identification of variables seems problematic.

_____EVERYTHING IS FINE—START WRITING!

Cliché: You can't teach an old dog new tricks.
Translation: Aging impairs information processing in humans.

Corsini, R.J. (Ed.). (1984). Middle age. Encyclopedia of psychology (Vol. 2). (pp. 372-373). New York: John Wiley & Sons, Inc.

The encyclopedia article suggested that motor skills become more difficult to learn with age, but that many forms of verbal learning are not influenced by age.

Cohen, G. & Faulkner, D. (1983). Age differences in performance on two information-processing tasks: strategy selection and processing efficiency. Journal of Gerontology, 38, 447-454.

Researchers investigated age differences in performance of a mental rotation task and a sentence verification task. Previous findings had suggested that visuospatial processing (represented by the mental rotation task) is more affected by aging than some other types of cognitive tasks. The present authors attempted to identify the processing strategies used to perform each task, age differences in type of strategy selected and then age differences in performance.

The dependent variables for both tasks were errors and reaction time. Age and number of trial blocks were independent variables for both tasks. For the mental rotation task view of the figure to be rotated was an independent variable (4 views). For the sentence verification task sentence type (affirmative or negative) and comprehension/verification were independent variables.

The authors found that older subjects were less efficient in the rotation task than young subjects, but both young and old subjects showed the same degree of improvement with practice. Practice was more beneficial for old subjects than young subjects in the sentence verification task. The authors concluded that older subjects were less efficient in processing information than young subjects when they adopted strategies that were complex. In other words, if the strategy adopted involved a great deal of information processing, older subjects were less efficient on the task (slower, more errors) than young subjects.

Moore, T.E., Richards, B., & Hood, J. (1984). Aging and the coding of spatial information. Journal of Gerontology 39, 210-212.

The purpose of this experiment was to test the hypothesis that spatial information which is automatically encoded is not affected by age in the way that more effortful forms of information processing are. The authors were particularly interested in testing this hypothesis with nonverbal materials.
The dependent variables were time to complete the task, number of block shapes correctly recalled, and number of block shapes correctly placed in position. The independent variable was age.

Both the number of shapes correctly recalled and the number correctly placed in position decreased with age. The authors concluded that the data do not support the notion that spatial information is automatically encoded and, therefore, not influenced by age. They speculate that the tactual nature of the task may explain this difference from previous work.

Harker, J.O. & Riege, W.H. (1985). Aging and delay effects on recognition of words and designs. Journal of Gerontology, 40, 601-604.

The authors hypothesized that aged subjects should have more difficulty with inter-item processing and should show deficits in a word recognition task, but should not have difficulty with the automatic intra-item processing and therefore should not differ from young subjects on a design recognition task. (No clear definitions of inter- and intra-item processing were given).

The independent variables in this experiment were age, type of task and delay interval between target presentation and response opportunity. The dependent variables were recognition accuracy (A'), a decision criterion measure (Z (FA)), and decision time.

Young subjects were superior to old subjects on word recognition but not on design recognition. Equivalent effects of practice and delay on performance were found. The authors concluded that their hypothesis was supported.

Conclusion

All three of these articles addressed information processing in young and aged subjects. Information that is automatically encoded like spatial information or intra-item information should not be affected by age since no effort or attention is required. However, Moore, Richards and Hood (1984) found a difference in the performance of aged subjects in a tactual task. The visual recognition task used by Harker and Reige (1985) did not produce a difference. The data presented by Cohen and Faulkner (1983) suggests that the complexity of information processing required by a task may determine whether age differences are detected. Of the two studies examining the influence of practice on performance, both found that practice improved the performance of elderly subjects as much or more than it improved the performance of young subjects. You can teach an old dog new tricks. They may not perform some types of new tricks as well as young dogs but some types of tricks can be performed as well when old as when young.

INSTRUCTOR'S COMMENTS ON THE SAMPLE ASSIGNMENT

I wanted to try out this assignment to see where some of the problems may lie for you and to see how well it will work. After I used the encyclopedia, I located information using PSYCHLIT. You will find that you may need to try several different search strategies to find the one that works best for you. Just for fun, I tried dog* and trick* and found a few fun things—Nancy Taylor will show you one of my finds. More reasonable strategies would include:

(aged in de) and (cognitive ability)
Or (age differences) and (skill learning)
or other combinations

Of the items I located I followed up 10 by going to the journals and reading the articles or at least the abstracts. A few of the articles were eliminated because we did not have the journal. NOTE: To minimize frustration, be sure to check the list on your library handout or the one next to the computer terminal for journals indexed in PsychLit that we have in our libraries. I read six articles and selected three for summarizing that seemed to relate to each other reasonably well.

You may need to do more skimming than I did because some of the articles you locate may be very complex and you may wish to find simpler ones to summarize. Some articles report the results of several experiments. If you like, you may report on only one of the experiments in a work of that type.

If you are using the current PsychLit disc and are not finding much, remember to try the backfile disc.

THE TAs AND I ARE THERE TO HELP YOU—ASK FOR HELP IF YOU NEED IT!! It took me approximately 4.5 hours to complete this assignment, including typing this report. You should anticipate spending 8-12 hours because you are less familiar with locating and reading articles of this type. The following questions should help you analyze the articles you choose.

How to Read Journal Articles

1. What is the problem the researchers address? What is the question they asking?
2. What have other researchers found that the authors of this paper are questioning?
3. To what extent does the dependent variable (what is measured) reflect the behavior the authors are interested in? What are the independent variables (i.e., what is manipulated)? CAUTION: If your article is one that examines correlations between variables, then you will probably not have an independent variable, only dependent variables. If you are not sure, check with me or with one of the TA's.
4. Are you satisfied that the changes that occur in the dependent variable are due to the independent variable? Are there control experiments or procedures?
5. What are the results?
6. What are some other interpretations of the results? Do the authors adequately address these other interpretations?
7. What is the theoretical significance of this study?
8. What is the practical significance?

Human Development/Social Relations

Dr. Nelson Bingham, Psychology Department, Earlham College

PROBLEM ANALYSIS

GENERAL PURPOSES

A. To provide an opportunity for HDSR majors to further integrate their understanding of the theoretical models, methodological strategies, and bodies of empirical data of the disciplines comprising HDSR;

B. To solidify the student's understanding of the distinctive paradigm which HDSR represents;

C. To allow students to gain confidence in and to demonstrate their ability to focus in on and clearly define a specific issue or problem, to utilize available resources to describe and explain that problem analytically and integratively, to draw effectively upon their own ethical and value commitments, and to propose effective and appropriate action in relation to that issue; and

D. To foster and/or demonstrate skills of oral communication.

OUTLINE OF PROBLEM ANALYSIS

The HDSR Comprehensive Exam consists, in part, of an oral presentation of a problem analysis. This presentation must be done to a group of three other students, the instructor of the Senior Seminar, and one other faculty member. Additional persons may also be invited to attend. This oral presentation should be approximately one hour in length and is to be arranged by the presenter with a scheduling form filled with the instructor by January 22nd.

Three major issues should be addressed in these presentations:

1. an interdisciplinary analysis of the problem (including definition, review of relevant theory, methodological considerations, etc.);

2. a consideration of the value questions and/or ethical issues inherent in this problem and in your approach to it; and

3. a proposed strategy or set of strategies for action.

SPECIFIC QUESTIONS TO BE ADDRESSED

A. What is the topic or issue upon which your paper will focus? Can you phrase this in terms of a specific policy question?

B. Why is that an important topic?

C. What empirical data can you present which will aid the listener in understanding this problem?

D. What critiques can you offer of this body of data?

E. What theoretical models and/or concepts seem most helpful in approaching this question? In what ways are those models complementary? In what ways are they in conflict?

F. What is the ideal vision of persons and systems which is guiding your thinking about this problem?

G. What information (not now available) would be needed in order to deal effectively with this problem? How could this be obtained?

H. What ethical theories and/or value commitments are relevant here? For example, which are most salient for the individuals and groups involved? Which are most important to you?

I. How does this specific issue relate to other problems or to the systematic context in which is it embedded?

J. How can you utilize the above analysis and synthesis to propose a plan of action to deal with the problem as you have presented it?

K. How can you evaluate the effectiveness of your intervention? What are the implications (direct and indirect) of your action?

CRITERIA FOR EVALUATION OF ANALYTICAL PRESENTATIONS

A. Familiarity with and understanding of basic concepts covered in HDSR courses (especially the Core);

B. Understanding of major theoretical perspectives and of the commonalities and distinctive features of the disciplines comprising HDSR;

C. Attention to and clarity of problem definition, methodological sophistication, and strategies of action;

D. Ability to utilize integrative/synthetic thinking as well as critical analysis; use of creative imagination as well as logical thinking;

E. Appreciation of ethics and values and of their use as a basis for making decisions (about theory and method as well as intervention);

F. Realism and practicality in one's proposed intervention, including recognition of obstacles to implementation;

G. A sense of coherence in one's approach to the topic; ability to define the topic clearly and to maintain a focus on that topic throughout the presentation;

H. Quality of communication effectiveness—includes style of speaking, organization, precision, logicality, etc.

Equilibrium and Analysis

Dr. Wilmer Stratton, Chemistry Department, Earlham College

Independent Laboratory Project

The laboratory time for approximately 3-4 weeks will be devoted to projects done individually or in small groups. You should begin planning immediately for this, so that you will be ready at the scheduled time and so that we can make sure that the necessary materials are available.

In general, the projects ought to feature the use of some kind of chemical analysis and should include (a) reading and/or library searching for relevant methods, (b) the problems of setting up a procedure and validating it, and most importantly (c) collecting and interpreting data. Where appropriate, the study ought to include an investigation of detection limits and the range of conditions over which the method works.

Spectrophotometric methods (including atomic absorption) are attractive for several reasons, but there are numerous possibilities for potentiometric, chromatographic, and titrimetric methods.

The most important criterion is that the study be something you want to do and in which you are willing to invest effort over the last part of the term. To be realistic about the time, the project needs to be relatively modest, involving no more than 4-5 afternoons of laboratory work (plus additional time in reading and data processing.) Groups of 2-3 persons may work together to good advantage but larger groups tend to become inefficient.

You are encouraged to come up with your own ideas for projects and to discuss them with me. Listed below are several suggested projects. These may stimulate you to think of others.

For whatever project you choose, you first need to do some reading and planning: (a) What analytical methods are available—what are their advantages and disadvantages? Which method seems best for the problem at hand? What difficulties do you anticipate? What precision and accuracy do you expect? What reference standards will you use? (b) What sampling strategy will you use? What samples? How many? Under what conditions will they be collected? etc. Once a project and analytical method have been decided upon, it is important that you acquire a thorough understanding of the chemistry of the analysis, as well as experimental procedures.

Important note regarding the written report: You will be asked to produce a complete, carefully-done report of your study, including background information on the problem and analytical methods, and to give me a copy to keep. I strongly urge you to do the report on a computer and to save the file until the end of the term. This will permit you to produce drafts of portions or all of the report for me to critique and will permit easy editing. The final result should then be something of which both you and I will be proud.

SUGGESTED LABORATORY PROJECTS

1. Studies of the chemical composition of rain and snow (pH, anions, metals, alkalinity).

2. Determination of fluoride in drinking water and aquatic samples.

3. Development of a method for determining sulfites in baked goods and other foods.

4. Determination of lead in drinking water.

5. Determination of trace metals in human hair.

6. Caffeine content of beverages or residual caffeine in various kinds of decaffeinated coffees and teas.

7. Determination of sugars (sucrose, glucose, fructose, lactose, etc.) in honeys, syrups, soft drinks, or other foods.

8. Metals in sewage sludge leachates from the sewage treatment plant.

9. Determination of lead in canned foods (it comes from the solder) or in maple syrup (from the solder in the evaporator pans).

10. Vitamin C in various foods. What foods are good sources? What about "fortified" foods? Does aeration of orange juice in the cafeteria destroy the Vitamin C?

REFERENCE BY APPOINTMENT:
WHY AND HOW ONE-ON-ONE INSTRUCTION WORKS

Susan D. Skekloff

In September of 1993 the Walter E. Helmke Library on the campus of Indiana University-Purdue University at Fort Wayne, Indiana (IPFW), implemented a two-tiered model of reference service. IPFW is a commuter campus of approximately 11,000 students. The campus offers two- and four-year degrees, as well as several masters level programs. Four out of the seven professional librarians on the staff were responsible for providing all reference service at the time of the model's implementation. My presentation today will focus on three areas: why our library implemented such a model, how the model was implemented, and how we tried to improve upon it after one semester in use.

The new model utilized paraprofessionals stationed at the library's first floor service desk who answered "level-one" reference questions, that is, the most commonly asked questions involving the most routinely used sources in the library. Reference librarians turned "desk hours" into "office hours" and library users who had "level-two" questions requiring more in-depth assistance were referred to a librarian who had open office hours. Librarians thus could provide one-on-one instruction to each library user who needed it.

There were three major reasons this model of service was implemented:

Skekloff is associate librarian, Walter E. Helmke Library, Indiana University-Purdue University at Fort Wayne, Indiana.

1. The library director had spoken of doing something more innovative with the traditionalreference desk for several years. He was happy neither with the fact that professionals staffed the desk whether library users needed assistance or not, nor with the fact that there were two service points on the first floor, the circulation desk and the reference desk. Library users were confused by the two service points; and when one service point was busy, those staffing the other service point were unable to help.

2. Reference service was not available after 9:00 p.m. or during certain hours on the weekend. Circulation desk staff were told for years not to answer reference questions during these times, even if they were able to. This created an awkward situation that many library staff members, both professional and nonprofessional, wanted to remedy.

3. The explosion of technology in our library put new degrees of stress on the traditional reference desk mode of library assistance. Users with in-depth library needs waited for assistance (or left) while librarians trouble-shooted hardware problems. Users unfamiliar with computers were offered only as much help as the librarian on duty could afford to give. The quality of service was

totally dependent on how many users needed assistance from moment to moment. Librarians were not satisfied with the level of assistance they were able to offer users, particularly those who needed to use several databases. While the demand grew for in-depth interviews involving teaching the use and content of one or more databases, as well as interpretation of search results and follow-up search strategy, we struggled with the idea that there must be a way to provide time for quality in-depth assistance for those who needed it, in a systematic manner.

In January of 1993, the library director created the Research Design Task Force, made up of the four reference librarians and the head of the circulation department. The group was charged with the implementation of a model of reference service which would allow paraprofessionals to screen incoming reference questions, answer those which we defined as "level one," and refer all others to a librarian. He also wanted the reference desk and the circulation desk combined into one service point, and, finally, he directed that "level-one" reference be available all hours the library was open. He reallocated money to fund two full-time paraprofessionals to be stationed at the new central service point. He also increased the duties of the three existing full-time circulation staff members to include answering "level-one" reference questions.

Steps in the implementation process were as follows:

1) Physical reconfiguration of the reference area.

2) Creation of the information assistant (paraprofessional) positions.

3) Training the information assistants (IAs).

4) Defining the librarian's role in the new service.

5) Evaluating the model and making needed adjustments.

The physical rearrangement of the reference area was accomplished using existing pieces of furniture. The Research Design Task Force was assisted in its planning by a student worker majoring in architectural design. He drew a floor plan complete with paper models drawn to scale of all first floor furniture involved in the move. The goal of deciding upon the new arrangement and instructing the campus physical plant personnel to move the furniture during the weekend the library was closed at the end of the Spring 1993

semester was met. The circulation desk and reference desk were now merged into the service desk.

The heads of reference and circulation created job descriptions for the two new information assistant positions. The overall breakdown of task percentages totalled 90 percent reference duties and ten percent circulation duties, though we stressed to job applicants that during quiet periods during the academic year, the breakdown would inevitably change. We also indicated that because these were new positions the job content might be subject to modification in the future.

Reference training sessions began during the last week in July, just after both IAs had begun working. Since one IA worked from Tuesday through Saturday from 9:00 a.m. until 6:00 p.m., and one from Sunday through Thursday from 1:30 p.m. until 10:30 p.m. some hours remained uncovered by a full-time IA. (The library opens at 8:00 a.m. and closes at 11:00 p.m.) The library director increased the duties of the three full-time circulation staff members to include answering level-one reference questions. One of the individuals was always present at the service desk; thus they were available when no IA was working and also as backups when necessary. The training sessions included all five individuals. Priority was given to familiarizing them with the most often-used ready reference sources now located behind the service desk; training them on Information Online, the library's online catalog; and instructing them on the most often-used databases on the library's CD-ROM local area network. With regard to training given in printed indexes, the physical reconfiguration of the reference area played a part in defining level-one indexes for the IAs. Only the Wilson indexes and several other core indexes were left on the index tables close to the service desk. Others, which were more sophisticated and not used as frequently, were relocated in the first floor reference stacks. Obviously each training session also had to include information on basic reference interview skills. IAs were expected to recognize level-one and level-two inquiries and also to encourage the user with a level-two question to make an appointment with the appropriate subject librarian. See the first paragraph on the handout "Scheduling Library Users with a Librarian: Guidelines" (see appendix 1) for a description of the referral process.

The four reference librarians handled level-two reference questions in their offices. They met to set office hours during a brief meeting at the beginning of each semester to insure that a great deal of overlap in hours did not occur. The director had emphasized that level-two service would not be available at all hours the library was open, but that level-one reference would be. He had, in fact, not filled a professional librarian's position, which occurred due to retirement earlier that spring, and had terminated the six part-time librarians who worked evenings and weekends on the traditional reference desk, and reallocated their salaries to fund the two information assistant positions. Thus, he indicated that while level-two service would henceforth be limited to certain hours, library users would have access to basic reference assistance anytime the library was open, something that had never been accomplished before. Nevertheless, several librarians did set evening appointment hours. Each librarian was also available for up to five hours per week of arranged appointments for library users who were unable to come during scheduled hours. Users were given the librarian's business card and contacted the librarian directly to arrange such an appointment.

Under normal circumstances, however, the user would be referred to the librarian currently available or he or she could sign up as far in advance as two weeks for a time slot with a librarian. Librarians recorded their open office hours in an appointment book at the service desk and most users initially signed up for 30 minutes. The majority of appointments involved instructing the user on one or more of the library's databases. All librarians had access to all of these databases at the workstations in their offices. When printed sources were needed, we took the patron into the reference area, or brought selected sources back to the office, especially if used in combination with a computer source. According to statistics gathered over a one-week period during the Spring 1994 semester, librarians answered approximately 22 percent of all reference inquiries. Since level-one questions had always significantly outnumbered in-depth questions, and since the model was implemented with little advance publicity, we felt encouraged by these statistics. "Comment cards" collected from users during spring semester documented only positive feedback from those who utilized level-two service.

During the winter break between fall and spring semesters, several meetings were held by the Research Design Task Force to look at how the model was working and decide whether or not we could improve upon the system. Several improvements were implemented during the spring semester, but since I know you are all anxious to ask questions, let me conclude my presentation by describing the major change we made as a result of these meetings. At certain times of the day, especially when the semester was in full-swing, IAs at the service desk might be extremely busy, while librarians were stationed in their offices with no level-two reference inquiries to be handled. It was decided that librarians were to be called to the service desk by the IAs to help provide level-one assistance during busy periods. Some librarians in fact, expressed a desire to automatically go and work at the service desk during their office hours if no library users were scheduled to see them. This is an option each librarian may choose to follow at the present time.

Excerpts from: "SCHEDULING LIBRARY USERS WITH A LIBRARIAN: GUIDELINES"

When a library user has a question which you do not know how to answer, or which requires in-depth reference assistance, you should:

1. Refer the individual to a librarian. Try to determine whether the question is of a more specialized nature and refer the library user to the appropriate subject specialist (See the Subject Specialist Chart). Asking a student the name of the course and the course level may aid you in determining whether or not the question is of a more general or specialized nature. If you determine that the question is specialized, actively encourage the user to make an appointment for in-depth assistance with the librarian who is the most familiar with the sources in that area. You may want to indicate that, for example, "Susan Smith is the liaison to the Business Department and she has developed the expertise with business sources." However, if the subject specialist is not immediately available, you may refer the user to a librarian who is currently free, if the user does not want to wait. Follow the instructions described under "The Referral Process" section of this document.

2. If you feel the question may be one you are able to answer after some brief, initial guidance from a librarian, you may contact the librarian currently "on duty" (provided he or she is not helping a library user), or the Head of Information Support Services, and consult her about the question.

The Referral Process

Check the appointment schedule to see if a librarian is immediately available. If so, fill in the librarian's name, room number, and the date and time of the appointment on the referral slip. Record the user's name in the appointment schedule. (If a library user does not want to give his or her name, record their status, for example, "undergraduate," in the schedule.) Hand the appointment slip to the user and give directions to the librarian's office.

When no librarian is immediately available, consult the appointment book and schedule an appointment for the user at a later time. Record the user's name and phone number in case the librarian becomes ill, etc. and rescheduling is necessary. Fill out the referral slip, and give it to the user. Tell the user the slip must be given to the librarian at the appointment session.

Arranged Appointments

When a user cannot return during any of the times there is a librarian "on duty," give the user the appropriate subject specialist's business card or the card of the ISS Head and indicate they must contact this librarian to arrange a mutually convenient appointment. Information Assistants should not take written reference questions and phone numbers from library users who refuse to wait.

REFERRAL DURING BUSY PERIODS: During busy periods at the Service Desk when Information Assistants are engaged in assisting library users you may refer a user waiting for assistance to any librarian who currently has open office hours. Check the appointment book to see that the librarian is available before sending the individual to the office.

TEAM TEACHING IN CYBERSPACE

Debbie Tenofsky

My name is Debbie Tenofsky, and I work for Loyola University Chicago as the coordinator of user instruction. I coordinate the instruction program for four of the Loyola campus libraries. A growing part of my position is teaching and coordinating the Internet instruction program.

I am going to assume that all of you have used the Internet, since I will be using some Internet jargon without much explanation. In this presentation I will outline the evolution of Loyola's faculty-oriented Internet workshops. I am going to spend the first portion describing the history of the program, and the history of our relationship with the information technologies department. Then, I will describe what we teach to the faculty and the methodologies we use. Lastly, I will describe the subject-specific Internet workshops we teach to faculty in the same discipline.

Loyola University Chicago has approximately 14,000 students included in the undergraduate, graduate, medical, law, social work, education, and business schools and about 1,000 faculty. It is a Jesuit Catholic institution. The library has over 1.4 million books and about 10,000 periodical titles. There are seven different libraries at Loyola, each with a different subject-specialty focus.

Traditionally, libraries and computer centers have been at odds with one another. Oftentimes, there is little communication between these departments. This lack of communication led to duplication of services,

---

Tenofsky is library instruction coordinator, Loyola University, Chicago, Illinois.

especially the duplication of workshops which taught the new technologies.

Loyola is fortunate in that the director of our library works closely with the director of information technologies, which is our computer center. This makes the development of our instruction program much stronger and easier than it might have been if we needed to negotiate with a new group of people who may or may not have been supportive of our efforts in the library. Also, there is no duplication of workshops, publicity, and staffing. We have been able to build a program where communication between departments actually works. The librarians, for example, refer questions about setting up modems in faculty offices to the information technologies staff, and the information technologies staff refer faculty to the librarians to answer specific questions about online resources.

In the spring of 1993, some of the information technologies staff knew that we were planning to start teaching the Internet, and they asked us to work with them in developing an Internet workshop. We formed an Internet committee including members of the information technologies and the library to develop these workshops.

The committee decided to teach these particular workshops only to the faculty, even though we realized that the students needed to learn the Internet as well. The reasoning came from one of the information technologies staff. He felt that the faculty do not want to feel intimidated in front of their students when it comes to learning new technologies. Faculty, like most people, enjoy learning in a peer environment. The librarians and the information technologies staff were considered colleagues, so the atmosphere would be one of colleague teaching colleague and not of teacher instructing student. The faculty also have different needs than the students. The faculty were interested in information regarding their own research, and the Internet gave them a new resource to find vast amounts of information in their disciplines. From the library's standpoint, we were interested in teaching the Internet as a resource tool, just like the other resources we owned in other formats. We were not as interested in teaching how to use the system as we were in showing the faculty how to search for the Internet information they needed. This also gave us an opportunity to show the faculty that the library was one of the university leaders in acquiring and implementing new technology.

We also decided that these workshops would be team taught by a member of the information technologies department, the instruction coordinator (myself), and/or another librarian. These workshops were entirely hands-on, which required a great deal of supervision for each person. If you have ever taught a hands-on class by yourself you understand how much time can be spent on just making sure that each person is not either falling behind or having technical difficulties or getting too far ahead. Only 12 to 14 faculty were taught at one time, since we wanted each participant to have his or her own terminal.

Each concept taught was divided evenly between the instructors. Since each person learns differently, the participants got to learn from a variety of teaching styles. If one instructor was not explaining a concept clearly enough, then the participant could ask for individual help from the other instructor. Changing instructors also broke up the pace of the workshop. The participants stayed focused because the workshop varied with each instructor's teaching style and methodology. This approach also gave us an opportunity to train other staff to become future instructors by asking them to watch one or two workshops and then teach a section on their own.

We wanted to save time during the workshops, so I got permission from information technologies to help create Internet addresses before the workshops. This enabled the faculty members to get addresses without going through the information technologies' application process. Information technologies did not automatically assign Internet addresses to members of the faculty, staff or students; one applied directly to information technologies for an address. I was able to check for problem addresses before the workshops.

Some of the goals of the workshops were to give the faculty a start at using the Internet, to give them some hands-on training, to answer their general Internet questions, and to have them become exposed to some

new library resources. The workshops were designed as a basic introduction to the Internet for beginning users.

For the rest of the presentation, I would like to focus on what we taught in the workshops. When we started teaching these workshops in Spring 1993, Loyola did not have its own gopher (we would get ours up and running in the summer of 1993). Therefore, we taught the faculty how to search using Telnet and ftp commands.

The workshops were three-hours long and were taught at one of the campus computer center labs. To make teaching easy and consistent, we created an agenda of the workshop. We also created a workshop packet containing explanations of the concepts and exercise examples. The faculty could follow along with the packet during the workshop and take it with them to use as a reference guide.

We started the workshop with a history of the Internet. We found that it was important to spend time on the conceptual aspects of the Internet in order to help the participants understand what the Internet was exactly, who paid for it, and why they were using it. Many of them, like ourselves when we started, were confused and this introduction helped to answer some of their questions.

We explained the various parts of their Internet addresses and how to identify other addresses around the world. Then, we went into an explanation of telnetting. As I mentioned before, a hands-on approach was used. The faculty followed along with us through a sample telnet session; then they were given time to practice on their own with examples from *Crossing the Internet Threshold: An Instructional Handbook*, by Roy Tennant, John Ober, and Anne Lipow.

After a break, we explained ftp using the same methodology, except this time they watched us perform a step-by-step sample search, then we walked them through another sample search, and then they had time to ftp their own files. We felt that since they were beginning users of the Internet they would not understand all of the concepts, symbols, or terminology within ftp. Using three different teaching methods—lecture and example; a handheld example; and working through on their own—should be enough to answer many of their questions. They could use the extra examples from *Crossing the Internet Threshold* from the packet as practice after the workshop.

Each faculty member was asked to evaluate the workshop. The faculty members were satisfied with what we taught, but they needed to practice on their own to become more comfortable with telnetting and ftping files. We taught two sessions that spring and 20 people.

Our workshops changed for the better when the information technologies department brought up the Loyola gopher and Usenet access that summer. The gopher and the Usenet reside on the Unix system we call Orion. Orion accesses the gopher, Usenet, and electronic mail much easier than did our older system on the IBM mainframe. On the Orion system, for example, many of the commands were written at the bottom of the screen. The mainframe system had poor help screens, which were difficult to use and understand.

The committee met again and an agenda was developed, but this time the committee decided to emphasize the gopher and the Usenet. We also revised the handout packet, and we decided to teach our new workshops to the library staff first as a test market.

As with the earlier workshops, we started the workshop with an historical and conceptual explanation of the Internet. We taught the gopher and the Usenet using the same methodology as the ftp and Telnet workshops. They were team taught, hands-on, using a handout packet.

We had one major complaint from the librarians about the workshops. They wanted to have individualized, one-page handouts describing each system, which they could refer to if they wanted help with a specific system. If they wanted help with the gopher, for example, they wanted to be able to refer to one page as opposed to a whole packet. At this time the packet was approximately 80-pages long, so you can understand their concern.

Based on their suggestion, we eliminated the packet and moved to a system of one-page handouts on each of the concepts we were teaching. The front side of the handout has some explanation about the system and the backside has the commands. We have gotten many compliments about the handouts from the librarians, the faculty participants, and other librarians outside of Loyola.

During the summer, the committee also met and devised a long-range plan to teach these workshops in three levels. The first level would be for any faculty member who wanted an introduction to the Internet; the second level would be for those faculty members who wanted more advanced training (Telnet or ftp); and the third level would be a workshop designed for faculty in a specific subject discipline.

The faculty who had taken the workshops had one overriding complaint: we did not teach electronic mail. Many of them, as beginning users, only wanted to learn electronic mail and they felt disappointed that we did not teach it. We did not teach electronic mail in these workshops because other of the information technologies staff taught workshops exclusively on electronic mail, and we did not want to overlap what they taught

in their workshops. However, since so many people complained about not learning electronic mail, and because our gopher system allows you to mail items to your mailbox, we decided to add a short, 30-minute section on electronic mail.

The revised workshops were still three hours long and taught in the computer center labs with one faculty member per terminal. They were considered our level-one workshops. The first 20 to 30 minutes of the workshop were used as a time to get the participants to explore the gopher. Participants who arrived early were not having to wait for latecomers to arrive. During this time they were handed a getting-started sheet, a gopher help sheet, and some sample gopher exercises to use while they were exploring the gopher system. We explained to them that this was just a time to explore and an explanation of the gopher would come later in the workshop.

After they had time to explore, we asked them to stop and we started the lecture portion of the workshop. We gave them a history of the Internet and explained about their Internet addresses.

Many people were confused about the addresses since they had at least two different Loyola Internet addresses, the Orion one we just assigned to them and their mainframe address, which was often called their "bitnet" address. Information technologies did not eliminate the mainframe addresses once the Orion system was installed, so it was possible for people to have more than one Internet address. We explained that the gopher on the Orion system was easier to use and to teach, so if they had never used the Internet, then they should use the easier Orion address.

We taught them about the gopher and the Usenet as we had done before, but we added a short section on how to send, receive, and reply to electronic mail. As part of the gopher exercises we had them send files to themselves, so they would have mail to view when we got to this portion of the workshop. We asked each participant to exchange addresses with another person, and then send that person an electronic message. They received the message and replied right back to the person. They really liked sending messages to each other. We explained about netiquette, and to remember that they were representatives of Loyola and should put any disclaimers on their messages if they felt it was necessary. This short introduction to the electronic mail system was enough to stop any criticism we previously received. We also encouraged them to take the longer electronic mail workshop taught by other information technologies staff.

We taught a few advanced, level-two workshops to faculty who at least knew how to send electronic mail and the gopher. We concentrated on teaching Telnet and NCFTP, a newer version of ftp, Unix, and advanced electronic mail commands. We also discussed downloading files, but the Orion system used different commands and software depending on how they accessed the system. We were not able to demonstrate how to download in the lab, but we gave them a few handouts, which they could use in their offices or homes.

Even though a majority of our efforts has been spent teaching general Internet introductions to the faculty, we have started to shift our focus to teaching subject-specific Internet workshops: the level-three workshops. These workshops are team taught by a subject bibliographer and another librarian, generally myself.

We felt that not only did the faculty enjoy learning within a peer environment, but they would be better served and more interested if they took workshops with other people in their field. The bibliographer was used as a liaison to the faculty members, since he or she already had ties with the department.

We taught these subject-specific workshops to faculty members in the psychology, mathematics, philosophy, physics, natural science, and law departments. We took special care to develop extra handouts, which focused on gopher and Usenet paths for that specific field. All of the gopher paths are laid out for the faculty, so they can find the resources back in their offices or homes.

The workshop structure was the same as with the introduction to the Internet workshops. We designed extra handouts for members of other departments, even though we have not been able to teach a workshop. These are distributed at department meetings as incentives for future workshops.

We advertised the Internet workshops in a variety of ways. We produced flyers, which we sent to all of the faculty at three of our campuses and the medical center. We wrote articles in the bibliographers' newsletter to the faculty. The bibliographers excited individual faculty members about the Internet at faculty meetings and one-on-one. The bibliographers arranged for the subject-specific workshops through the specific department chair. Notices were posted in the campus faculty newspaper with the dates and times. Also, the faculty approached us wanting to learn about the Internet.

Beyond the workshops, the library has developed several different training tools to teach the library staff and students how to search the Internet, for example, one of the science librarians designed a weekly Internet hunt for the science staff based on the national Internet hunt run by Rick Gates. The library staff loved this so much that they want more questions each week. The "winner" of their hunt was one of the other librarians at the science library. She is probably in her seventies and before this hunt she was not extremely computer

literate, but now she is on the Internet all the time, and she is one of their best searchers! She is a good example of how to convince the faculty to come to the library and use the new resources. The science librarian also revised the hunt as a contest for students during National Library Week. We recently brought up a series of Gateway 2000 workstations that have H-gopher loaded on them. H-gopher is a Windows-based version of gopher. I taught the graduate students to use this system, and they teach daily workshops on the new terminals.

Teaching these workshops has been exciting and successful, and has brought some great publicity to the library. We have taught over 200 faculty and almost all of the library staff in 32 workshops since Spring 1993. Working with information technologies has been rewarding. Although it was not as rosy as I presented it, which was expected I enjoy the eventual open communication we in the library have with them, especially when I have questions, since I now know exactly whom to ask and I do not need to get transferred to several people before getting my question answered. Also, I do not feel that we are duplicating the efforts of others on campus. The team teaching approach allows each member of the team to teach what he or she understands best, and breaks up the momentum of the workshop. The participants always have someone to ask if they have questions or problems and the rest of the class does not need to be stopped to fix one person's problem. We have gotten several compliments about this.

We will continue to teach these workshops as hands-on sessions, but we met again as a committee and we decided to broaden the workshops to students as well as faculty. We will be teaching more of the workshops, which will involve more of the staff, and we will be breaking some of the workshops into smaller sessions, for example, a one and a half hour workshop just on the gopher and Usenet.

The Internet is another tool to information resources, and we librarians should view it this way. In the subject-specific and advanced workshops we get an opportunity to teach the how-to search for Internet resources and not just the mechanics of the system. I would like to work with the bibliographers and have us teach more of these workshops to specific groups of faculty and students. Also, I would like to pursue the idea of teaching the Internet to our first-year students in their composition classes.

I recommend that you consider teaching subject-specific workshops to the faculty. They want to learn about the new technology, but they do not want to feel embarrassed in front of their students. I also recommend that you try to develop ties with your computer center. Faculty require a great deal of help and having

— DEBBIE TENOFSKY —

allies at the computer center cannot hurt when it comes to answering their questions. The library has been able to capitalize on these workshops as a public relations venture, since we have been able to introduce our faculty to new library resources. As I said above, these Internet workshops might be the way to solve one problem of getting older faculty into the library again.

Internet Workshop Level I

LOEX CONFERENCE, 1994

TEAM TEACHING IN CYBERSPACE

Tips for Teaching Faculty the Internet

1. Team teach with at least one other person.

2. Try to develop a partnership with the Computer Center staff.

3. Use a hands-on approach.

4. Teach specific workshops to faculty in the same department.

5. Offer a variety of workshop lengths.

6. Create handouts which:

    a. give subject specific examples.
    b. give tips on the system.
    c. show how to dial into the system from their offices or homes.
    d. give the phone numbers and electronic mail addresses of staff they can contact for help.

Appendix 2:

Internet Workshop Level I

GOPHER INTRODUCTION

I. What is the gopher? The gopher was designed at the University of Minnesota. It is a tool which navigates you through the Internet via menus. The gopher retrieves and "dials" the addresses of the Internet sites. Loyola's gopher resides on the UNIX system which uses your Orion id (yourname@orion.it.luc.edu).

II. Why would I use a gopher? The gopher makes login into other institutions' computers easy. You do not:

> **need to find the address of the Internet sites.
> **need to "dial" the FTP or Telnet address.

Some of the gopher's features allow you to:

> **use natural language to retrieve information.
> **save files directly to your directory or electronic mailbox.
> **log directly into other universities' catalogs.
> **read electronic journals, for example, The Chronicle of Higher
>   Education.

III.   How do I connect to the gopher?

1.   If you are at the **telecommunications menu**, highlight the **gopher** choice.

2.   If you are at the **orion >** prompt, type **gopher**

IV.   Help

1.   Ho Joo Kim
      Information Technologies
      Crown Center 104
      508-3999
      hkim@orion.it.luc.edu

2.   Jack Corliss
      Information Technologies
      Administration Building, Room 4702
      708-216-8012
      jcorlis@luccpua.it.luc.edu

3.   Debbie Tenofsky
      Cudahy Library
      508-2778
      dtenofs@luccpua.it.luc.edu

4.   Help Desk
      4-4444
      gopher@orion.it.luc.edu

GOPHER INFORMATION

I.   TYPES OF INFORMATION ON THE GOPHER

	Type	Symbol
1.	directories	/
2.	text file	.
3.	search index	< ? >
4.	Telnet sessions	< TEL >
5.	phone books	< CSO >

II.   HELPFUL HINTS

Command/Key	Meaning
up arrow	move to a previous line
down arrow	move to the next line
return/enter	view current item
spacebar	view next page
b	view previous page
=	display address of item
/	natural language search
a	set a bookmark
d	delete a bookmark
v	view personal gopher
u	exit one layer at a time
m	mail item
s	save item
p	print item to local printer
o	change options
q	quit
^]	escape out of the system
quit	at telnet > exits telnet to orion
elm	read orion mail
exit	exit orion
h	help

Appendix 3:

Internet Workshop Level I

AGENDA

I.   Set up/getting started (30 minutes)
    A.   Set up terminals, so participants can login to their orion accounts
    B.   Put a copy of the "Getting Started" handout at each terminal
    C.   Pass out "Gopher" handout
    D.   Wander around the room helping participants as needed

II. Internet overview (15-20 minutes)
    A.   Introductions
    B.   History of the Internet
        1. Global network of networks
        2. Started in 1969 in the Defense Department
        3. 1.5 million computers and 50/60 nations
        4. Superhighway example (Internet is like a superhighway)
    C.   Things you can do on the Internet
        1. Look at things like online catalogs, etc.
        2. Connect to other computers and get things like graphics, files, etc.
        3. Communicate with others by sending and receiving electronic mail
    D.   Addresses
        1. Hard to navigate without the address
        2. What is an Internet address
        3. What do ours look like (write on the board some examples)
    E.   Review what the Internet is and does

III. Gopher (20-30 minutes)
    A.   Navigational tool to get things
    B.   History of the gopher
        1. Started at Univ. of Minnesota
        2. 100s of universities set aside computer space for their gophers
        3. CWIS at Loyola with topics of interest to the community like White House policies, weather, local restaurants, etc.
    C.   Explain what you find on gopher (what does the / mean, etc.)
    D.   Methods of using the gopher
        1. browsing (what they were doing)
        2. searching using veronica (explain)
    E.   As a group, have class perform some of the gopher exercises (Loyola gopher and finding catalogs)
    F.   Explain bookmarks
        1. Have the class try creating some(use the "Exercises" handout)
    G.   Explain veronica
        1. Hands-on with the "Exercises"

BREAK

IV.   Elm (15 minutes)
- A.   Orion's e-mail system
- B.   Pass out "Elm" handout
- C.   Hands-on
  1. How to send a message (send a message to neighbor)
  2. How to receive a message
  3. How to reply to a message

V.   Tin (30-45 minutes)
- A.   Pass out "Tin" handout
- B.   Explain Tin and Usenet
  1. Global list of news files where people discuss a common topic
  2. Describe hierarchies (comp, sci, alt)
- C.   Hands-on with the "Exercises" sheets

VI.   Questions

VII.   Wrap up
- A.   What is:
  the Internet
  Gopher
  Tin

VIII.   Evaluations

Handouts

1. Introduction to gopher
2. Introduction to Tin/Usenet
3. Introduction to elm/e-mail
4. Evaluation
5. Exercises
6. Getting started

Appendix 4:

Internet Workshop Level I

GETTING STARTED

1.   At the **login >** type the **first letter of your first name** and the **first six letters of your last name**   (this is your orion login id)
                for example: dtenofs (my name is debbie tenofsky)
      Press **< return >**

2.   At the **password >** type **123abc** (this is your password)
      Press **< return >**

3.   You will want to change your password, since everyone in the class has the same one. To change your password, type **passwd** at the **orion >**   and follow the instructions on the screen.

      Your new password must have: at least two non-alphabetic characters, three alphabetic characters and at least five characters total.

4.   At the **orion >** type **gopher**

5.   You are now in the Loyola gopher. Please spend the next 30 minutes or so searching the gopher. To search, type the **number** of the choice you would like and press **< return >**.

      A formal presentation on the Internet and the gopher will begin in approximately 30 minutes.

Please do not hesitate to ask questions. Thank you very much.

Internet Workshop Level I

Exercises

Gopher Exercises:

<u>Loyola gopher.</u>

1. Check your entry in the University telephone directory.

2. Locate the weather forecast for Chicago.

3. Locate the menu for Dave's Italian Kitchen in Evanston.

4. What are the Cudahy Library hours?

<u>Gophers outside of Loyola.</u>

1. Find a gopher that would have information on Japan.

2. Locate and obtain the full electronic version of <u>Aladdin's Lamp.</u>

3. Find a gopher with information that is of interest to you.

<u>Bookmarks.</u>

1. Locate the online library catalog at Harvard University and mark that item for inclusion on your personal gopher menu.

2. Locate the electronic phone directory and include that item on your personal gopher menu.

3. View your personal gopher menu.

4. Exit the gopher and orion, and log back on to test out your new personal menu.

<u>Veronica.</u>

1. Locate information about the recent Vatican Library exhibit.

2. Locate a copy of the <u>Gettysburg Address.</u>

3. Connect to the CARL (Colorado Alliance of Research Libraries) system.

4. Connect to the online library catalog at Northeastern University in Boston and locate works by John J. Piderit, S.J.

4. Locate information that interests you.

Appendix 6:

Loyola University of Chicago
Searching for Internet Materials in Philosophy

Some Gopher Paths for Philosophy Materials

Below are some paths through the Internet gopher leading to online resources in Philosophy. These can be incorporated into assignments for advanced Philosophy students or used in research.

1. Internet Resources (in Philosophy)
   --Start at the root gopher server: gopher.luc.edu
      --Connecting to other gopher servers/
      --All the gopher servers in the world (via U of M)/
      --American Philosophical Association

2. Wittgenstein in Electronic Facsimile
   --Start at the root gopher server: gopher.luc.edu
      --Connecting to other gopher servers/
      --Search titles in gopherspace using veronica/
      --Search gopherspace in PSINet/
      --Type Wittgenstein at the prompt

3. Postmodern Culture: An Electronic Journal
   --Start at the root gopher server: gopher.luc.edu
      --Library services and resources/
      --Humanities resources/
      --Philosophy and religion/
      --Postmodern Culture (e-journal) (U Mich)/

4. Harvard University's Online Catalog (HOLLIS)
   --Start at the root gopher server: gopher.luc.edu
      --Library services and resources/
      --Library catalogs around the world/
      --Library catalogs beyond Yale (via the Internet)/
      --Catalog search by keyword/
      --Type Harvard at the prompt

5. Social Ethics. A Forum for Interdisciplinary Approaches to Social Ethics
   --Start at the root gopher server: gopher.luc.edu
      --Library services and resources/
      --Directory of Scholarly Electronic Conferences/
      --Type Ethics

R. Stalzer 12/93

Appendix 7:

Internet Workshop Evaluation

Date_____

Status: ___Faculty ____Staff ____Graduate ____Undergrad

1.   How worthwhile was the workshop?

        not worthwhile   1-----2-----3-----4-----5   very worthwhile

2.   Were the presenters clear?   ____Yes   ___No

3.   Which best describes your Internet skill level?

    a. before the workshop: ___freshman   ___sophomore ___junior ___senior

    b. after the workshop: ___freshman   ___sophomore ___junior ___senior

4.   What else would you like to know about the Internet?

5.   Do you have any suggestions which will help us improve the workshop?

6.   If we offer follow-up workshops, what time of the day would be most convenient
     for you?

    Which method works best to contact you?   ___phone ___write ___flyer
    ___electronic mail   ___other (be specific)

Thank you very much.

POSTER
SESSIONS

INTERNET INSTRUCTION: ELECTRONIC AND CLASSROOM WORKSHOPS

At the Oscar A. Silverman Undergraduate Library at the University of Buffalo, we undertook the responsibility of creating two distinctly different approaches to Internet instruction.

The first program was a group effort of the Instructional Resources Group at the University at Buffalo. "Internet Basics Online" was designed for beginning Internet users and covered a wide variety of topics. The workshop was conducted via electronic mail, through the Libraries' Distribution list. Participants worked on the lessons independently, but were encouraged to ask for help electronically if needed.

The second series of workshops took place in our Bibliographic Instruction rooms within our library. The rooms are equipped with computer terminals having Internet accessibility. These workshops were designed by the Reference/Instruction librarians as a hands-on program, with demonstrations and a chance for the participants to explore the lessons with the instructing librarian. The emphasis in this series was on locating resources on the Internet.

Poster session by
Lara Bushallow-Wilbur and Mary Glazier
Reference/Instruction Librarians
SUNY at Buffalo -- Undergraduate Library

Poster session 1 (Bushallow-Wilbur and Glazier): Part 1 - Internet Instruction Introduction

VIA ELECTRONIC MAIL

Topics

The first lesson sent out was an introduction acquainting staff with the function commands needed for the Internet sessions along with a glossary. Next, in succession, came:

* FTP   * Electronic Journals
* Telnet   * Gopher
* Listservs   * World Wide Web
* NNR   * WAIS

Marketing

Since this was designed specifically for faculty and staff within the University Libraries, we did not have to publicize the workshop. We did however, post two messages prior to the start of the course informing people of the upcoming lessons.

Registration

There was no registration for the course. Faculty and staff were automatically sent the lessons. An announcement was posted on the distribution list prior to the start of the course
informing people who were not interested in the course to delete the messages entitled: Internet Basics Lesson 1, etc..

Times and Dates

Internet Basics Online lessons were distributed electronically every Monday and Thursday over a six week period. The session began November 18 and ended December 21. This was a self-paced course with each lesson requiring approximately one hour to complete.

Poster session 1 (Bushallow-Wilbur and Glazier): Part 2 - Internet Instruction via Electronic Mail

INTERNET INSTRUCTION

Things to keep in mind if you are planning an Internet workshop
via electronic mail:

Planning

- Create a distribution list of participants
- Who will be your audience
- What Internet components would you like to cover
- Which platform(s) will you use - IBM, VAX/VMS, UNIX
- How often will the lessons be distributed - daily, weekly
- On an average, how long will each lesson be

Suggestions

- Have participants send in completed lessons (this way you know how many are actually participating)
- Don't overwhelm people - keep lessons to about an hour in length, you can always add more lessons

Disadvantages
- Keeping up to date with changes on the Internet
- Interaction is not spontaneous, nor do others benefit from hearing a question answered
- Knowledge of electronic mail functions varies with participants
- Files take up space on hard drive
- Different learning styles are not able to be accommodated

Advantages

- Reach many people at once, not restricted by class size
- A training room and additional equipment is not needed
- Self-paced workshop allows participants to proceed at their own pace; beginners do not feel rushed, advanced users can move on
- No problems with live demonstration not working
- Accommodates everyone's schedule
- Provokes questions from those who wish not to speak up in class

Poster session 1 (Bushallow-Wilbur and Glazier): Part 2 - Internet Instruction via Electronic Mail (continued)

VIA CLASSROOM PRESENTATION

Topics
We designed a series of four Internet workshops and arranged the topic content according to individual participating librarians' strengths. The topics covered were:
* Internet Basics: An Introduction to the Internet
* Campus Wide Information Systems
* Locating Employment Sources on the Internet
* Electronic Discussion Groups

Marketing
To ensure thorough media coverage, we advertised in all three of the University of Buffalo's student newspapers and put up flyers around the campus. We also targeted specific user groups such as the School of Information and Library Science department, and the Career, Planning and Placement Office informing the faculty and staff of our program, hoping that they pass it on to students.

Registration
Registration was on a call in basis. Applicants called the Undergraduate Library's secretary, and she kept the registration records in order. Registration was kept to a maximum of 15 people for each session, the maximum amount of terminals available in the classroom. Participants' only prerequisite was that they have an electronic mail account.

Times and Dates
The workshops took place over a one-month time period. The workshops continued from March 1 - March 23, with two sessions of each topic taking place on each consecutive Wednesday. Trying to cater to people's differing time schedules, we offered one session in the morning at 11am, and one in the evening at 7pm. The duration of each workshop ran for one and a half hours.

Poster session 1 (Bushallow-Wilbur and Glazier): Part 3 - Internet Instruction via Classroom Presentation

Things to keep in mind if you are planning an Internet workshop
via classroom presentation:

Planning

- When will the workshops take place, how long will each session be
- What Internet topics would you like to cover
- Who will be presenting the workshops
- Which platform(s) will you use - IBM, VAX/VMS, UNIX
- How will you advertise your workshops
- Will there be handouts to be distributed
- How will you handle registration procedures

Suggestions

- Limit registration to number of terminals available in your instruction room, or to classroom size
- Don't overwhelm people - keep lessons to about an hour in length
- Leave lots of time for questions throughout the lesson
- Have easy to follow handouts -- keep handouts user-friendly
- Advertise your workshops extensively
- Hand out evaluation forms, and learn from peoples' comments for future workshops

Disadvantages

- Number of workshop participants is limited by classroom size
- Problems with equipment or connections may interrupt flow of session
- May not accommodate everyone's schedule
- Knowledge of electronic mail functions varies with participants
- An instruction room with additional equipment is necessary

Advantages

- An instructor is there to ask questions or solve problems
- Questions arise and group discussions follow
- Participants get to practice the lessons within the workshop
- Can accommodate different learning styles (visual, lecture, hands-on, etc.)
- You get immediate feedback from the participants

Lara Bushallow-Wilbur and Mary Glazier
Reference/Instruction Librarians
SUNY at Buffalo -- Undergraduate Library
107 Capen Hall, Buffalo, NY 14260

lbw@ubvm.cc.buffalo.edu   mglazier@ubvm.cc.buffalo.edu

Poster session 1 (Bushallow-Wilbur and Glazier): Part 3 - Internet Instruction via Classroom Presentation (continued)

Electronic Chemical Data Resources: Impacts and Implications for BI and Reference Services

Jane Keefer, Resource Services Librarian (Science), Johns Hopkins University,
Baltimore, Maryland

Introduction

Science reference in academic settings has always included a certain amount of reference point-of-use teaching and tutoring. Particularly in the chemical sciences, with its vast accumulation of data about compounds and reactions, students cannot just pull a handbook or compilation such as Beilstein off the shelf and expect to quickly and easily find data in it. In the past couple of years, however, several major chemical data reference resources have made their electronic debuts in the marketplace. These include the Chapman-Hall publications such as the ever popular *Dictionary of Organic Compounds* and its corresponding relatives for inorganic chemistry and natural products, Beilstein's *Current Facts* Series, and CRC's *Properties of Organic Compounds*.

When compared to the print versions of these classic reference resources, the CD-ROM products represent considerable enhancement with respect to searching for chemical property and reaction data. With this expanding searching ability, however, comes complexity and the problems of navigating different interfaces and learning and teaching new search terminology and techniques.

Chemical Workstation

For the past nine months the Eisenhower Library at Johns Hopkins University has had a "chemical/science workstation" loaded with all three of the products listed above on this site and available to users in the science reference area. The chemical workstation uses OCLC Gateway. This poster session outlines some of the instructional problems and teaching techniques and materials we have developed to assist students in using these new reference resources.

Instructional Aids--All of these CD-ROMs come with manuals which are kept at the workstation desk. Additionally, single sheet help aids for each of the three handbook CD-ROMs and the STN Online enduser searching access were developed and made available to users at the desk (see handouts, Appendixes 1-4).

Staff Training Sessions--Introductory sessions for non-science reference librarians and paraprofessional information assistants. These included both one-on-one tutorials and sessions for several librarians at once.

One-Shot User BI Sessions--Single topic science reference sections were held weekly during the spring semester to introduce graduate students and faculty to electronic resources in general. One session of this series was devoted to the chemical workstations' electronic handbook data. These sessions will be repeated during the summer when both graduate students and faculty have more time.

Menuing Systems--Two of the three CD-ROMs require Microsoft Windows to run, thus making it relatively easy to set up a Windows based menu system, as shown in figure 1. To maintain security, the Windows "file" menu and exit options were completely disabled. This in combination with a "hardwired" password protected computer system, prevents users from accidentally damaging vital files. However, the Windows menu system is not without its own problems, since there is no consistent way to return to this main menu. Thus patrons may still need some help getting started.

Poster session 2 (Keefer): Part 1 - Science Reference at an Electronic Workstation

Documentation--The workstation documentation gives brief descriptions of the items displayed on the station along with some of the more common problems that may occur and how to solve them. A copy is kept at the science reference desk along with password information for the STN Academic account that is available to users in the evening. It is also available to the general reference librarians via an icon on the computer in the main Resource Services Research Consultation Office.

Conclusions

Electronic Products require both more and less teaching in the reference setting. Although the electronic reference databases are relatively easy to use, just as with OPACs and other electronic database systems, it is also very easy to get erroneous negative results. Thus students initially need both point of use guidance and when that is not available, quick and easy help aids such as the single sheet handouts included here. (see Appendixes)

One interesting side effect is an increases use of the older *Beilstein* material. In recent years the Beilstein *Handbook*, traditionally the organic chemist's "bible" for property and preparation data, has been neglected by students who prefer not to struggle with the German language volumes and the complex Beilstein classification system. Now, however, the *Beilstein Current Facts* disks, which are in English, are beginning to reverse this trend because the data for compounds listed on these disks includes citations to the prior Beilstein volumes. This motivates students to learn how to use these older resources which they then discover are not as hard to use as they had thought. As an added benefit, they begin to gain a sense of the history and evolution of organic chemistry and the vastness of the chemical literature base they are searching.

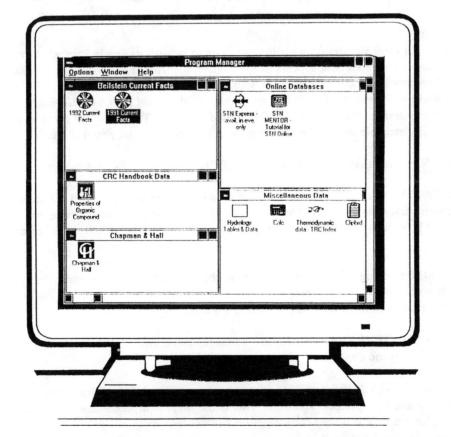

Figure 1: Chemical Workstation Menu Milton S. Eisenhower Library, Johns Hopkins University

Poster session 2 (Keefer): Part 1 - Science Reference at an Electronic Workstation (continued)

Print Volumes. The Beilstein Handbook of Organic Chemistry [QD251.B43], called "Beilstein" for short, has long been considered the premier reference source for organic property and preparation data. Two important characteristics of this resource are that data are not just compiled but also evaluated, and the coverage is complete.

Data in Beilstein are organized by compound and date. Compounds are assigned to certain classes, which then appear in the same volume number regardless of the publication date. Each volume has it's own substance & molecular formula index and there is a Centennial Index for the Basic & first four supplement editions.

Broad Class	Volumes
Acyclic	1-4
Carbocyclic	5-16
Heterocyclic	17-27

See Sci. Ref. Wall Chart for
  more precise classification

Literature Covered	Series	Abbrevation Print(CD-ROM)
1830-1909	Basic Ser.	H (00-)
1910-1919	Suppl. I	E I (01-)
1920-1929	Suppl. II	E II(02-)
1930-1939	Suppl. III	EIII(03-)
1940-1959	Suppl. III/IV	EIII/IV(03-)
1960-1969	Suppl. IV	E IV(04-)
1970-1979	Suppl. V	E V (05-)
1980-1989	Online only	
1990-	Current Facts (CD ROM annual)	

CD ROM Volumes.

A. Database contents. In 1990, the Beilstein Institute decided to publish its yearly harvest of organic compound data in electronic form only. This data now appears in the Beilstein Current Facts CD ROM disks, some of which are mounted on the Chemistry/Science workstation located in the Science Reference area. Although the number of compounds on the disks is limited, the CD-ROMs not only provide recent data and references, but also give volume and page number information for the older data in the printed editions. Thus they can serve as a relatively quick and painless entry to the Beilstein Handbook data that has been collected for the past 150 years.

B. Ways to Search. There are four distinct ways to SEARCH the Current Facts database;

* IDENTIFICATION - For known compounds, this is the quickest way to find information. You can search by name, name fragment, molecular formula, etc. Furthermore, you can browse and select on these items using the LIST feature. Additional access points include the CAS Registry number and atom and element counts.

* FACTS - FACT seaching allows you to search on the properties of compounds; thus you can search for all compounds with certain ranges of property values. Beilstein has more than 150 distinct property categories and many of these also have the LIST browsing feature.

* CITATION - CITATION SEARCHING can be useful when you want to find papers by a given author or you have an incomplete citation.

* STRUCTURE - STRUCTURE searching feature gives you the ability to draw a structure with both exact or generic aspects and then perform a search. This is the most complex feature in the Current Facts software and is best pursued only if other search avenues have failed.

Poster session 2 (Keefer): Part 2 - Handout for Beilstein on Workstation—Appendix 1

Strategies and Uses for the Beilstein CD-ROMs

* To gain entry to the older printed Beilstein literature and/or online Beilstein for known organic compounds.

* To find a Chemical Registry Number for known compounds for the purposes of doing an on-line search in Chemical Abstracts or other databases.

* To find the latest literature on an organic compound, including preparation, reactions and properties.

* To find recent papers by individual researchers.

* To determine alternative names for a compound to use in searching other chemical resources such as Chemical Abstracts or Science Citation.

* To identify and unknown organic compound by searching for property data

Caveats and Troubleshooting! Although the name indexing on these discs is quite rich, the spelling of some entries still reflects Beilsteins German language tradition. Never accept a negative result without question. Try to think of other ways to name the compound you are looking for and/or use a combination of IDENTIFICATION search features (molecular formula, name fragments, etc.) to attempt to find the compound. Use the LIST feature to browse many different possibilities and use truncation if necessary. For example, searching for aspirin as a compound will result in 0 hits in the 1992 Current Facts, but searching for aspirin* leads to one hit or alternatively by browsing on the word aspirin in the LIST featur reveals that the spelling for this compound is Aspirine. In the 1991 Current Facts, however, the compound is listed under the spelled Aspirin.

If a search retrieves too many hits, as is often the case with common compounds with lots of substituted derivatives, there are two strategies that can be useful.

a. Put the molecular formula in the formula entry box using the Hill system as explained on the summary sheet and repeat the search using both the name and formula.

b. Transfer the structure of one of the retrieved hits to the structure editor (Click on the EDIT HIT menu option; Click on the SEARCH option of the top menu bar; and then use the right mouse button to remove substitutions from the basic compound that you are searching for. Two rapid clicks on the right button removes any atom. Once you have the structure you want, start the structure search, by clicking on the START.

Below are some compounds listed in Beilstein Current Facts 1991 & 1992 that illustrate some of the problems noted above.

1. Benzaldehyde

2. Phenylcyclopropane

3. Coumarin

4. n-Decanol

Poster session 2 (Keefer): Part 2 - Handout for Beilstein on Workstation—Appendix 1 (continued)

Summary Sheet for Seaching Beilstein Current Facts

Click on the Beilstein CD-ROM icon in the Windows Main Menu.

To find data for a known organic compound

1. Click on the Search Menu (or press Alt S)

2. Click on the Identification choice (press Alt I)

3. If you know the name of the compound, put the blinking cursor in the Chemical Name box. If you are sure of the name, type it in. This tends to work best with common names, like aspirin for acetyl sacilylate. You may use truncation symbols: ? for a single character, ?? for two characters, and * for unlimited characters. Punctuation, such as dashes or commas, should be omitted. Both name fragments and full names are indexed.

4. Start your search by clicking on the START menu choice on the bottom menu line, and follow the prompts.

5. If you are unsure of the name or not having any success, click on the LIST menu choice on the menu line at the bottom. This brings up the begining of the index list of chemical names and fragments. At the bottom of the list is a blank line waiting for you to type in some characters. It will take a couple of seconds to move to the area of the list corresponding to the characters you type in. Once you see an entry you want to search, highlight it and then click on the START menu choice to bring up the data.

6. Molecular formula searches can be utilized to narrow searches that return a large number of hits. Enter formulas using the Hill system. That is, Carbon comes first, then Hydrogen, then all other elements in alpha order. Be sure to use capital letters for single letter symbols, so the system can distinguish between the C of Carbon and the Cl of Chlorine, etc. Molecular formulas can also be browsed using the LIST facilty.

To find compounds that have certain properties.

1. At the Main Menu, click on the SEARCH option and then choose the FACT item on the menu.

2. Click on the LIST option on the bottom menu, to bring up the list of properties you can search on. You can browse on either the abbreviations (eg. MP) or the full property name (Melting Point.)

3. Highlight the desired item and press enter to bring the field name into the search box. Put your cursor into the property value box and type in the value or range of values you wish to find. Most fields also allow you to browse the actual values, so if you are not sure of units, click on the LIST option to display the values.

To find out what compounds a researcher has been studying recently.

Click on the CITATION option of the SEARCH Menu.

Move the Cursor to the AUTHOR box and type in the last name first or click on the LIST option to browse on the Author Index.

Click on the START option to retrieve compounds with data published by this author.

Poster session 2 (Keefer): Part 2 - Handout for Beilstein on Workstation—Appendix 1 (continued)

PROPERTIES of ORGANIC COMPOUNDS(POC) - CD ROM

POC, a CD-ROM reference product from CRC, is meant to be a quick look-here first source of organic property and spectral data. It contains data on nearly 27,000 compounds, including CAS registry numbers and Beilstein references. Click on the POC Icon and then follow the prompts to the main menu screen. If the system gives you an out of memory message or says that POC is still running then click on the Windows Program Manager button in the far upper left hand corner. Next select the Switch Applications to display the active programs list and click on the POC entry there. This should take you directly to the POC main menu.

KNOWN COMPOUNDS: To find data for a known organic compound.

* Click on the Name action button at the Main Menu Screen

* Type in the name of the compound: Omit all spaces, numerals, punctuation, greek letters and/or prefixes such as tert, o, m, p, etc. Then press Enter or Click on the Find Button.
  Examples:

NAME	ENTER
cis-2-Butene	butene
Benzene, 1-chloro-3-nitro	benzenechloronitro
D-(+)-Alanine	alanine
N-Methyl-N'-acetylurea	methylacetylurea
CFC-123a	CFC
n-decanol	decanol

* Troubleshooting. If you get no results, shorten the name or try another name form. Search on the molecular formula, by clicking on the MolForm action button at the main screen and typing in the molecular formular using the Hill ordering scheme (C first, H next, all other elements in alphabetical order; Capitalize the first letter of every element.) Perform the search using the Chemical Abstracts Registry Number (Click on the CASRN action button and type in the registry number with or without hyphens.)

UNKNOWN COMPOUNDS: To identify an unknown organic compound for which you have property or spectral data.

Physical Property Data - Click on the Props Action Button to do combined searching on four distinct physical properties: Boiling Point, Melting Point, Density and Molecular Weight. Single item searches with a narrow or single range are fastest while complex multivalued searches can take several minutes to complete. Examples:

    Boiling Point between 100 and 120
    Molecular Weight = 120.2 and density < 1
    Boiling Point between 100 and 200 and (Melting Point between 10 and 20)

Spectral Peak Data - Click on the Peaks Action Button and then on the type of spectra you want to search for. Enter desired peaks separated by commas or spaces (but not both.) Click on the Find button to start the search. Searches on more than 3 peaks can take several minutes. Example: Under Infrared Spectral Peaks

    2900 1600 1510

Comments: The entire users manual is available thru the help system. This includes abbreviations used, information about units and other property specific information.

Poster session 2 (Keefer): Part 3 - Handout for POC CD-ROM on Workstation—Appendix 2

The Chapman Hall Dictionaries on CD ROM

The Chapman Hall Dictionary series have long been regarded as a major of source of references and data for particular compounds. Syntheses, identification, isolation and reaction data can all be located here. These Windows based CD-ROM's, now mounted on the Chemistry Workstation in the Science Reference area, include the following.

> **Dictionary of Organic Compounds** - A database of over 150,000 organic compounds.
> **Dictionary of Natural Products** - A database of approximately 100,000 substances derived from or based on natural products. Many physiologically active compounds can be found here.
> **Dictionary of Inorganic Compounds** - A database of over 41,500 inorganic compounds.

Searching can be either TEXT or STRUCTURE based. The structure searching module has the same interface as STN express. TEXT searching is relatively straight-forward and it is recommended for all known item or concept searching.

GETTING STARTED: Click on the Chapman Hall Icon and follow the prompts to the Database Menu. Double Click on the database of your choice.

To Find Information on a known compound.

> Click on TEXT SEARCH in the Main Menu; then Click on the QUICK SEARCH option

> Click on the CHEMICAL NAME option

> Type in the name and then Click on the SEARCH option at the top menu bar (or press Enter) - The system looks for your term exactly as you type it and thus you may get a negative answer.

> If you get no results, Click on the BROWSE option at the top menu bar. Then start the name index display by typing in the first few letters of the chemical name. Within a 2 to 10 seconds, the letters you typed will appear at the bottom entry box and the browse list will be displayed. You can browse up and down the list or click on the CLEAR option to start browsing in some other part of the list.

> When you see the item you want, highlight it and click on the SELECT menu option. This will transfer the item to the chemical name entry box. You can edit this entry and use an asterisk(*) to indicate truncation where appropriate; e.g., vitamin* will bring up all entries starting with vitamin.

> Click on the SEARCH menu option at the top menu bar.

> Display the first item on a retrieved list by clicking on the SELECT menu option. Within a display you can move to the NEXT item, display a STRUCTURE, or return to the SUMMARY list.

Some sample searches to try: Aspirin, Vitamin C.

Poster session 2 (Keefer): Part 4 - Handout for Chapman-Hall Dictionaries on Workstation—Appendix 3

Online Searching: STN, the Online Version of *Chemical Abstracts* and More

Searching for information in print abstracts is tedious and slow. Furthermore, only a single concept can be searched at a time. Searching in the cumulative electronic version of *Chemical Abstracts* is much faster and more efficient. It also is more complex and costs more money. There are a number of companies that provide access to chemical information. STN, a joint venture of ACS with their German and Japanese counterparts, is the most comprehensive.

For a small fee, one signs up for an account, acquires a modem or internet connections, and then logs on to the database service. STN has several hundred databases, mostly in the sciences. There are two basic types of accounts; regular and academic. Regular accounts have access to all the STN databases, at any time and at the full prices. Academic accounts have access to *Chemical Abstracts*, some learning files, Inspec (Physics), Compendex (Engineering), and a miscellaneous collection of European databases covering a variety of topics.

Until recently the entire searching process was through a command language. Now, however, there are several options a user can invoke to make the commands easier, and with the use of STN Express, a "front-end" for logging on and searching STN files, it is now possible to draw a structure or substance and then have the searching done more or less automatically. The science reference room in the library now has this system installed on its chemistry workstation and the limited access academic account is available to students and faculty in the evening, currently by appointment and at present without charge.

Generally before starting a search on-ine, you will want to search off-line just to get a feel for what is out there and what kind of terminology is used. The *Chemical Abstracts Index Guide* is particularly useful in this respect. If you are searching for information about a known compound, then getting the CAS registry number is the fastest, cheapest and most effective way to search. Registry numbers are becoming increasingly available in other sources, including both print and electronic reference sources. All three of the Chemistry Workstation reference resources contain registry numbers. When you can't find a registry number, because of naming difficulties, it is possible to search the registry file by molecular formula and/or structure if known.

When you are ready to go "on-line," contact one of the science librarians for a final consultation and to arrange for your evening search session.

Jane Keefer (keefer@jhunix.hcf.jhu.edu/x4156)
Karla Pearce (karla@jhunix.hcf.jhu.edu/x4153)

Poster session 2 (Keefer): Part 5 - Online STN Searching Information—Appendix 4

Examples of some basic searching commands for STN.

Selecting a File
File CA - puts you into the Chemical Abstracts file

File Registry - puts you into the Registry file

File LCA or File LRegistry - puts you in the Chemical Abstracts or Registry Learning files.

Browse an Index
E or Expand coumarin - examine the index surrounding a search term in the basic index. Displays 12 items in the index.

E Back coumarin/cv - browse backwards in the controlled vocabulary.

Search for Citations
S or Search coumarin - finds all documents with the term coumarin in the basic index,

S E6 - Find documents that contain the term listed as E6 in the displayed index.

S coumarin/cv - finds documents with the term coumarin in the controlled vocabulary. This will narrow your search results.

S coumarin and fluorescence - finds documents on the fluorescence of coumarin

S coumarin and C9H8O2/mf - finds all documents with the term coumarin and a molecular formula of C9H8O2 in the basic index

S coumarin? - finds documents on coumarin, coumarins, coumarinates, etc.

S coumarin and (toxic? or poison?) - finds documents on the toxicity of coumarin.

Display Results
D or Display 1-5 Ti - displays the first 5 titles of the most recent search

D L3 1,4 cbib - display the 1st and 4th titles of the results of search #3 in the compact bibliographic(CBIB) format

Display History or D His - Displays a list of all previous searches

Display Cost or D Cos - Displays the cost of the current session

Log Off
Logoff - end the online session

Logoff Hold - suspend session - retains results of seaches for 1 hour

All searches default to the basic index field, unless otherwise specified. This includes single words from the title, registry numbers, keyword phrases, controlled vocabulary and terms, and abstracts. To indicate an author search you must append /AU to your search terms. Standard nesting and boolean operations are available. The chemistry workstation in the Science Reference Area includes a short tutor program (STN MENTOR) in using the commands directly as shown above. The tutor logon ID is: STN, and the password is: MENTOR.

Poster session 2 (Keefer): Part 5 - Online STN Searching Information—Appendix 4 (continued)

PIECES OF THE PUZZLE: THE LIBRARY BUILDING AS A BI TOOL
--ENVIRONMENTAL PSYCHOLOGY--

ABSTRACT

A major problem for students is accessing information when the librarian is not available. In our absence the library itself communicates with them through signs, pathways, placement of material, and handouts. What messages does our library convey to students? How do we improve the effectiveness of those messages? When did you last walk around your library to see what it looks like? Would you want to use it if you were a student? Since technology is changing the library's physical environment and the way we think about information access, we must be creative in using that environment to our advantage and that of our students.

Environmental psychology in libraries is the study of the effect the built environment has on its users. It is our responsibility to ensure that users find the information they want without much difficulty, especially when a librarian is not available for assistance. To do this, we must understand wayfinding, that is, the manner in which students react to the cues they are given for finding information.

How does a person react when he enters the library? Does he look for the information desk immediately, or just try to find the book section to browse? Are there enough signs, or are there too many? In order to create an environment that will facilitate the patron's visit, must answer these questions, among others.

Librarians need to spend more time looking at the library from a student's point of view, from the building entrance, to the placement of signs, to the arrangement of furniture. We cannot assume that everyone interprets signs and instructions the same way. In examining a library guide, for example, we should ask the following questions: Is the guide too detailed? Is the print too small? Does the paper color provide good reading background? Is too much jargon used? Are definitions provided? To whom is the guide directed? Does it need graphics? Does the guide need to be personalized? Does it have an appropriate title? What is the psychological impact of the guide?

C.M. Deasy, in <u>Designing Places for People</u> says that studying human behavior and planning for space, furnishings, lighting, etc., is directly related to the value we place on people. In sum, a supportive environment gives a patron clearer choices for action and saves him from spending hours searching for information when he could be interpreting and learning instead. It also gives him a feeling of control, increases his self-confidence and makes him more self-sufficient.

Poster session 3 (Glikin): Part 1 - The Library Building as a BI Tool

REFERENCES

1. Deasy, C.M. DESIGNING PLACES FOR PEOPLE: A HANDBOOK ON HUMAN
BEHAVIOR FOR ARCHITECTS, DESIGNERS, AND FACILITY MANAGERS (NY:
Whitney Library of Design, 1985).
2. ERIC Publication #ED266791. Steffenson, Martin B. and Larry D.
Larason, Eds. "The User Encounters the Library. An
Interdisciplinary Focus on the User/System Interface.
[Proceedings of] a Library Training Institute (Monroe, Louisiana,
July 31-August 3, 1978)." 123 pp. Papers presented include:
"Environmental Psychology: Factors in Library Environments,"
William H. Ittelson; "Personal Space and Facilities Usage,"
Robert Sommer; "Architectural Approaches to Design and Behavior,"
Nancy McAdams; "Question-Negotiation at the Reference Desk,"
Judith Braunagel. Wrap-up session includes selected participant
questions and comments.
3. Issues of ENVIRONMENT AND BEHAVIOR, Sage Periodicals Press.
4. Johnson, Carolyn. "Signs of the Times: Signage in the Library"
in WILSON LIBRARY BULLETIN, November 1993, pp. 40-42.
5. Kinder, Jackie and Catherine Eckman. "Where Do I Go From
Here?" in COLLEGE AND RESEARCH LIBRARIES NEWS, February 1993, pp.
79-80.
6. Marks, Barbara S. "The Language of Signs" pp. 89-97, in Pollet
(see next reference).
7. Sherman, Claire Richter. "Wayfinding in Research Libraries: a
User's View" pp. 167-178, in Pollet, Dorothy and Peter C.
Haskell, SIGN SYSTEMS FOR LIBRARIES (NY: Bowker, 1979).
8. Sommer, Robert. SOCIAL DESIGN: CREATING BUILDINGS WITH PEOPLE
IN MIND (Englewood Cliffs, NJ: Prentice-Hall, 1983).
9. Yeaman, Andrew R.J. "Vital Signs: Cures for Confusion" in
LIBRARY JOURNAL, November 1989, pp. 23-27.

Poster session 3 (Glikin): Part 1 - The Library Building as a BI Tool (continued)

The Library Collage

Presented by Kelley McHenry and Jean Kent

The "Library Collage" is a hands-on experience which brings students into the library with their instructors to discover a diverse range of resources that directly pertain to their course of study. It introduces them to the library services and collection by requiring them to actively participate in locating materials which they will be able to use and which should appeal to their interests. It can be tailored to the specific requirements of the instructor and the research projects that the instructor has assigned.

This model was developed by Kelley McHenry a librarian at Seattle Central Community College, to take the place of the 50 minute library tour, and it has been enthusiastically adopted by the librarians at North Seattle Community College, too.

Goal: To teach students that their college library has a wide variety of information sources and services of interest to them.

Objectives: Students will:

Meet a librarian and hear the s/he is there to help them;

Actively identify materials that interest them and are relevant to their course of study;

Work in a small group to accomplish a task;

Present their findings to their classmates;

Evaluate the process

Procedure:

1. A librarian consults with the instructor to plan the orientation. During this interview, they identify the specific tools and subject areas to be covered. The librarian may elect to create a brief handout listing the tools, reference materials, and classification numbers that would be useful to the students after consulting with the instructor.

2. The librarian produces a set of tasks for the students to accomplish. These tasks might include using the online catalog and other computerized research tools, finding specific reference works or circulating books or selecting titles of interest from a range of call numbers, locating journal, magazine, and newspaper titles, investigating the

Poster session 4 (McHenry and Kent): Part 1 - The Library Collage pamphlet collection, requesting audiovisual items from the media center, etc. (Examples of the tasks used at North Seattle Community College are attached.)

3. Each group should have 2 to 4 tasks to work on and should be able to complete the tasks in about 5 minutes.

4. The actual orientation begins with a brief overview of the handouts and an examination of major library services. Each student receives a map, a basic library information handout, and a brief bibliography on the subjects to be covered if one has been created.

5. The procedure is explained as follows:

    The librarian breaks the class up into groups of 2 to 4 students.

    Each group is given their tasks.

    The groups are instructed to use their maps to locate the materials they have been asked to retrieve.

    Each group appoints a record-keeper to document their progress and a time-keeper to keep them on track.

    The groups are encouraged to work together on all the tasks rather than dividing them up and working on them individually.

6. The suggested timetable is:

    10 minutes for the introduction
     5 minutes for accomplishing the tasks
    30 minutes for the group presentations
     5 minutes for evaluation, questions, and closing
        remarks

7. When the students return to the classroom, the groups take turns coming to the front of the room to report on their tasks. The librarian gives the first report to model the type of presentation desired.

8. Students display an interesting example of their selections or explain the purpose and use of resources that can't be brought into the classroom. Each group is given a round of applause after its presentation.

9. Finally, students are given an opportunity to give feedback

Poster session 4 (McHenry and Kent): Part 1 - The Library Collage (continued)

on the process and ask questions that remain.

10.   The librarian thanks them for coming, asks them to give
      themselves a round of applause, and invites them to return
      to the library in the near future.

Attached you will find an example of a formal evaluation
instrument that has been used at North Seattle Community College
to evaluate theses types of orientations, examples of the various
tasks that students are given, and comments from students and
faculty about the "library collage".

If you have questions or suggestions, please contact the
presentors at the following addresses:

Kelley McHenry, Librarian   Jean Kent, Librarian
Seattle Central Com Col   North Seattle Com Col
1701 Broadway Ave E   9600 College Way North
Seattle, WA 98102   Seattle, WA 98103

(206) 587-4072   (206) 527-3835
kelley@seaccd.ctc.edu   jkent@seaccd.ctc.edu

David Gronbeck from North Seattle Community College created the
photographs and signs for our presentation and we'd like to thank
him for all his hard work.

Poster session 4 (McHenry and Kent): Part 1 - The Library Collage (continued)

Go to the **Magazines (Back Issues)** (to the left as you leave the classroom) and select an issue for each of the following titles:

Examine these publications and be prepared to briefly tell the rest of the class about them.

BRING A COPY OF EACH TITLE BACK TO THE CLASSROOM

    ****

Go to the **Inlex Online Catalog** and look up the following SUBJECT / AUTHOR / TITLE:

A step-by-step guide is located near one of the catalogs - use it if you need help!

Be prepared to tell the class the results of your search.

    ****

Go to the **Newspapers** (straight ahead and on the opposite wall from the classroom) and select an issue for each of the following titles:

Examine these publications and be prepared to briefly tell the rest of the class about them.

BRING A COPY OF EACH TITLE BACK TO THE CLASSROOM

    ****

Go to the **Map File** and try to understand how this collection is organized. Find a map of the following area:

BRING THE MAP YOU FIND BACK TO THE CLASSROOM

Be prepared to briefly tell the rest of the class about the **Map File**.

Poster session 4 (McHenry and Kent): Part 2 - Examples of Tasks Given to Students—Appendix 1

— KELLEY MCHENRY AND JEAN KENT —

Go to the **Library LAN** and choose the following database from the menu:

Try a subject heading search / key word search with the following:

PRINT A FEW CITATIONS OR BRIEF ARTICLE FROM THE DATABASE.

Be prepared to tell the rest of the class the results of your search.

          ****

Go to the **Periodical Index** area and find a copy of the "North Seattle Community College Magazine and Newspaper List". **BRING THIS LIST BACK TO THE CLASSROOM.**

Be prepared to tell your classmates about this list.

          ****

Go to the **Pamphlet File** (yellow filing cabinets near the Reference Desk). Find the file titled:

BROWSE THROUGH THE FILE AND RETURN TO CLASS WITH AN ITEM TO USE AS AN EXAMPLE.

Be prepared to share what you have learned with the class.

          ****

Go to the **Reference Collection** and browse the shelf with the call number range:

Select a book from this area that interests you and notice what other books are on the shelf nearby. **BRING THIS BOOK WITH YOU TO THE CLASSROOM.**

Be prepared to share what you have learned and a little about the book you have chosen.

Poster session 4 (McHenry and Kent): Part 2 - Examples of Tasks Given to Students—Appendix 1 (continued)

Go to the **Main Collection** (upstairs on the second floor) and browse the shelf with the call number range:

Select a book from this area that interests and notice what other books are on the shelf nearby. **BRING THIS BOOK WITH YOU TO THE CLASSROOM.**

Be prepared to share what you have learned and a little about the book you have chosen.

        ****

Go to the **Magazines (Back issues)** on the left as you leave the classroom.

Select an issue of the following **scholarly journal(s):**

Select an issue of the following **popular magazine(s):**

BRING AN ISSUE OF EACH TITLE BACK TO THE CLASSROOM.

Carefully examine these publications and be prepared to explain some of the differences between them to your classmates.

        ****

Go to the **Reference Collection** and find the following book:

Examine the book to get an idea of what is important about it. Notice what other books are on the shelf around it. **BRING THE BOOK WITH YOU TO THE CLASSROOM.**

Be prepared to share what you have learned with the rest of the class as well as a little about the book you have found.

        ****

Go the the **Main Collection** (upstairs on the 2nd floor of the library) and find the following book:

Examine the book to get an idea of what is important about it. Notice what other books are on the shelf around it. **BRING THE BOOK WITH YOU TO THE CLASSROOM.**

Be prepared to share what you have learned with the rest of the class as well as a little about the book you have found.

Poster session 4 (McHenry and Kent): Part 2 - Examples of Tasks Given to Students—Appendix 1 (continued)

Student and Faculty Comments
Spring 1994

"Using small groups with mini-assignments stimulates learning and gets students actively involved in the research process."

Clara Smith, Faculty

"My students are enthusiastic about this approach and really enjoy and learn from this hands-on, active introduction to library services and resources."

Partick Bouker, Faculty

"I'm so excited about the Negro Almanac. I never knew one source could have so much information about African Americans."

Student at SCCC

"Before when I came into the library I was confused and wandered around. Now I know where to start and who to ask. I feel really good about myself."

Student at SCCC

"I never knew there were so many kinds of information."

Student at SCCC

"The most important thing I learned was what a variety the reference section offers and to allow plenty of time for research."

Student at SCCC

"I've never really explored the Reference section before. Now I know where to go when I need information."

Student at SCCC

"I learned to question my sources and to watch for subtle bias."

Students at SCCC

Poster session 4 (McHenry and Kent): Part 3 - Feedback from Students and Faculty—Appendix 2

Library Faculty Evaluation
(Librarian's name)

I need your help in evaluating my performance and improving library training for the future. Please complete this form by marking the choice that best represents your opinion about the questions below. Then answer the written response questions at the end.

1. I learned about the information resources that will help me succeed in the work for this class.

| I strongly agree | I agree | I'm uncertain | I disagree | It was a waste of time |

2. This library training session was well organzied.

| I strongly agree | I agree | I'm uncertain | I disagree | It was a mess |

3. My explanations and answers to questions were clear.

| I strongly agree | I agree | I'm uncertain | I disagree | Your explanations confused me |

4. The handout for this session seems well organized and useful.

| I strongly agree | I agree | I'm uncertain | I disagree | It's a waste of paper |

5. The most useful MAGAZINE or NEWSPAPER resource that I learned about was:

6. The most useful REFERENCE BOOK that I learned about was:

7. The INLEX Online Catalog tells me how to find:

8. A change that would improve this training is:

Poster session 4 (McHenry and Kent): Part 4 - Evaluation Form—Appendix 3

BIBLIOGRAPHY

LIBRARY ORIENTATION AND INSTRUCTION—1993

Hannelore B. Rader

The following is an annotated list of materials dealing with information literacy including instruction in the use of information resources, research, and computer skills related to retrieving, using, and evaluating information. This review, the twentieth to be published in *Reference Services Review*, includes items in English published in 1993. A few are not annotated because the compiler could not obtain copies of them for this review.

The list includes publications on user instruction in all types of libraries and for all levels of users, from small children to senior citizens and from beginning levels to the most advanced. The items are arranged by type of library and are in alphabetical order by author (or by title if there is no author) within those categories.

Overall, as shown in figure 1, the number of publications related to user education and information literacy decreased by 14 percent from 1992 to 1993.

These figures are approximate and are based on the published information that was available to the reviewer; however, since the availability of this information does not vary greatly from year to year, these figures should be reliable.

Publications dealing with user instruction in academic libraries continue to be the largest number, although they decreased by six percent. The number of publications about user instruction in public and school libraries decreased; special library publications increased as did items for all levels.

Rader is director, University Library, Cleveland State University, Cleveland.

User education publications in libraries continue to deal with teaching users how to access and organize information, including online searching, online system use, and bibliographic computer applications. An increasing percentage deal with evaluative research of user education. It is noteworthy that in 1993 articles dealing with instruction in the use of CD-ROMs, online catalogs, and the Internet increased substantially as did articles dealing with information literacy, resource-based and active learning, and integrating information literacy into the curriculum.

ACADEMIC LIBRARIES

Adalian, Paul T., Jr. "Use of Media News in Bibliographic Instruction: An Application in a Biological Literature Course." In *What Is Good Instruction Now? Library Instruction for the 90s*. Ed. by Linda Shirato, 31-36. Ann Arbor, MI: Pierian Press, 1993.

Explores new approaches in providing user instruction to undergraduate biology majors at California Polytechnic State University at San Luis Obispo.

Adkins, Susan L. "CD-ROM: A Review of the 1992 Literature." *Computers and Libraries* 13 (September 1993): 20-21, 24-53.

Provides overview of CD-ROM technology and its implication for academic librarians including information and how to instruct users on that.

Type of Library	# of 1992 Publications	# of 1993 Publications	% Change
Academic	140	131	- 6%
Public	04	03	- 25%
School	56	28	- 50%
Special	11	12	+ 9%
All Types	06	12	+ 100%
TOTAL	217	186	- 14%

Allen, Susan. "Designing Library Handouts: Principles and Procedures." *Research Strategies* 11 (Winter 1993): 14-23.

Explores design principles and procedures to help librarians create more effective, attractive handouts for instruction and promotion using desktop publishing systems.

Armstrong, Allison, and James McFee. "Technology's Impact on Library Instruction." In *What Is Good Instruction Now? Library Instruction for the 90s*. Ed. by Linda Shirato, 37-45. Ann Arbor, MI: Pierian Press, 1993.

Discusses technology's impact on the instructor, on the students, and on instruction. Provides examples from University of Nevada's library instruction program.

Barclay, Donald. "Evaluating Library Instruction: Doing the Best You Can with What You Have." *RQ* 33 (Winter 1993): 195-202.

Describes a successful library instruction evaluation effort for freshmen writing students. Provides a model for evaluating library instruction addressing major learning goals for beginning students.

Becker, Karen A. "The Characteristics of Bibliographic Instruction in Relation to the Causes and Symptoms of Burnout." *RQ* 32 (Spring 1993): 346-357.

Examines bibliographic instruction librarians' burnout in the 1990s and reviews burnout symptoms with reported definitions from the library literature. Discusses coping strategies such as developing more realistic goals, reducing workloads, decreasing criticism and increasing feedback, rewards, and recognition.

Becker, Karen A. "Individual Library Research Clinics for College Freshmen." *Research Strategies* 11 (Fall 1993): 202-210.

Discusses a program at Northern Illinois University that teaches freshmen English students library skills. Compares two groups: the educationally disadvantaged and honor students.

Behrens, Shirley J. "Obstacles to User Education for Off-Campus Students: Lecturers' Attitudes to Library Skills." In *Off-Campus Library Services Conference Proceedings*. Mount Pleasant, MI: Central Michigan University Press, 1993.

Describes the library instruction experience at the University of South Africa, which educates a large off-campus student population.

Bevilacqua, Ann P. "Research Assistant." In *Bibliographic Instruction in Practice*. Ed. by Larry Hardesty, et al., 77-87. Ann Arbor, MI: Pierian Press, 1993.

Discusses the software program "Research Assistant" in terms of user-initiated library skills instruction.

Blacker, Marilyn, et al. "Library Orientation: A Model for Support Personnel on an Urban Campus." *Research Strategies* 11 (Summer 1993): 150-155.

Presents ideas developed by library school students at Emporia State University for planning and implementing a library orientation program specifically for support personnel.

Blumenthal, Caroline, et al. "The Impact of CD-ROM Technology on a Bibliographic Instruction Program." *College and Research Libraries* 54 (January 1993): 11-16.

Examines the effect of CD-ROM technology on the bibliographic instruction program at Georgia State University. Predicts what changes will occur in the program due to the technology.

Brown, Jeanne M. "The Multi-file OPAC Environment: A Manageable Approach to Developing an Instruction Program." *Art Documentation* 12 (Fall 1993): 119-122.

Describes guides to search remote databases developed by University of Nevada librarians.

Burnam, Paul. "Fine-Tuning Classroom Technique: A Peer Coaching Experience." *Research Strategies* 11 (Winter 1993): 42-46.

Discusses how peer coaching at Ohio Wesleyan University improved instruction librarians' presentation techniques.

Butler, H. Julene. "Library Instruction in an Electronic Classroom." In *What Is Good Instruction Now? Library Instruction for the 90s*. Ed. by Linda Shirato, 123-126. Ann Arbor, MI: Pierian Press, 1993.

Describes Brigham Young's library instruction room, equipped with state-of-the-art technology, where students are instructed in information and library skills on a 24-hour basis.

Cameron, Lynn. "Assessment of Library Skills." In *What Is Good Instruction Now? Library Instruction for the 90s*. Ed. by Linda Shirato, 47-50. Ann Arbor, MI: Pierian Press, 1993.

Reports the results of a three-year attempt to assess the library skills of freshmen, sophomores, and seniors at James Madison University, describes how to conduct an assessment, and discusses some of the benefits of a formal assessment of library skills.

Carroll, Elizabeth. "Open House for Researchers." In *What Is Good Instruction Now? Library Instruction for the 90s*. Ed. by Linda Shirato, 127-130. Ann Arbor, MI: Pierian Press, 1993.

Describes an open house for graduate students to introduce them to library and research facilities in the Washington, DC area.

Cavalier, Rodney. "Why Worry? I'm Not!" In *Information Literacy. The Australian Agenda*. Ed. by Di Booker, 19-27. Adelaide: University of South Australia Library, 1993.

Provides an information literacy perspective from the language professor's point-of-view. Discusses the complexity of information structures in various disciplines and compares it to serendipity.

Chapin, Lloyd D. "Bibliographic Instruction from an Administrative Point-of-View." In *Bibliographic Instruction in Practice*. Ed. by Larry Hardesty, 123-128. Ann Arbor, MI: Pierian Press, 1993.

A vice president of instruction advocates that librarians become full participants in the educational enterprise in higher education.

Chu, Felix T. "Bibliographic Instruction at the Scholarship of Integration." *Research Strategies* 11 (Spring 1993): 66-72.

Librarians can facilitate the scholarship of integration by teaching students how to access, gather, and synthesize information from a variety of disciplines and viewpoints.

Collins, K.L.K. "Information Technology in the Teaching Role of the College Librarian." *Reference Librarian* 39 (1993): 41-52.

Promotes the role of reference librarians in the development of life-long, self-directed, information-seeking skills for college students.

Cooper, John E. "Using CAI to Teach Library Skills." *College and Research Libraries News* 54 (February 1993): 75-78.

Uses a computer-assisted instruction program to provide library orientation to beginning biology students at the University of California, Riverside.

Coupe, Jill. "Undergraduate Library Skills: Two Surveys at Johns Hopkins University." *Research Strategies* 11 (Fall 1993): 188-201.

Presents and compares results from two surveys of basic library skills administered to students at Johns Hopkins University. Compares freshmen to upperclassmen in several areas of library instruction.

Davis, Dorothy F. "A Comparison of Bibliographic Instruction Methods on CD-ROM Databases." *Research Strategies* 11 (Summer 1993): 156-163.

Reports on a study of four methods used to instruct students on searching PsychLIT on CD-ROM: lecture/demonstration, lecture/demonstration with an LCD, video, and computer-based tutorial. Outcomes are analyzed and suggestions are made for developing a CD-ROM instruction program.

Eckman, Cathy. "We Are Thomas Cooper Library." In *What Is Good Instruction Now? Library Instruction for the 90s*. Ed. by Linda Shirato, 131-132. Ann Arbor, MI: Pierian Press, 1993.

Discusses the use of music video to enhance library instruction for first-year college students.

Eckwright, Gail Z. "Evaluating the Library BI Program." *College and Research Libraries News* 54 (January 1993): 13-16.

Describes the evaluation program of library instruction at the University of Idaho. The program involves a written assignment and the cooperation of the English faculty.

Ellis, David. "Modeling Information-Seeking Patterns of Academic Researchers: A Ground Theory Approach." *Library Quarterly* 63 (October 1993): 469-486.

Farber, Evan. "Bibliographic Instruction at Earlham College." In *Bibliographic Instruction in Practice*. Ed.

by Larry Hardesty, et al., 1-14. Ann Arbor, MI: Pierian Press, 1993.

Provides rationale for bibliographic instruction in terms of undergraduate instruction. Provides a detailed history and case study of the bibliographic instruction program at Earlham College.

Farber, Evan. "The Reference Interview." In *Bibliographic Instruction in Practice*. Ed. by Larry Hardesty, et al., 97-102. Ann Arbor, MI: Pierian Press, 1993.

Models a reference interview with a faculty member in order to promote and plan course-integrated bibliographic instruction.

Feinman, Valerie J. "Bibliographic Instruction: A Basic Guide." *Computers and Libraries* 13 (January 1993): 63-67.

Presents the summary of a survey of library user education programs with an emphasis on preparing for instruction sessions, recordkeeping, and actual instruction.

Feinman, Valerie J. "Computers and Library Instruction: Expert Systems." *Computers and Libraries* 13 (March 1993): 53-55.

Reviews expert systems and their impact on library instruction. Advocates that instruction librarians should be involved in the development and applications of such systems.

Fister, Barbara. "Teaching the Rhetorical Dimensions of Research." *Research Strategies* 11 (Fall 1993): 211-219.

Examines the importance of teaching the rhetorical dimensions of research to help students to gain college-level inquiry skills at Gustavus Adolphus College.

Forys, Marcia, et al. "Library Navigator: An Electronic Orientation to the University of Iowa Libraries." *Research Strategies* 11 (Winter 1993): 39-41.

Describes the Library Navigator, a computerized introduction to the libraries, which is the product of a team effort.

Fowler, Richard H., et al. "A Hypermedia System to Explain Library Use." *Computers in Libraries* 13 (November/December 1993): 14-16+.

Describes a computer-assisted instruction system at the University of Texas Pan American to teach students library use.

Fox, Lynne M., and Lee Weston. "A Course-Integrated Instruction for Nursing Students: How Effective?" *Research Strategies* 11 (Spring 1993): 89-99.

Describes a library user survey/test at the University of Northern Colorado, which found that students who received formal bibliographic instruction had higher levels of self-assessed and actual knowledge of library skills than students who did not receive formal instruction.

Garcha, Rajinder, and Patricia Y. Russell. "Bibliographic Instruction for International Students in Academic Libraries." *Library Review* 42 (1993): 14-22.

Describes a user instruction program for foreign students at the University of Toledo to help them become library and information literate in the United States, based on a study of 63 students.

Gilchrist, Debra. "Collaborative Teaching through Inquiry-Based Instruction." In *What Is Good Instruction Now? Library Instruction for the 90s*. Ed. by Linda Shirato, 51-56. Ann Arbor, MI: Pierian Press, 1993.

Inquiry as a method to teach how to ask questions and find answers is used at Pacific Lutheran University to teach library and information skills to students. Provides practical examples.

Gonzalez, Nelly S. "Term Paper Counseling in Academic Libraries: The Caribbean Studies Example." *Collection Building* 12 (1993): 27-33.

Gives information on user instruction in a term paper workshop session using Caribbean Studies as an example at the University of Illinois.

Graves, Gail T., and Barbara Adams. "Library Instruction and Cultural Diversity: Programming in an Academic Library." *Mississippi Libraries* 57 (Winter 1993): 99-101.

Describes a program at the University of Mississippi Library to help prospective African-American graduate students gain research skills. Gives details about a special information literacy program for international students to help them become productive users of information.

Hall, Barbara W. "Bibliographic Instruction in the Social Sciences." In *Bibliographic Instruction in Practice*. Ed. by Larry Hardesty, et al., 51-62. Ann Arbor, MI: Pierian Press, 1993.

A political science professor from Earlham College discusses her view of bibliographic instruction.

Hanson, Donna M. "Library Instruction: Using the Internet, Hypertext, Export Systems." *PNLA Quarterly* 58 (Fall 1993): 35.

Describes a workshop using computer-assisted instruction to teach the Internet and other information searching techniques.

Hardesty, Larry L. "Collection Development and Bibliographic Instruction: A Relationship." In *Bibliographic Instruction in Practice*. Ed. by Larry Hardesty, et al., 129-136. Ann Arbor, MI: Pierian Press, 1993.

Surveyed collections in 473 college libraries to assess the relationship between the collection strength and assignments resulting from library instruction.

Hardesty, Larry L. "Student Response to Bibliographic Instruction: A Student Panel." In *Bibliographic Instruction in Practice*. Ed. by Larry Hardesty, et al., 117-122. Ann Arbor, MI: Pierian Press, 1993.

Summarizes students' opinions regarding their experience with bibliographic instruction.

Hardesty, Larry L. "Working with the Classroom Faculty: A Panel Discussion. A Library Director's Perspective." In *Bibliographic Instruction in Practice*. Ed. by Larry Hardesty, et al., 107-113. Ann Arbor, MI: Pierian Press, 1993.

Offers a library administrator view of library instruction in cooperation with faculty; a professor from psychology and one from sociology provide their views.

Harrington, Jane E., and Debra O. Spindle. "Cooperative Planning for Service and Instruction." In *Off-Campus Library Services Conference Proceedings*. Mount Pleasant, MI: Central Michigan University Press, 1993.

Discusses the development of a bibliographic instruction course developed by the library school faculty for University of Oklahoma distance education students.

Harrington, J.P. "Reference Assistant: A HyperText Touch Screen Program to Assist Users of a Learning Resource Center." *The Journal of Education Media and Library Science* 30 (Spring 1993): 221-230.

Reviews the development and use of a software program called "Reference Assistant" to provide brief directional information to users at various service levels.

Harrison, Chris. "Technical and Further Education." In *Information Literacy. The Australian Agenda*. Ed. by Di Booker, 46-49. Adelaide: University of South Australia Library, 1993.

Talks about the importance of teaching information literacy skills in vocational education.

Heaton, Gwynneth, et al. "A HyperCard Program to Assist Users at a Self-Paced Periodicals Information Center." *Technical Services Quarterly* 11 (1993): 55-70.

Describes how librarians at the University of Toronto developed a user instruction program using HyperCard so that students could become self-sufficient in using periodicals.

Hixon, Charles, III. "CD-ROM and the Graduate: Reference and Instruction at Risk." *Reference Services Review* 21 (Fall 1993): 31-34.

Argues that the new technology has moved reference librarians from their traditional duties and has also increased the need for both an in-depth reference interview and bibliographic instruction.

Holmes, Colette, et al. "Something Old, Something New: Using Professional Journals to Teach Language and Culture." *Research Strategies* 11 (Summer 1993): 180-184.

Describes a three-credit writing course to teach students at Rensselaer Polytechnic how to analyze the language and culture of professional literature; team-taught by librarians and library instructors.

"Immodest Rebuttle: A Community College Perspective." *Research Strategies* 11 (Spring 1993): 100-105.

Describes a review of Tom Eadie's controversial proposals regarding the ineffectiveness of bibliographic instruction, by community college librarians. Stresses the importance of providing effective library instruction to diverse, part-time student populations.

Isbell, Dennis, and Carol Hammond. "Information Literacy Competencies." *College and Research Libraries News* 54 (June 1993): 325-327.

At Arizona State University West librarians developed course-integrated library instruction with the faculty that focused on information literacy competencies for students. Provides information about the planning and publicity processes used.

Jackson-Brown, G. "The Academic Librarian's New Role as Information Provider." *Reference Librarian* 39 (1993): 77-84.

Discusses the impact of electronic information resources such as CD-ROM on academic libraries and how librarians must work more closely with faculty to bring about user instruction.

Jacobson, Trudie, and Lynne M. Martin. "Merging Critical Thinking and the Electronic Library: A Visionary Perspective of SuperPAC, an Enhanced OPAC." *Research Strategies* 11 (Summer 1993): 138-139.

Proposes the development of SuperPAC, an enhanced online public access catalog that would allow users to better evaluate a wide range of information resources. Discussed are two enhancements: the integrated availability of electronic evaluation resources and use of improved and augmented MARC records.

Jaggers, Karen E. "No Site Is Too Remote: Taking the Technology to the Classroom." In *Off-Campus Library Services Conference Proceedings*. Mount Pleasant, MI: Central Michigan University Press, 1993.

Describes how Northern Arizona University librarians provide library instruction in the use of ERIC on CD-ROM to distance education students.

Jurgens, Jane C., and Dario J. Villa. *Academic Libraries as Dynamic Classrooms*. ERIC Reproduction Service, 1993. ED 349014.

Discusses the problems encountered by nontraditional university students in doing library research and shows how librarians at Northeastern Illinois University teach students information literacy skills.

Keefer, Jane A., and Stuart A. Karabenick. "Help-Seeking and the Library Reference/Instruction Setting: A Social Psychological Perspective." In *What Is Good Instruction Now? Library Instruction for the 90s*. Ed. by Linda Shirato, 63-71. Ann Arbor, MI: Pierian Press, 1993.

Seeks to examine the linkages between the information search process and help seeking to illustrate how interaction can enhance the delivery of reference and instruction services in academic libraries.

Keefer, Jane. "The Hungry Rats Syndrome: Library Anxiety, Information Literacy, and the Academic Reference Process." *RQ* 32 (Spring 1993): 333-339.

Offers process models of information seeking to examine information use and the purpose of library instruction in relation to library users. Author reflects on students' interaction with library systems in her discussion of content versus process-oriented instruction programs. If students are taught information searching they will begin to develop creativity and critical thinking skills to help them become information literate.

Kesselman, Martin. "Is a Personal Digital Assistant in Your Future?" *Wilson Library Bulletin* 67 (April 1993): 81-83.

Advocates additional resources to purchase and learn in order to use CD-ROMs.

Kinder, Jackie, and Catherine Eckman. "Where Do I Go from Here?" *College and Research Libraries News* 54 (February 1993): 79-80.

Stresses the need for good signage, and includes a checklist of criteria for signage.

Kissane, Emily C., and Daniel J. Mollner. "Critical Thinking at the Reference Desk: Teaching Students to Manage Technology." *RQ* 32 (Summer 1993): 485-489.

Discusses how critical thinking skills can be taught at the reference desk especially in the electronic environment. Stresses the importance of setting goals that bring together reference service and library instruction for the good of the students' learning.

Klein, Gary M. "Helping Students Find Sensitive Materials: A Guide to the Literature on Homosexuality." In *What Is Good Instruction Now? Library Instruction for the 90s*. Ed. by Linda Shirato, 57-62. Ann Arbor, MI: Pierian Press, 1993.

Describes a project at the University of Toledo where librarians and faculty members in various disciplines are using assignments in the area of gender and sexuality to help students gain valuable research skills.

Kussrow, Paul G., and Helen Lawrence. "Instruction in Developing Grant Proposals: A Librarian Faculty Partnership." *Research Strategies* 11 (Winter 1993): 47-51.

Describes a course at Florida Atlantic University that teaches students how to apply for grant funding and to write proposals. The course is team-taught by an instructor and a librarian and covers library search tools, government documents, and literature surveys.

LaGuardia, Cheryl, et al. "A Group Approach to Teaching a Library Research Course." *Research Strategies* 11 (Spring 1993): 111-115.

Describes how a group of librarians revised and taught a two-credit course in library research. The team-teaching involved mentoring assignments as well as a variety of teaching modes.

LaGuardia, Cheryl, et al. "Learning to Instruct on the Job: Team-Teaching Library Skills." *Reference Librarian* 40 (1993): 53-62.

Describes a team-teaching approach to bibliographic instruction at the University of California, Santa Barbara.

Leach, Bruce. "Computer-Based CD-ROM Tutorials Provide Effective On-Demand Instruction." *CD-ROM Professional* 6 (July 1993): 113-114+.

Describes a program developed at Ohio State University to teach biology students end-user searching and other information skills.

Learning to Teach: Workshops on Instruction. Chicago: Association of College and Research Libraries, Bibliographic Instruction Section, Learning to Teach Taskforce, 1993.

Provides excellent ideas for teaching librarian information skills to students.

Levene, Lee-Allison, and Polly Frank. "Peer Coaching: Professional Growth and Development for Instruction Librarians." *Reference Services Review* 21, no. 3 (Fall 1993): 35-42.

Explains peer coaching and shows how librarians can use it to become more reflective about their teaching and how it helps them to grow as instructors. As peer coaches, librarians can support their partners by giving them specific descriptive feedback.

Libutti, Patricia. *Library Support for Graduate Education, Research and Teaching.* ERIC Reproduction Service, 1993. ED 349007.

Summarizes data from three studies at Fordham University Library for graduate education scholarship. One study focused on student information literacy needs and how library staff responded to these needs.

Litzinger, Mary Ellen, and Bonnie Osif. "Accommodating Diverse Learning Styles: Designing Instruction for Electronic Information Sources." In *What Is Good Instruction Now? Library Instruction for the 90s.* Ed. by Linda Shirato, 73-81. Ann Arbor, MI: Pierian Press, 1993.

Instructional programs should provide opportunities to complement students' individual cognitive learning styles to help them perceive, conceptualize, and analyze diverse pieces of information. Includes practical instructional design examples.

Loomis, Abigail, and Deborah Fink. "Instruction: Gateway to the Virtual Library." In *The Virtual Library. Visions and Realities*, 47-69. Westport, CT: Meckler, 1993.

Defines the virtual library and discusses how bibliographic instruction will occur in this environment. Provides four components of instruction, describes the teaching/learning environment, the learners including remote users, and the changing landscape.

Loomis, Abigal, and Patricia Herrling. "Course-Integrated Honors Program—Pros and Cons." In *What Is Good Instruction Now? Library Instruction for the 90s.* Ed. by Linda Shirato, 83-102. Ann Arbor, MI: Pierian Press, 1993.

Discusses a course-integrated instruction program at the University of Wisconsin-Madison in biology education.

Mandernak, Scott B., and John M. Tucker. "Selected Readings on Bibliographic Instruction, 1980-1992." In *Bibliographic Instruction in Practice.* Ed. by Larry

Hardesty, et al., 139-152. Ann Arbor, MI: Pierian Press, 1993.

Provides a selective and evaluative bibliography on bibliographic instruction during the past 12 years.

Markee, K.M. "Searching for Such-and-Such: The Key Is Instruction." In *Proceedings of the Fourteenth National Online Meeting*, 301-305. Medford, NJ: Learned Information, 1993.

Suggests techniques for cost-effective library instruction programs in the academic environment.

McKinzie, Steve. "Bibliographic Instruction or Research: What's in a Name?" *College and Research Libraries News* 54 (June 1993): 336-337.

Discusses the name change for the ACRL Bibliographic Instruction Section.

Mensching, Glenn. "A Simple, Effective One-Shot for Disinterested Students." In *What Is Good Instruction Now? Library Instruction for the 90s.* Ed. by Linda Shirato, 133-141. Ann Arbor, MI: Pierian Press, 1993.

Acquaints new high-risk students with library and information skills at Eastern Michigan University.

Metter, Ellen, and Elizabeth Willis. "Creating a Handbook for an Academic Library: Rationale and Process." *Research Strategies* 11 (Fall 1993): 220-232.

Describes the rationale, the development production, and distribution of the library handbook to supplement library instruction.

Mullins, Gerry. "Higher Education." In *Information Literacy. The Australian Agenda.* Ed. by Di Booker, 42-45. Adelaide: University of South Australia Library, 1993.

Indicates facts and issues that will affect appropriate changes within higher education to raise the level of information literacy.

Mullins, Lynn S. "Partnerships in Information Teaching and Learning: Building a Collaborative Culture in the University Community." *New Jersey Libraries* 26 (1993): 18-22.

Discusses how faculty and librarians work together at Rutgers University to provide students with library and information skills.

Nahl-Jakobovits, Diane, and Lean J. Jakobovits. "Bibliographic Instructional Design for Information Literacy: Integrating Effective and Cognitive Objectives." *Research Strategies* 11 (Spring 1993): 73-88.

Bibliographic instructional design is described as a systems analysis approach. Information skills are defined as integrated behavioral objectives within critical thinking, information evaluation, and learning to learn.

Nichols, Jan. "Library Orientation: A Workable Alternative Re-Worked." *Library Review* 42 (1993): 5-14.

Describes a workbook program at the University of the West in Bristol, England.

Nolf, Marcia L. "Information Literacy: What Every Honors Student Needs to Know." In *What Is Good Instruction Now? Library Instruction for the 90s*. Ed. by Linda Shirato, 103-107. Ann Arbor, MI: Pierian Press, 1993.

At California University of Pennsylvania, an honors program has been established to promote and reward outstanding intellectual achievement. Included in this program is a library instruction component to help these students gain valuable information skills.

Norlin, Dennis A., and Joyce C. Wright. "The Electric Undergrad: An Interactive Library Program." *College and Research Libraries News* 54 (July/August 1993): 398-399.

Describes a high-tech multimedia introduction to the Undergraduate Library at the University of Illinois at Urbana.

Nowakowski, Frances C. "Faculty Support Information Literacy." *College and Research Libraries News* 54 (March 1993): 124.

Osif, Bonnie A. "Science Fiction Futures and Bibliographic Instruction." *Research Strategies* 11 (Spring 1993): 116-119.

Describes the use of science fiction literature in a library research methodology course where students explored issues relating to the changing information environment at Pennsylvania State University.

Partello, Peggy. "First-Year Students and Cheating: A Study at Keene State College." *Research Strategies* 11 (Summer 1993): 174-179.

Presents findings from a survey of freshmen regarding cheating behavior and suggests ways to educate the entire academic community about the problem.

Penhale, Sara J. "The Role of Bibliographic Instruction in the Improvement of Undergraduate Science Education." In *Bibliographic Instruction in Practice*. Ed. by Larry Hardesty, et al., 63-66. Ann Arbor, MI: Pierian Press, 1993.

Discusses the pros and cons about using computer-assisted instruction teach information skills to undergraduate science students.

Petrowski, Mary Jane, and Betsy Wilson. *Research Guide*. Champaign, IL: Stipes Publishing Co., 1993.

This is the revised edition of the 1984 publication used in the bibliographic instruction program at the University of Illinois Undergraduate Library. It is based on a conceptual three-step research strategy to help students acquire valuable research and information management skills. Provides practical teaching methodology and worksheets.

Piette, Mary I., and Betty Dance. "A Statistical Evaluation of a Library Orientation Program for Graduate Students." *Research Strategies* 11 (Summer 1993): 164-173.

Reports the results of evaluating a library orientation program for graduate students at Utah State University and suggests improvements for the program based on the evaluation results.

Poirier, Gayle, and Susan Hocker. "Teaching Critical Thinking in a Library Credit Course." *Research Strategies* 11 (Fall 1993): 233-241.

Describes how critical thinking skills are taught in a four-credit seven-week library resources course. Gives exercises and assignments.

Prorak, Diane, and Margaret von Braun. "Teaching Students to Use Electronic Information Sources to Research Chemical Toxicity." *Research Strategies* 11 (Spring 1993): 106-110.

Presents tested library-based assignments that meet mutual goals for students needing to use TOXNET. Gives specifics on assignments, library instruction, and evaluation as used at the University of Idaho, Moscow.

Rader, Hannelore. "From Library Orientation to Information Literacy: Twenty Years of Hard Work." In *What Is Good Instruction Now? Library Instruction for the 90s*. Ed. by Linda Shirato, 25-28. Ann Arbor, MI: Pierian Press, 1993.

Gives an overview of the past 20 years and a state-of-the-art as well as future predictions for bibliographic instruction.

Reed, Lawrence L. "Locally Loaded Databases and Undergraduate Bibliographic Instruction." *RQ* 33 (Winter 1993): 266-273.

Challenges librarians to identify and teach effective strategies to and for users in an environment that includes too much information.

Reese, J. "CD-ROM End-User Instruction: Issues and Challenges." *MicroComputers for Information Management* 10 (June 1993): 131-154.

Addresses the challenges of CD-ROM end-user instruction and various methodologies that could be used.

Reichel, Mary. "Information Use and Projections: The Importance for Library Instruction (and Doctor Seuss)." In *What Is Good Instruction Now? Library Instruction for the 90s.* Ed. by Linda Shirato, 19-24. Ann Arbor, MI: Pierian Press, 1993.

Discusses information use including information resources and scholarly communication in terms of a recent research project conducted by the author. Also discusses how learners become informed in the context of academic librarianship and library instruction.

Reichel, Mary. "Twenty-Five-Year Retrospective: The Importance of What We Do." *RQ* 33 (Fall 1993): 29-32.

Shares thoughts on library instruction from a 25-year perspective. Reassesses public services, librarians' role in the educational process, and the importance of evaluating library instruction.

Richardson, G., and J.A. De-Vris. "HyperCard Library Research Methods Simulation at the University of Minnesota (St. Paul Campus) Library." *Journal of Agricultural and Food Information* 1 (1993): 59-62.

Describes a course on the HyperCard library research methods simulation at the University of Minnesota Library.

Rockman, Ilene F. "Teaching about the Internet: The Formal Course Option." *The Reference Librarian* 39 (1993): 65-75.

Discusses a formal course on the Internet in cooperation with faculty at the California Polytechnic State University-San Luis Obispo.

Rodriguez-Talavera, LeTica. *A Semiotic Interpretation of the Business Communication in Today's Global Economical Trend.* ERIC Reproduction Service, 1993. ED 362931.

Presents theoretical and educational perspectives on communication and how it becomes a tool to promote social economic expansion and international cultures. Recommends objectives for business communication educators to integrate information literacy into communication courses.

Rogers, Steven, et al. "Slide/Tape Presentations: Cost-Effective Library Instruction." *Research Strategies* 11 (Winter 1993): 4-8.

Argues that slide/tape productions using computer-enhanced graphics can be superior to video in terms of expense, visual clarity, and simplicity of production.

Ruscella, Phyllis L. "Scoring: Bibliographic Instruction Helps Freshman Athletes Compete in Academic League." *Journal of Academic Librarianship* 19 (September 1993): 232-236.

Describes a library-based instructional module developed at the University of Central Florida for freshmen athletes; gives details about the planning and implementation of this module.

September, Peter E. "Promoting Information Literacy in Developing Countries: The Case of South Africa." *African Journal of Library, Archives and Information Science* 3 (April 1993): 11-22.

Defines information literacy and considers it in relation to developing communities; advocates integrated information literacy programs.

Shonrock, Diana, and Craig Mulder. "Instruction Librarians: Acquiring the Proficiencies Critical to Their Work." *College and Research Libraries* 54 (March 1993): 137-149.

Based on a survey of instruction librarians who are members of ACRL Bibliographic Instruction Section, instruction librarians must possess many proficiencies. Especially needed are communication, instruction, and planning skills; these skills are preferably acquired in library schools. More studies are needed to assess the role continuing education can play in the acquisition of the more than 25 skills listed as the top needs for instruction librarians.

Silva, Marcos, and Glenn F. Cartwright. "The Design and Implementation of Internet Seminars for Library Users and Staff at McGill University." *Education for Information* 11 (June 1993): 137-146.

Describes an Internet workshop given by librarians at McGill University for students, faculty, and staff to teach them end-user searching.

Slack, Frances. "Library Instruction and OPACs: Who Needs Help?" In *What Is Good Instruction Now? Library Instruction for the 90s.* Ed. by Linda Shirato, 109-115. Ann Arbor, MI: Pierian Press, 1993.

Discusses how instruction in the use of OPACs is handled in British Academic Libraries.

Son, Inhye K., et al. "Lessons for the Teacher and Student. Developing a HyperCard Tutorial." *Computers and Libraries* 19 (May 1993): 18-20.

Demonstrates the usefulness of computer-assisted instruction by using the University of Virginia's Health Sciences Library program as an example.

Staines, Gail M., and Sheryl L. Knab. "Supplemental BI: Developing an OPAC Self-Help Guide." *Research Strategies* 11 (Winter 1993): 33-38.

Reports on supplementing course-integrated library instruction related to the OPAC at Niagara County Community College.

Stephenson, William K. "A Departmental Approach to Bibliographic Instruction." In *Bibliographic Instruction in Practice*. Ed. by Larry Hardesty, et al., 27-32. Ann Arbor, MI: Pierian Press, 1993.

Describes the science library instruction program at Earlham College from the point of view of the biology professor.

Stewart, Linda. "Helping Students During Online Searches: An Evaluation." *The Journal of Academic Librarianship* 18 (January 1993): 347-351.

Presents an evaluation of student online searches and the value of staff assistants using tape recordings, questionnaires, and post-search interviews. It was found that students required extensive assistance and that the coaching program was helpful.

Surprenant, Thomas T. "Welcome to Obsolescence: What Is Good Instruction Now?" In *What Is Good Instruction Now? Library Instruction for the 90s*. Ed. by Linda Shirato, 1-6. Ann Arbor, MI: Pierian Press, 1993.

Provides three possible scenarios for the future of bibliographic instruction in terms of scholars', students', and teachers' needs.

Swinney, Victoria K. "Interactive Video at Cameron University Library." *College and Research Libraries News* 54 (February 1993): 81-82.

Describes a video projection system used for bibliographic instruction at Cameron University in Lawton, Oklahoma. Gives details for the equipment used.

Taylor, Susan K. "Successful Bibliographic Instruction Programs at Three Small Liberal Arts Colleges." *Research Strategies* 11 (Fall 1993): 242-247.

Describes three small college library instructional programs and how they have been successful: Earlham College, Berea College, and Sterling College.

Thompson, Gordon W. "Faculty Recalcitrance about Bibliographic Instruction." In *Bibliographic Instruction*

in Practice. Ed. by Larry Hardesty, et al., 103-105. Ann Arbor, MI: Pierian Press, 1993.

Discusses how to overcome faculty resistance in working with librarians and planning course-integrated bibliographic instruction.

Thompson, Gordon W. "Sequenced Research Assignments for the Undergraduate Literature Student." In *Bibliographic Instruction in Practice*. Ed. by Larry Hardesty, et al., 41-50. Ann Arbor, MI: Pierian Press, 1993.

Describes Earlham College's bibliographic instruction program from the humanist's point-of-view. Discusses four different stages of library instruction for literature students.

Tiefel, Virginia. "Innovative Applications of Technology to Library User Services." In *What Is Good Instruction Now? Library Instruction for the 90s*. Ed. by Linda Shirato, 7-18. Ann Arbor, MI: Pierian Press, 1993.

Discusses library user education in the future in terms of Ohio State's gateway to information and a survey of 13 academic libraries' programs in the area of user instruction.

Trail, Marianne, and Carolyn Gutierrez. "Spruce up Your Teaching Techniques: A Two-Day Seminar for Revitalizing a BI Program." *Research Strategies* 11 (Winter 1993): 9-13.

Describes an in-house seminar to evaluate the library's instruction program and its effectiveness in meeting planned objectives.

Tumlin, M.D. "Point-of-Use Instruction on CD-ROM: How Much Is Too Much?" In *Proceedings of the Fourteenth National Online Meeting*, 415-421. Medford, NJ: Learned Information, 1993.

Considers point-of-use instruction on CD-ROM in order to balance reference desk demands with electronic reference sources.

Turner, Diane. "What's the Point of Bibliographic Instruction, Point-of-Use Guides, and In-House Bibliographies?" *Wilson Library Bulletin* 67 (January 1993): 64-67.

Discusses the importance of bibliographic instruction as part of the curriculum and teaching process. Advocates national goals for the profession in the area of information literacy and user instruction.

Vakili, Mary Jane. "Revamping a Required BI Course for Adult Students." *Research Strategies* 11 (Winter 1993): 24-32.

Discusses the development of a required library use course for nontraditional students at Iowa State

University. Provides evaluation of the course through local reactions and comparison to other programs described in the literature.

VanBrakel, Pieter A. "Teaching Online Searching in a LAN Environment." *The Electronic Library* 11 (August/October 1993): 289-293.

Describes how the limited concept of "online searching" is broadened when a LAN and local databases are incorporated into the online teaching process.

Wallace, Patricia M. "How Do Patrons Search the Online Catalog When No One's Looking? Transaction Log Analysis and Implication for Bibliographic Instruction and System Design." *RQ* 33 (Winter 1993): 239-252.

At the University of Colorado public access terminals were electronically monitored to analyze users' behavior regarding online catalog searching. Findings indicate that 66 percent of subject and name searches produce ten or fewer results, user persistence in scanning titles is high, and emphasis on improved system design is needed to help searchers become more effective.

Warmkessel, Marjorie M., and Frances M. Carothers. "Collaborative Learning and Bibliographic Instruction." *Journal of Academic Librarianship* 19 (March 1993): 4-7.

Reviews history and philosophy of collaborative learning and describes a strategy called "pairing" to help undergraduates learn the art of electronic database searching.

Warren-Wenk, Peggy, and Anita Cannon. "Project Outline." In *What Is Good Instruction Now? Library Instruction for the 90s.* Ed. by Linda Shirato, 143-151. Ann Arbor, MI: Pierian Press, 1993.

Identifies and evaluates library research guides for academic library users.

Weil, Carol. "Support Staff in Bibliographic Instruction." *Library Mosaics* 4 (May/June 1993): 17.

Discusses the use of support staff in user instruction at California State University, Long Beach, Library.

Westbrook, Lynn, and Robert Waldman. "Outreach in Academic Libraries: Principle into Practice." *Research Strategies* 11 (Spring 1993): 60-65.

Library outreach services have gained in importance through new developments in information technologies and changes in campus populations. User needs, campus environment, and available resources are analyzed.

Westbrook, Lynn, and Dee Decker. "Supporting User Needs and Skills to Minimize Library Anxiety: Considerations for Academic Libraries." *Reference Librarian* 40 (1993): 43-51.

Suggests guidelines for use by academic librarians to evaluate facilities, services, and staff in order to become more effective in helping students with their information needs.

Wiggins, Marvin E., and Donald H. Howard. "Developing Support Facilities for BYU's BI Program." *Journal of Academic Librarianship* 19 (July 1993): 144-148.

Discusses the importance of appropriate instructional facilities in the library to support bibliographic instruction programs. Describes how librarians at Brigham Young University planned, designed, and obtained funding for such a facility.

Witucke, A. Virginia. "Bibliographic Instruction without Being There: Using Job Aids for Off-Campus Needs." In *Off-Campus Library Services Conference Proceedings.* Mount Pleasant, MI: Central Michigan University Press, 1993.

Discusses bibliographic instruction experiences in bibliographic instruction for distance education students at Central Michigan University.

Wolf, Carolyn, and Richard Wolf. *Basic Library Skills* Jefferson, NC: McFarland, 1993.

This is a text designed for students in library skills courses or in classes that have fully integrated library components. It is updated to reflect current technology and includes objectives, exercises, and terminology.

Young, Vicki. "Applying the Principles of Adult Learning to the Design of a Two-Hour Workshop for Adult and Part-Time Students." In *What Is Good Instruction Now? Library Instruction for the 90s.* Ed. by Linda Shirato, 117-120. Ann Arbor, MI: Pierian Press, 1993.

Explains the ten principles of learning and describes how they can be applied to an instruction program for part-time and undergraduate students.

Zahner, Jane E. *Thoughts, Feelings and Actions: Integrating Domains in Library Instruction.* ERIC Reproduction Service, 1993. ED 362215.

Presents a framework for library instruction that integrates learning into the cognitive and effective domains. Compares the effects of two methods of academic library instruction on the research process, library anxiety, student performance, and attitudes about library instruction.

Zambella, BethAnn, and Catherine Geddies. "Information Literacy and Undergraduate Libraries in New Jersey: Trends and Observations." *New Jersey Libraries* 26 (1993): 14-17.

Summarizes information literacy programs in three-year and four-year institutions in New Jersey.

PUBLIC LIBRARIES

Bowers, John W., and Catherine C. Childs. "Cunning Passages, Contrived Corridors; Mobilizing Volunteers for a Public Library Tour." *Public Libraries* 32 (May/June 1993): 143-147.

Describes how volunteers are used at the Boulder Public Library to orient the public to the library.

Cram, Jennifer. "Public Libraries." In *Information Literacy. The Australian Agenda*. Ed. by Di Booker, 50-53. Adelaide: University of South Australia Library, 1993.

Discusses the role information literacy can play in public libraries in the area of empowerment for citizens and the importance of well-educated librarians.

Harlow, Marilyn. "Industry and Business." In *Information Literacy. The Australian Agenda*. Ed. by Di Booker, 58-59. Adelaide: University of South Australia Library, 1993.

Discusses the importance of business information for the community and the role public libraries should play to further economic development.

SCHOOL LIBRARIES

ACCESS PENNSYLVANIA Curriculum Guide. ERIC Reproduction Service, 1993. ED 355963.

This curriculum guide is used to teach students in Pennsylvania schools the purpose and function of the ACCESS PENNSYLVANIA database within the concept of information literacy.

Allen, Christine. *Skills for Life: Library Information Literacy for Grades K-6*. Worthington, OH: Linworth Publishers, 1993.

Beer, J. "Equipping Children with Life-Long Skills." *Cape Librarian* 37 (January 1993): 16-17.

Defines and describes information skills and suggests that they should be taught by both teachers and librarians.

Bird, Jane, and Judith Libby. "Stimulating Higher-Order Thinking with Database Searching." *Indiana Media Journal* 15 (Spring 1993): 15-19.

Discusses the use of microcomputers in schools and how they can help teach media and information skills to students in elementary schools.

Breivik, Patricia S., and J.A. Senn. *Information Literacy. Educating Children for the 21st Century*. New York: Scholastic, Inc., 1993.

Defines information literacy within the information age and discusses the importance for educating young people to become information literate. Addresses elementary school principals and challenges them to become leaders in the movement to educate an information-literate population.

Breivik, Patricia S., and J.A. Senn. "Information Literacy: Partnerships for Power." *Emergency Librarian* 21 (September/October 1993): 25-28.

Summarizes the efforts in New York and Pennsylvania to bring information literacy education into the school and college environment by creating partnerships with principals, teachers, community members, and businesses.

Burnheim, Robert. *Curriculum Delivery Is Changing—Responding to the Change*. ERIC Reproduction Service, 1993. ED 355946.

Presents the competency-based training style of curriculum delivery in the Technical and Further Education Program in Queensland, Australia.

Callison, Daniel. "The Impact of New Technologies on School Library Media Center Facilities and Instruction." *Journal of Youth Services in Libraries* 6 (Summer 1993): 414-419.

Summarizes aims and objectives for automating school libraries and its impact on media skills instruction.

Collicutt, Cathy. "Technology, Young People, and the Library." *North Carolina Libraries* 51 (Summer 1993): 75-76.

Discusses library instruction for elementary and high school students in the context of automation.

Cox, Helen, and Eva Long. "Introducing Resource-Based Learning. The Practicalities." *Access* 7 (August 1993): 19-21, 28.

Illustrates how a successful team learning experience involving teachers and librarians can help bring about initiated resource-based learning in the school setting. The case study described is from Queensland, Australia, and provides actual plans.

Dobson, Barbara. "The Demise of the Project; Information Skills Meet Genre: Implications for the Teacher-Librarian." *Access* 7 (August 1993): 23-25.

Describes how the English curriculum in elementary education in Australia is used to emphasize the importance in other genres in order to teach information skills.

Doyle, Christina. "Designing for 21st Century Success." *CMLEA Journal* 16 (Spring 1993): 13-16.

Information literacy in the context of elementary and high school education will teach students critical thinking and problem-solving skills. This will be most important in the context of the information age economy where citizens will need to have access to information and be able to evaluate information sources.

Eisenberg, Michael B., and Donald P. Ely. "Plugging into the Net." *ERIC Review* 2 (Winter 1993): 2-8.

Gives an overview for K-12 teachers about educational users for the Internet. Includes a glossary of network terms and a useful bibliography.

Eshpeter, Barry, and Judy Gray. *Preparing Students for Information Literacy. School Library Programs and the Cooperative Planning Process.* ERIC Reproduction Service, 1993. ED 357766.

Discusses the development of a school library program for Canadian schools that focuses on teacher/librarian cooperation to teach information literacy.

Handy, Alice E., et al. "Teaching Research Skills." *Book Report* 12 (November/December 1993): 13, 15-25, 27-29.

Includes nine articles that discuss the teaching of research skills to junior and senior high school students using a variety of projects, cooperative learning, and board games.

Jacobson, Frances F., and Michael J. Jacobson. "Representative Cognitive Learning Theories and BI: A Case Study of End User Searching." *Research Strategies* 11 (Summer 1993): 124-137.

Examines an online searching program for high school seniors from the perspective of cognitive learning theories and proposes a synthesized approach to apply learning theory to bibliographic instruction.

Kehoe, Louise. "Lost in the Library: A Middle School Orientation." *The School Librarian's Workshop* 14 (September 1993): 7.

Describes medial skill instruction in middle schools in Michigan.

Kuhlthau, Carol. "Implementing a Process Approach to Information Skills: A Study Identifying Indicators of Success in Library Media Programs." *School Library Media Quarterly* 22 (Fall 1993): 11-18.

Describes a study that evaluated implementing a constructivist process approach to learning information skills in the school setting. Discusses training for media specialists, identification of inhibitors, and enablers for successful programs and gives a longitudinal case study.

Lupton, Paul. "The School Perspective." In *Information Literacy. The Australian Agenda.* Ed. by Di Booker, 38-41. Adelaide: University of South Australia Library, 1993.

Outlines the history and development of information literate students within the Australian school systems based on existing national documents and other materials.

McNally, Mary Jane. "Current Projects in Information Literacy in School Libraries." *New Jersey Libraries* 26 (1993): 7-10.

Provides an overview of information literacy programs in five New Jersey schools.

Munns, Sec, and Megan Perry. "Learning, Thinking and Research in the Age of Information and Technology: An Approach in a Pre-School to Year 12 School." *Access* 7 (1993): 13-18.

Describes how the introduction of personal computers in the school setting helps teach students problem solving, critical thinking, and research skills.

Pappas, Marjorie. "Information Skills for Electronic Resources." *Ohio Media Spectrum* 45 (1993): 11-15.

Reviews information skills curricula presently under revision in Ohio as library media specialists and teachers focus on the challenges within the information age and the need to prepare students for effective life-long learning.

Small, Graham. "Integrating Information Skills into the Mainstream Curriculum: The Evolution of a Model." *School Librarian* 41 (February 1993): 142-144.

Describes an information skills program for secondary education students in London.

Swim, Patty. "Teaching Critical Thinking through Library Research." *Indiana Media Journal* 16 (Fall 1993): 63-70.

Discusses how critical thinking skills can be learned through the use of appropriate learning strategies in the elementary level. Provides practical examples for five different levels.

Thompson, Debra M. "Library Jeopardy: A Fifteen-Minute Orientation for Teachers." *School Library Media Activities Monthly* 10 (September 1993): 36+.

Describes library instruction for teachers and administrators in the school setting.

Todd, Ross J., et al. "Information Skills and Learning: Some Research Findings." *Access* 7 (March 1993): 14-16.

Reports on a research project in Sydney, Australia, to place information literacy at the center of the school's curriculum. Research program began in 1991.

Todd, Ross J., et al. *The Power of Information Literacy: Unity of Education and Resources for the 21st Century*. ERIC Reproduction Service, 1993. ED 354916.

Describes an approach for promoting information literacy and establishing an integrated information skills program in secondary schools in Sydney, Australia.

Werner, Mary Jane, and Gaylyn Stone. "Library Access for All Limited English Proficient Students: One School's Approach." *Emergency Librarian* 20 (May/June 1993): 20-23.

Describes a library media skills instruction program for students with limited English skills in San Diego High School in Garden Grove, California.

SPECIAL LIBRARIES

Clinch, Peter. "Legal Research Skills Training in Universities and Polytechnics in England and Wales: Report of a Study." *Law Librarian* 24 (September 1993): 137-140.

Summarizes two surveys conducted in 1992/93 of law librarians to assess their needs regarding education in the area of legal literature.

Cohen, Eileen. "Teaching Legal Research to a Diverse Student Body." *Law Library Journal* 85 (Summer 1993): 583-590.

Asserts that student learning in law schools can be improved by expanding our teaching methods to incorporate a variety of learning styles in a diverse law student population.

Dunn, Donald J. "Why Legal Research Skills Declined, or When Two Rights Make a Wrong." *Law Library Journal* 85 (Winter 1993): 49-70.

Discusses issues relating to the poor quality of legal research in the context of legal writing programs. Illustrates that legal research is not a course but a

concept. Proposes changing the way legal research instruction is offered in law schools.

Fishman, D.L. "The Maryland Model Statement of Objectives for Bibliographic Instruction." *Medical Reference Services Quarterly* 12 (Summer 1993): 91-98.

Discusses how academic librarians in Maryland developed a bibliographic instruction plan for the state. Includes major objectives and relative competencies.

Frank, P.P. "Active Library Instruction for Art Educators: Addressing Every Day Concerns." *Art Services Quarterly* 1 (1993): 11-20.

Emphasizes the importance of library instruction for art education. Gives practical problem-solving examples.

Johnson, Deborah S. "An Integrated Bibliographic Instruction Program for the Architectural Studies Program at Clemson University: Planning and Early Implementation." *Art References Services Quarterly* 1 (1993): 21-28.

Describes a restructuring of the bibliographic instruction program for architectural students at Clemson University in response to changing teaching approaches in architecture.

Likness, C.S. "Can We Talk? Or, What Do Art History Undergraduates Really Know about the Library?" *Art Services Quarterly* 1 (1993): 29-36.

Presents a conceptual model that goes beyond traditional instructional frameworks and proposes a cooperative instruction program for undergraduates having librarians and art historians in partnership.

Mincow, Rochelle L., et al. "Breaking New Ground in Curriculum-Integrated Instruction." *Medical Reference Services Quarterly* 12 (Summer 1993): 1-18.

Describes a course-integrated library instruction program at the University of California, Irvine.

Prince, William W., et al. "Project-Focussed Library Instruction in Business Strategy Courses." *Journal of Education for Business* 68 (January/February 1993): 179-183.

Rankin, Jocelyn A., and Jean W. Sayre. "The Educational Role of Health Sciences Librarians." *Library Trends* 42 (Summer 1993): 45-61.

Discusses how the educational role of health sciences librarians in universities and hospitals is expanding due to new technology and new educational models. Health sciences librarians now teach access to the literature, other information resources, and technology to manage information.

— HANNELORE B. RADER —

VanJacob, ScottJ. "Integrating Library Instruction into an Undergraduate Art Historical Methods Class." *Art Reference Services Quarterly* 1 (1993): 53-59.

Describes the teaching of bibliographic tools in an art historical research methods course at Dickinson College and an applied research project.

Widziniski, L. "How Hyper Are We? A Look at Hyer-Media Management in Academic Health Sciences Libraries." *Bulletin of the Medical Library Association* 81 (January 1993): 58-61.

Summarizes an informal survey to determine the extent to which academic health sciences libraries support hyper-media applications. Includes a copy of the survey questionnaire.

ALL LEVELS

Bean, Robert. "Workplace Education." In *Information Literacy. The Australian Agenda*, 54-59. Adelaide: University of South Australia Library, 1993.

Discusses the training needs of the Australian workforce in regard to literacy and information skills. Places these issues in the context of lifelong learning.

Breivik, Patricia S., and Barbara J. Ford. "Promoting Learning in Libraries through Information Literacy." *American Libraries* 24 (January 1993): 98, 101, 102.

The American Library Association is leading the way in promoting information literacy through a diverse coalition of organizations.

Breivik, Patricia S. "Information Literacy: What's It All About?" In *Information Literacy. The Australian Agenda*. Ed. by Di Booker, 6-18. Adelaide: University of South Australia Library, 1993.

Gives history and overview of information literacy movement in the United States. Explains the concept of resource-based learning, cultural diversity, and the relationship to library instruction. Discusses the National Forum on Information Literacy and its accomplishments.

Breivik, Patricia S. "What Can We Learn from the US Experience?" In *Information Literacy. The Australian Agenda*. Ed. by Di Booker, 155-165. Adelaide: University of South Australia Library, 1993.

Advocates that action is needed now if information literacy is to become a reality. Gives a prescription for action now.

Foster, Stephen. "Information Literacy: Some Misgivings." *American Libraries* 24 (April 1993): 344-353.

Examines the concept of information literacy and defines information-literate people as those who have learned how to learn.

George, Mary W. "Information Literacy: A Selective Review of Recent Literature." *New Jersey Libraries* 26 (1993): 3-5.

Summarizes the information literacy literature from 1989 to the present.

Hattery, M. "Canadian National Summit on Information Policy." *Information Retrieval and Library Automation* 28 (January 1993): 1-2.

Reports on the National Summit on Information Policy in Canada in order to form partnerships between information science components. Stresses the importance of an information literate population for Canada.

Hazell, Anne. "What the Government's Saying: Information Literacy in Recent Government Reports." In *Information Literacy. The Australian Agenda*. Ed. by Di Booker, 28-36. Adelaide: University of South Australia Library, 1993.

Provides an overview of 13 key federal government reports from 1990-1992 in the area of education in Australia and highlights the importance of information literacy for all Australian citizens.

Humes, Barbara, and Carol C. Lyons. *Library Literacy Program: Analysis of Funded Projects, 1991, Title VI, Library Services and Construction Act*. ERIC Reproduction Services, 1993. ED 357764.

This booklet analyzes FY 91 adult literacy projects funded under LSCA Title VI and discusses major developments in the program, including library instruction.

Millsap, Larry, and Terry E. Furl. "Searching Patterns of Remote Users: An Analysis of OPAC Transaction Logs." *Information Technology and Libraries* 122 (September 1993): 321-343.

Owen, Richard. "Establishing the Agenda for Change." In *Information Literacy. The Australian Agenda*. Ed. by Di Booker, 149-154. Adelaide: University of South Australia Library, 1993.

Summarizes outcomes and recommendations from the Australian Conference on Information Literacy. Issues to be addressed include staff development, research, library profession training, economic development, social justice, advocacy, and curriculum development.

Whitmore, Marilyn P., and Elizabeth N. Kenney. "Aims of User Education in School Libraries: Results of a Nation-wide Survey." *Library Instruction Roundtable News* 16 (December 1993): 19-23.

Summarizes a survey of libraries to ascertain the purpose and character of formal and informal user education in school, academic, special, and public libraries.

— HANNELORE B. RADER —

PARTICIPANTS

ROSTER OF PARTICIPANTS

Diana Accurso
Library
Denison University
Granville, OH 43023
accurso@max.cc.denison.edu

Michael Aked
Carlson Library
University of Toledo
Toledo, OH 43606-3399

Jan Alexander
Wolfgram Library
Widener University
Chester, PA 19013
oajealexander@cyber.
   widener.edu

Sallie J. Alger
James White Library
Andrews University
Berrien Springs, MI 49104
alger@andrews.edu

Connie Anderson
Library
Southern Oregon State
Ashland, OR 97520
anderson@sosc1.sosc.osshe.edu

Judith Arnold
Byrne Memorial Library
Saint Xavier University
Chicago, IL 60655
arnold@sxu.edu

Teresa Ashley
Library
Austin Community College
Austin, TX 78758
tashley@austin.cc.tx.us

Mary Beth Aust-Keefer
Library
Edison Community College
Piqua, OH 45356
austkeefer@edison.cc.oh.us

Margaret Bailey
Fondren Library
Southern Methodist University
Dallas, TX 75275-0135
mbailey@sun.cis.smu.edu

William Baker
King Library
Miami University
Oxford, OH 45056
baker_bill@msmail.
   muohio.edu

Aggie Balash
South Campus Library
Manatee Commmunity College
Venice, FL 34293

Promilla Bansal
Library
Roosevelt University
Chicago, IL 60605
axvrubp.vicvmc.bitnet

Mary Barton
Lord Library
Moorhead State University
Moorhead, MN 56563
bartonm@mhd1.moorhead.
   msus.edu

Abbie Basile
King Library
Miami University
Oxford, OH 45056
abbie@watson.lib.muohio.edu

Lisa Baures
Memorial Library
Mankato State University
Mankato, MN 56002

Larry Benson
Lee Library
Brigham Young University
Provo, UT 84602
larry_benson@byu.edu

Joan Bewley
Hunt Library
Carnegie Mellon University
Pittsburgh, PA 15213
jbcx@andrew.cmu.edu

Goodie Bhullar
Ellis Library
University of Missouri
Columbia, MO 65201
ellisgb@mizzoul.missouri.edu

Cheryl Blackwell
Stockwell-Mudd Library
Albion College
Albion, MI 49224
cblackwell@albion.bitnet

Lisa Blankenship
Michener Library
University of Northern Colorado
Greeley, CO 80639
lblank@slinky.univnorthco.edu

Sonia Bodi
Library
North Park College
Chicago, IL 60625
npcts@class.org

Mary Bopp
Library W121
Indiana University
Bloomington, IN 47405
boppm@indiana.edu

Barbara Bowley
Library
Union County College
Cranford, NJ 07016
bowley@hawk.ucc.edu

Jane T. Bradford
duPont-Ball Library
Stetson University
DeLand, FL 32720
jbradfor@suvax1.stetson.edu

Ann Breitenwischer
Timme Library
Ferris State University
Big Rapids, MI 49307

Carla Brooks
Mardigian Library
University of Michigan-Dearborn
Dearborn, MI 48128
cbrooks@ml-f1.umd.umich.edu

Chester Bunnell
Library
St. Louis University
St. Louis, MO 63108
bunnellcs@sluvca.slu.edu

Lara Bushallow-Wilbur
Undergraduate Library
SUNY-Buffalo
Buffalo, NY 14260
lbw@ubvm.cc.buffalo.edu

Karen L. Byrne
Library
Delaware Valley College
Doylestown, PA 18901
dlvcollib@hslc.org

Suzanne Byron
Library
University of North Texas
Denton, TX 76201
sbyron@library.unt.edu

Hilde Calvert
Bracken Library
Ball State University
Muncie, IN 47306
oohocalvert@bsuvc.bsu.edu

Lynn Cameron
Library
James Madison University
Harrisonburg, VA 22807
fac_scam@vax1.acs.jmu.edu

Elizabeth Carroll
Library
American University
Washington, DC 20016-8046
carroll@american.edu

Diane Chladil
Library
University of Texas-Pan
 American
Edinburg, TX 78539-2999
chladil@panam.edu

Lee Christner
Boatwright Library
University of Richmond
Richmond, VA 23173
christner@urvax.urich.edu

Denise L. Clark
Library
North Idaho College
Coeur d'Alene, ID 83814

Charlotte Cohen
Thunderbird Library American
Graduate School of International
 Management
Glendale, AZ 85306
cohenc@mhs.t-bird.edu

Ron Colman
Eastern Michigan University
 Library
Ypsilanti, MI 48197
lib_colman@emunix.emich.edu

Susan Cooperstein
Harford Community College
 Library
Bel Air, MD 21015

Rosanne Cordell
Schurz Library
IU-South Bend
South Bend, IN 46634
rcordell@indiana.edu

Karen Croneis
Olin Library
Washington University
St. Louis, MO 63130
kcroneis@library.wustl.edu

Mary Cummings
Library
Shawnee State University
Portsmouth, OH 45662
mcummings@shawnee.edu

Jeanne Davidson
Library
Augustana College
Rock Island, IL 61201
alijrd@augustana.edu

Katherine M. Dickson
Nimitz Library
U.S. Naval Academy
Annapolis, MD 21402
dickson@nimitz.nadn.navy.mil

Kathleen Donovan
Gutman Library
Harvard University
Cambridge, MA 02138
donovaka@hugsel.harvard.edu

Linnea Dudley
Library
Marygrove College
Detroit, MI 48221-2599

Diane Duesterhoeft
Academic Library
St. Mary's University
San Antonio, TX 78228
diane@vax.stmarytx.edu

H. Minnie Dunbar
Library
Florida International University
Miami, FL 33199

Carmen Embry
Ekstrom Library
University of Louisville
Louisville, KY 40292
cfembr01@ulkyvm

Margaret Fain
Coastal Carolina University
Library
Conway, SC 29526
r201039@univscvm.csd.
 scarolina.edu

Elaine Filsinger
Library
Lock Haven University
Clearfield, PA 16830
efilsing@eagle.lhup.edu

Peggy Firman
University of Puget Sound
   Library
Tacoma, WA 98416
firman@ups.edu

Cynthia Foulke
Library
Millikin University
Decatur, IL 62522
cfoulke@mail.millikin.edu

Susan Frey-Ridgway
Helmke Library
IU-PU at Fort Wayne
Fort Wayne, IN 46805

Margaret Gardner
Wallace Library
Wheaton College
Norton, MA 02766
mgardner@wheatonma.edu

Virginia Gillette
Library
Butler University
Indianapolis, IN 46220

Mary Glazier
Silverman Library
SUNY at Buffalo
Buffalo, NY 14260
mglazier@ubvm.cc.buffalo.edu

Ronda Glikin
Eastern Michigan University
   Library
Ypsilanti, MI 48197

Gail Gradowski
Orradre Library
Santa Clara University
Santa Clara, CA 95053
ggradowski@scuacc.scu.edu

Esther Grassian
College Library
UCLA
Los Angeles, CA 90024
ecz5esg@mvs.oac.ucla.edu

Denise Green
Beeghly Library
Ohio Wesleyan University
Delaware, OH 43015
ddgreen@cc.owu.edu

Rosemary Green
Library
Shenandoah University
1460 University Dr
Winchester, VA 22601

Elizabeth Gulacsy
Scholes Library
New York State College of
   Ceramics
Alfred, NY 14802
gulacsy@bigvax.alfred.edu

Josephine Gurira
Library PO Box MP 45
University of Zimbabwe
Harare, Zimbabwe

Nancy Haas
Library
South Dakota State University
Brookings, SD 57007-1098
li15@sdsumus.sdstate.edu

Barbara Hamel
Steenbock Library
University of Wisconsin
Madison, WI 53706
bhamel@macc.wisc.edu

Doreen Harwood
Alverno College Library
Milwaukee, WI 53234-3922

Terese Heidenwolf
Skillman Library
Lafayette College
Easton, PA 18042
ht#o@lafayacs

Cynthia Mae Helms
Library
Andrews University
Berrien Springs, MI 49104-1400
helms@andrews.edu

Patricia Herrling
Steenbock Library
University of Wisconsin
Madison, WI 53706
pherrling@macc.wisc.edu

Judith Hesp
Library
Hahnemann University
Philadelphia, PA 19102
hespj@hal.hahnemann.edu

Connie Hildebrand
McDermott Library
University of Texas-Dallas
Richardson, TX 75080
connie@utdallas.edu

Beth Hillemann
DeWitt Wallace Library
Macalester College
St. Paul, MN 55105
hillemann@macalstr.edu

Patricia Hinegardner
Health Sciences Library
University of Maryland at
   Baltimore
Baltimore, MD 21201
phinegar@umab.umd.edu

Jill Hobgood
Cushwa-Leighton Library
St. Mary's College
Notre Dame, IN 46556
jhobgood@saintmarys.edu

Patricia Hogan-Vidal
Moellering Library
Valparaiso University
Valparaiso, IN 46307
phogan@exodus.valpo.edu

Martha Hooker
McKeldin Library
University of Maryland
College Park, MD 20742
mh@umail.umd.edu

Charlene Hovatter
207 Hillman Library
University of Pittsburgh
Pittsburgh, PA 15260
cehova@vms.cis.pitt.edu

Sue Huff
Lewis Towers Library
Loyola University
Chicago, IL 60611
shuff@luccpua.it.luc.edu

Jon Hufford
Library
Texas Tech University
Lubbock, TX 79409

Sandra Hussey
Lauinger Library
Georgetown University
Washington, DC 20057
shussey@guvax.georgetown.edu

Rebecca Jackson
Gelman Library
George Washington University
Washington, DC 20052
rjackson@gwuvm.gwu.edu

Elaine Jayne
Undergraduate Library
University of Michigan
Ann Arbor, MI 48109

Melba Jesudason
College Library
University of Wisconsin
Madison, WI 53706
jesuda@macc.wisc.edu

Anita Johnson
Roesch Library
University of Dayton
Dayton, OH 45469-1360
johnson@data.lib.udayton.edu

Jane Keefer
Eisenhower Library
Johns Hopkins University
Baltimore, MD 21218
keefer@jhunix.hef.jhu.edu

Veronica Kenausis
Franklin & Marshall College
    Library
Lancaster, PA 17604
v-kenausis@fandm.edu

Jean Kent
North Seattle Community
    College Library
Seattle, WA 98103
jkent@seaccd.ctc.edu

Elys L. Kettling
Wayne College Library
University of Akron
Orrville, OH 44667
elkettling@uakron.edu

Stacey Kimmel
King Library
Miami University
Oxford, OH 45056
skimmel@miamiu.acs.
    muohio.edu

Kathleen Kroll
Olson Library
Northern Michigan University
Marquette, MI 49855-5376
faka@nmumus.bitnet

Michael Kruzich
Mardigian Library
University of Michigan-Dearborn
Dearborn, MI 48128-1491
mkruzich@ml-f1.umd.
    umich.edu

Cheryl LaGuardia
Library
University of California at Santa
    Barbara
Santa Barbara, CA 93106

Kathleen A. Lance
Dayton Memorial Library
Regis University
Denver, CO 80221
katlance@regis.edu

Phyllis Lansing
Health Sciences Library
University of Maryland at
    Baltimore
Baltimore, MD 21201
plansing@umab.umd.edu

Deborah Lauseng
Public Health Library
University of Michigan
Ann Arbor, MI 48109
deborah-lauseng@um.cc.
    mich.edu

Anne R. Lawhorne
Monteith Library
Alma College
Alma, MI 48801
lawhorne@alma.edu

Sally Lawler
Purdy/Kresge Library
Wayne State University
Detroit, MI 48202
slawler@cms.cc.wayne.edu

Erica Lilly
Brill Science Library
Miami University
Oxford, OH 45056
elilly@miamiu.acs.muohio.edu

Xiaoyang Liu
Bracken Library
Ball State University
Muncie, IN 47304
00x0liu@bsu.edu

Abigail Loomis
Memorial Library
University of Wisconsin at
    Madison
Madison, WI 53706
loomis@macc.wisc.edu

Kathleen Lovelace
Library
Barat College
Lake Forest, IL 60045
baratlib@class.org

Bridget Loven
Health Sciences Library
University of North Carolina-
    Chapel Hill
Chapel Hill, NC 27599
bakl@med.unc.edu

Linda Maddux
Newman Library
Virginia Tech
Blacksburg, VA 24062
lmaddux@vt.edu

Gail Marradeth
Cleveland State University
   Library
Cleveland, OH 44115
ro544@vmcms.csuohio.edu

Lauren Matacio
James White Library
Andrews University
Berrien Springs, MI 49104
matacio@andrews.edu

Kelley McHenry
Library
Seattle Central Community
College
Seattle, WA 98122
kelly@seaccd.ctc.edu

Susan McMillan
Schmidt Library
York College of Pennsylvania
York, PA 17405
mcmillan@marvin.yorcol.edu

Sharyl McMillian-Nelson
Miller Nichols Library
University of Missouri
Kansas City, MO 64110
samcmillian@vax1.umkc.edu

Virginia McQuistion
Library
Millikin University
Decatur, IL 62522
vmcquistion@mail.
   millikin.edu

Glenn Mensching
Eastern Michigan University
   Library
Ypsilanti, MI 48197
lib_menschin@emunix.
   emich.edu

Heidi Mercado
Eastern Michigan University
   Library
Ypsilanti, MI 48197
lib_mercado@emunix.emich.edu

Marian I. Miller
Library
Augustana College
Rock Island, IL 61201
alimm@augustana.edu

Marsha Miller
Library
Indiana State University
Terre Haute, IN 47809
libmill@cml.indstate.edu

Mary Lynn Morris
Musselman Library
Gettysburg College
Gettysburg, PA 17325
mmorris@gettysburg.edu

Sharon Munro
Leddy Library
University of Windsor
Windsor, Ontario
Canada N9B 3P4

Melissa Muth
Bracken Library
Ball State University
Muncie, IN 47306
00mamuth@bsuvc.bsu.edu

Sue Norman
Dickinson College
Carlisle, PA 17013
norman-s@dickinson

Judy Olsen
Falvey Library
Villanova University
Villanova, PA 19085
olsen@ucis.vill.edu

Jan Orf
Library
University of St. Thomas
St. Paul, MN 55105
jmorf@stthomas.edu

Gina Overcash
Library
Davidson College
Davidson, NC 28036
giovercash.little.davidson.edu

Nancy Palma
Library-Venango Campus
Clarion University of, PA
Oil City, PA 16301
palma@vaxa.clarion.edu

Amy Parenteau
Library Media Center
Alverno College
Milwaukee, WI 53234-3922

Joan Parks
Smith Library
Southwestern University
Georgetown, TX 78626
parksj@ralph.txswu.edu

Karen Pearson
Byrne Memorial Library
Saint Xavier University
Chicago, IL 60655
mjpzkbp@aol.com

Sara Penhale
Wildman Science Library
Earlham College
Richmond, IN 47374
sarap@earlham.edu

Martha Peterson
Goshen College Library
Goshen, IN 46526
marthajp@cedar.goshen.edu

Mary Jane Petrowski
Case Library
Colgate University
Hamilton, NY 13346-1398
mpetrowski@center.colgate.edu

Lori Phillips
Coe Library
University of Wyoming
Laramie, WY 82070
lphil@uwyo.edu

Margaret Phillips
The Teaching Library
University of California
Berkeley, CA 94720
mphillip@library.berkeley.edu

Robert Phillips
Library
Southwestern Baptist Seminary
Fort Worth, TX 76122
rphillips@lib.swbts.edu

Nancy K. Piernan
University of Detroit-Mercy
MCN Library
Detroit, MI 48219
pierna@wayst1

Jane Ploughman
Griswold Library
Green Mountain College
Poultney, VT 05764

Michael Poma
Reinert/Alumni Library
Creighton University
Omaha, NE 68178
mapoma@creighton.edu

Mary Pagliero Popp
Library
Indiana University
Bloomington, IN 47405
popp@indiana.edu

Jenny Presnell
Miami University Library
Oxford, OH 45056
presnell_jenny@msmail.
   muohio.edu

Diane Prorak
Library
University of Idaho
Moscow, ID 83844-2361
prorak@raven.csrv.uidaho.edu

Cristine Prucha
Murphy Library
University of Wisconsin-
   LaCrosse
LaCrosse, WI 54601
prucha@uwlax.edu

Marea E. Rankin
Lupton Library
University of Tennessee
Chattanooga, TN 37403
mrankin@utcvm.utc.edu

Dan Ream
Library
Virginia Commonwealth
University Richmond, VA
23284-2033
dream@ruby.vcu.edu

Carol Reed
Carlson Library
University of Toledo
Toledo, OH 43606
creed@uoft02.utoledo.edu

James Rettig
Swem Library
College of William
   and Mary
Williamsburg, VA 23187
jrrett@mail.wm.edu

Elizabeth Retzel
Eastern Michigan University
   Library
Ypsilanti, MI 48197
lib_retzel@online.emich.edu

Lorraine Ricigliano
Collins Library
University of Puget Sound
Tacoma, WA 98416
ricigliano@ups.edu

Evelyn Rosenthal
Library
Dutchess Community College
Poughkeepsie, NY 12601

Patricia Rothermich
Courtright Library
Otterbein College
Westerville, OH 43081

Janell Rudolph
McWherter Library
University of Memphis
Memphis, TN 38152
rudolphn@memstvxi

Diane Ruess
Rasmuson Library
University of Alaska-
   Fairbanks
Fairbanks, AK 99775
ffder@alaska

Carol Rusinek
Library
Indiana University-NW
Gary, IN 46408
crusinek@ucs.indiana.edu

Marilyn Russell-Bogle
Library
University of Minnesota-Duluth
Duluth, MN 55812
mrussell@ua.d.umn.edu

Michele Russo
Schurz Library
IU-South Bend
South Bend, IN 46634
mrusso@vines.iusb.indiana.edu

Sherri Saines
Dawes Library
Marietta College
Marietta, OH 45750

Linda St. Clair
Zimmerman Library
University of New Mexico
Albuquerque, NM 87131
lstclair@carina.unm.edu

Bruce Sajdak
Neilson Library
Smith College
Northampton, MA 01063
bsahdak@smith.edu

Laurie Sauer
Pickler Library
Northeast Missouri State
   University
Kirksville, MO 63501
lm2290nemomus@academic.
   nemostate.edu

Ann Scholz
Library
University of Wisconsin-Parkside
Kenosha, WI 53141-2000
scholza@cs.uwp.edu

Lawrence Schwartz
Libraries
North Dakota State
    University
Fargo, ND 58105-5599
lschwart@plains.nodak.edu

Linda Shirato
Eastern Michigan University
    Library
Ypsilanti, MI 48197
lib_shirato@emunix.emich.edu

Arlie Sims
Library
Columbia College
Chicago, IL 60640
axvclas@uicvmc.bitnet

Vaswati Sinha
Skillman Library
Lafayette College
Easton, PA 18042
sv#3@lafayacs

Susan Skekloff
Helmke Library
IU-PU at Fort Wayne
Fort Wayne, IN 46805
skekloff@cvax.ipfw.indiana.edu

Carol Smith
Library
Kalamazoo College
Kalamazoo, MI 49006
csmith@kzoo.edu

Donna Soltermann
Library
St. Louis Community
College-Meramec
St. Louis, MO 63122

Marie Speare
Science Library
University of Manitoba
Winnipeg, Manitoba
CANADA R3T 2N2
speare@bldgdafoe.lanl.
    umanitoba.ca

Keith Stanger
Eastern Michigan University
    Library
Ypsilanti, MI 48197
lib_stanger@emunix.emich.edu

Glenn Ellen Starr
Belk Library
Appalachian State University
Boone, NC 28608
starrge@conrad.appstate.edu

Louisa Straziuso
Newark Campus Library
Ohio State University
Newark, OH 43055-1797
straziuso.l@osu.edu

Terry Taylor
Richardson Library
DePaul University
Chicago, IL 60614
libtat@orion.depaul.edu

Debbie Tenofsky
Cudahy Library
Loyola University
Chicago, IL 60626
dtenofs@luccpua.it.luc.edu

Charles Terbille
Carlson Library
University of Toledo
Toledo, OH 43606
lbr0013@uoft01.utoledo.edu

Nena Thomas
Curtis Laws Wilson Library
University of Missouri
Rolla, MO 65401
nenat@umr.edu

Kathleen Tiller
Roesch Library
University of Dayton
Dayton, OH 45469-1360
tiller@data.lib.
    udayton.edu

Lily Torrez
Library
University of Texas-Pan
    American
Edinburg, TX 78539-2999
lily@panam.edu

Nancy T. Totten
Library
Indiana University Southeast
New Albany, IN 47150

Winnie Tseng
Learning Resources Center
Sinclair Community College
Dayton, OH 45402
wtseng@lear.sinclair.edu

A. Alex Wachsler
Sandor Teszler Library
Wofford College
Spartanburg, SC 29303
wachsleraa@wofford.edu

James E. Ward
Library
David Lipscomb University
Nashville, TN 37204
jward@dlu.edu

Red Wassenich
Austin Community College LRS
Austin, TX 78701
redwass@austin.cc.tx.us

Sally Weston
Mardigian Library
University of Michigan-Dearborn
Dearborn, MI 48128
sweston@ml-f1.umd.umich.edu

Susan Whyte
Northup Library
Linfield College
McMinnville, OR 97128
swhyte@linfield.edu

Helene Williams
Snell Library
Northeastern University
Boston, MA 02115
hwilliam@lynx.neu.edu

Deborah Wills
Leddy Library
University of Windsor
Windsor, Ontario
CANADA N9B 3P4
dwills@uwindsor.ca

Victoria Witte
Olin Library
Washington University
St. Louis, MO 63130
vwitte@library.wustl.edu

Susan Wortman
King Library
Miami University
Oxford, OH 45056
shwortman@miavxl.acs.
  muohio.edu

Paul R. Wright
Library
Miami University
Oxford, OH 45056
wright_paul@msmar.muohio.
  edu.edu

Barbara S. Wurtzel
Springfield Technical
  Community College
Springfield, MA 01101
bwurtzel@rcnvms.rcn.mass.edu

Sandra Yee
Eastern Michgan University
  Library
Ypsilanti, MI 48197
lib_yee@emuvax.emich.edu

Jan Zauha
Hatcher Library
University of Michigan
Ann Arbor, MI 48109-1205
janz@umich.edu

Jayne Zetts
Dunbar Library
Wright State University
Dayton, OH 45435
jzetts@desire.wright.edu